McGraw-Hill
ENGLISH

Authors

Dr. Elizabeth Sulzby
The University of Michigan
Dr. Marvin Klein
Western Washington University
Dr. William Teale
University of Texas at San Antonio
Dr. Timothy Shanahan
University of Illinois at Chicago

Literature Consultant

Sylvia Peña
University of Houston

Contributing Authors

Lois Easton
Arizona Department of Education, Arizona
Henrietta Grooms
Tyler ISD, Texas
Miles Olson
University of Colorado, Colorado
Arnold Webb
New Jersey Department of Education, New Jersey

McGraw-Hill School Division

New York   Oklahoma City   St. Louis   San Francisco   Dallas   Atlanta

Cover Photograph: © Mark E. Gibson 1986/The Stock Market

Grateful acknowledgment for permission to reprint copyrighted material, illustrations and photographs appearing in this book is made on page 464 of this manual, which is hereby made a part of this copyright page.

ISBN 0-07-042270-2

McGraw-Hill Publishing
1200 Northwest 63rd Street
Oklahoma City, Oklahoma 73116-5712

1 2 3 4 5 6 7 8 9 0   8 9 7 6 5 4 3 2 1 0 9 8

McGraw-Hill
ENGLISH

CONTENTS

UNIT
2

Composition · Writing Directions

Grammar · Nouns

UNIT 3

Composition · Tall Tale

Grammar · Verbs I

Composition • Letter

UNIT
5

Composition • Descriptive Writing

Grammar • Pronouns

Composition · Book Report

Grammar · Adjectives

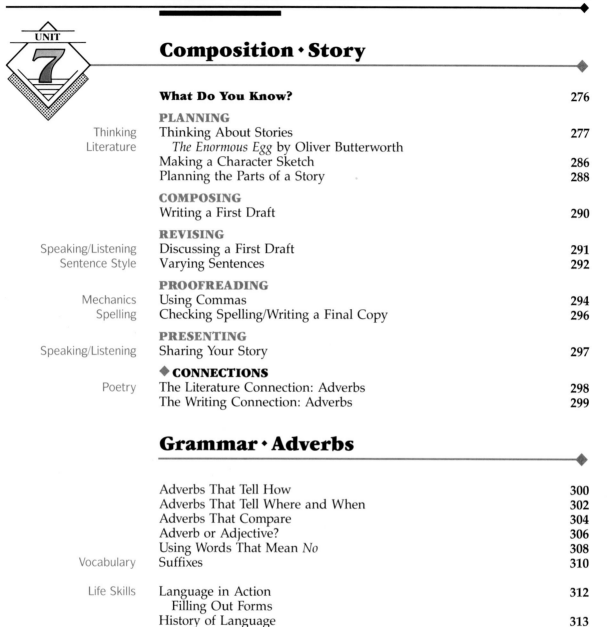

UNIT
7

Composition • Story

Grammar • Adverbs

UNIT 8

Composition · Research Report

Grammar · Sentences II

A Letter to the Student

You are beginning a new school year. You are meeting new people, including your teacher and classmates. This book is also new—at least to you.

As the authors of this book, we want you to know why we wrote it as we did. We planned this book so that you can make the best possible use of your time.

We are sure you will learn to write better this year. In this book, you will follow a clear, step-by-step plan as you write. You will also learn how knowledge of grammar makes you a better writer.

To help you get the most from this book, you will need to keep three types of journals or logs:

- **a personal journal**—in which you will write down your thoughts and feelings on many subjects during the year. You may use these notes to find ideas for your writing. This journal is for your eyes only.
- **a spelling log**—in which you will list the words you spell wrong in your writing. Keep it in a special place and go over the words before you do any new writing.
- **a learning log**—in which you will write about skills you found difficult and how you learned them, or skills you understood easily. By going over your learning log, you can do better next time.

Remember that we thought about you while writing this book. Let us know if we have helped you to improve your writing.

The Writing Process

English: Write a brief story. At least two pages.
Due Friday. Reminder: Book report due
next Monday.
Social Studies: Research report on state capitals
due Thursday.
Science: Complete report on science experiment.
Due Tuesday.

Do you write a lot in your class? This book will help you write reports, stories, and letters. However, good writing takes planning. It starts long before you put pencil to paper.

In each unit, you will complete your own work by following a step-by-step plan called the *writing process*. Here, briefly, are the steps:

Planning

◆ First, you must know the features of the kind of writing you will do. You will read a literature model of that type.
◆ Next, you must know your purpose and audience for writing.
◆ Choose a topic that interests you and that you know about.
◆ Then, take notes, make lists, draw a chart, or plan an outline to help you organize your ideas.

Choose a topic you *care* about.

Composing

- Use your notes to write a first draft. Include any new ideas you get, too.

> Every word does not have to be right. You can always make changes later.

Revising

- Have a partner read your draft. Discuss how you can make your ideas clearer or more interesting. Make changes in the content.
- Revise for style or organization. Decide where to combine sentences or move them around so they will read better. Add details or take out extra words.

> Now is the time to make your draft say *exactly* what you want it to say. Focus on your message.

Proofreading/Writing a Final Copy

- Read over your draft for mistakes in punctuation, capitalization, and spelling.
- Write a final copy, making all your changes.

> It takes a little time to check mistakes, but it's *important*. Tiny errors can get in the reader's way.

Presenting

- Find interesting ways to share your work with other people.

> Make your writing *fun* to read!

The more you practice the writing process, the easier it will be for you to write each time. Your work will improve steadily throughout the year.

Our Approach to Grammar

Some students like to study grammar. Others do not. We wrote this book for both kinds of students. We will explain how we did it.

First we asked ourselves this question: What is easy about grammar for students your age, and what is not? We gave special tests to students around the country. The results helped us plan the grammar parts of this book.

Every grammar lesson has a section called Strategy. It gives you a hint to help you understand a hard part of the grammar skill.

The instruction and exercises are divided into **A** and **B** sections. Use the **A** part of the instruction to help you with the **A** part of the exercises; do the same with the **B** parts.

You may sometimes wonder if there is a good reason to study grammar. In this book, we show how grammar can improve your writing.

We hope you will find this English book interesting and helpful. We worked hard to make it right for you!

PART ONE

Changes

I took today to bed with me
When I turned out the light,
And held it very closely
Through the cool, dark night. . .
I held it very close to me—
It could not get away—
And yet when morning came again
It was another day.

> from "Time"
> by Patricia Hubbell

◆

Changes are happening all around you, day after night after day. Some changes are made by people; other changes happen naturally. Sometimes changes may seem scary, but they are almost always exciting. In these units, think about how changes make you look at yourself and the world in new and different ways.

17

Personal Narrative

Sentences I

What Do You Know?

"Guess what happened to me!"

How often do you start telling a story with those words? If you've done something new or exciting, you want to tell your friends about it. Maybe something has changed in your life or maybe *you've* changed. You probably want to let your friends or family know.

Whenever you tell a story about yourself, it's a **personal narrative**. *Personal* means "about one person," and *narrative* means "story." A personal narrative tells a story about one person . . . you! A personal narrative is a story about the person you know best, yourself.

Thinking About Personal Narratives

What is a Personal Narrative?

A personal narrative has the following features:

- It tells about an event that involved the writer and usually tells about how the writer felt about the event.
- It can be funny or serious.
- It mentions the characters, time, and place of the event.
- The parts of the event are listed in time order.

Everywhere you look, on TV, in magazines, in books, and at home, you will find people telling and writing stories about themselves. Have you ever watched a talk show on TV and heard the guests tell what they have done? Have you read an article in a magazine in which your favorite stars tell how they got started? You have probably read a book by an author who told about his or her life. These are examples of personal narratives. Whenever people tell about something they did or thought, they are telling a personal narrative.

Things that happen to you are always important to you. They are often important to the people you know, too. If you tell about a mistake you made, that can help another person avoid making the same mistake. If something funny happened to you, you can tell other people to make them laugh.

Discussion

1. What was the last story you told about yourself?
2. Do you prefer reading or hearing other people's stories about themselves?
3. Did you ever tell a story that made someone say, "The same thing happened to me"?

Reading a Personal Narrative

Now that you know what a personal narrative is, read this story. In it, Lotty, the narrator, is too sick to go to school. Her mother has just started working outside the house. Lotty is mad at her mother for going to work and not staying home to take care of her.

On My Own
by
Susan Shreve

The story is told by the main character.

At that point in my daydream the telephone rang. It was my mother.

"Have you had your juice?" she asked.

"No," I said.

"Then have some," she said, "and look under your pillow."

We know that the story is taking place in her home.

I went downstairs and got a glass of grape juice. I made toast and read the front page of the newspaper with all the bad news. I fed our yellow-striped cat, Marzipan, and dragged Fleetwood off the velvet couch where he was sleeping. Then I went back to my room, climbed into my non-canopy bed, and looked under the pillow. There was a note on my mother's best stationery.

Dear, dear Lotty,

This morning I remember very clearly the first time you walked away from me across the living room floor on your own, so full of pleasure because you would not have to be carried any longer. It made me cry because you were my last baby and I wanted to be able to carry you longer.

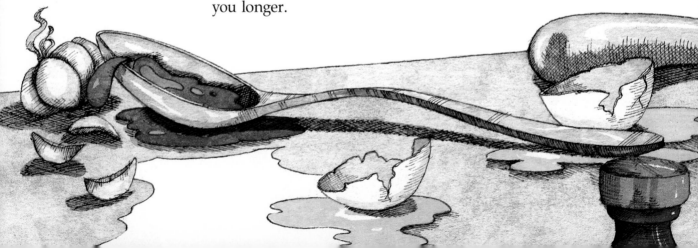

Changes are difficult, whether you are forty-two, like me, or eleven. This morning I would like to call my office and stay home with you. But change is also good once you get used to it. Wouldn't I be in fine shape and you, too, if you had not learned to walk and I still had to carry you—back and forth to school, up and down stairs, over to your friends' house?

I love you. M.

At lunchtime, I went downstairs and made a tunafish sandwich with a lot of onion, which Mama never uses. Then I did the breakfast dishes and vacuumed the living room rug. I turned the stereo on top volume and made the beds, even my parents'. I looked up a recipe for spaghetti, which I made and burned, and a cake for dessert, which was very thick at one end and very thin at the other. It looked quite good, I thought.

Twice my mother called, once to see what my temperature was and I'd forgotten to take it, and once to see if I'd had more juice, which I had. Both times, I didn't mention that I'd found her note and she didn't ask me.

We know what time of day the events take place.

21

The parts of the story are told in the order they happened.

But I was feeling much better. In fact, quite good, except for the sore throat. The house looked cleaner than it had that morning. I even brushed all of Fleetwood's black hair off the sofa. And dinner, a little burned but okay otherwise, was almost ready. I was sitting at the desk in the library doing the homework my friend Benny Diggs had brought me when Nicho and Philip walked into the house.

"You look better," Nicho said.

"Was it lonely?" Philip asked.

"Nope, not really," I said.

"Were you scared?" Nicho asked. "I thought you might be scared."

"With Fleetwood here?" I said, and we all laughed.

We know the main character's feelings about her experience.

When I finished my homework, I cut out a red construction-paper heart the size of an apple. Then I wrote, "I love you, too—Love, Lotty." I put the note on my mother's pillow where she couldn't miss it.

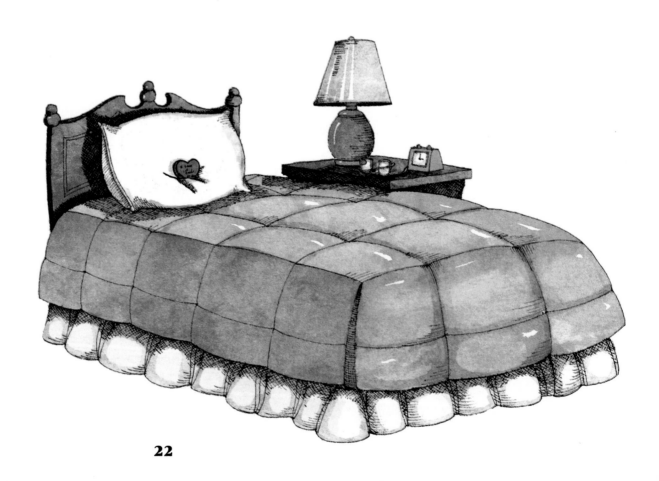

22

Understanding What You've Read

Answer the questions about the story you read.

1. Where did Lotty's mother put the note?
2. What was Lotty doing when Nicho and Philip came in?
3. Name three chores Lotty did.
4. Is this basically a funny or a serious personal narrative?
5. Who are the two most important characters?
6. If you were Lotty, what would you have written in the note to your mother?

Writing Assignment

What would you do if your teacher came in one day and said, "I'm bored. I want each of you to tell me a story." Would you have a good story ready to tell? In this unit, you will prepare a one-paragraph personal narrative. Your **audience** will be your teacher and class. Your **purpose** will be to inform or entertain them. You will also see how Aiko, another student, prepares her personal narrative.

Choose Your Topic

What kind of story would you like to tell about yourself? You might want to tell a funny story, or one that will teach something. To start, you need a topic. You can use a topic from the list below, or use one of your own. It's your choice.

growing up
learning from a brother or sister
a good lesson for me
new friends I've made
a funny surprise
a summer project
a class trip

After you choose your topic, write it down. Save it for the next lesson.

Narrowing a Topic

Aiko just moved to a new town. She wanted to tell her classmates something she had done. Then they would know something about her. Aiko decided to write about the camp she went to last summer. She learned a lot about herself at camp.

She realized that her topic was too broad. So she decided to draw an upside-down triangle to help her narrow it. Then she wrote her topic at the top, like this:

Next, Aiko thought of what she did at camp. She decided to write about her favorite activity, sports. She wrote *Sports* in the narrower part of the triangle, below *Summer Camp*. She knew that was still too broad a topic for one paragraph. Finally, Aiko narrowed her topic down to one special game of softball.

Look at Aiko's finished triangle. The topic at the top is very broad, too broad to cover in one paragraph. The next topic is one part of the first. The last topic is still part of the first topic, but it is narrow enough to cover in one paragraph.

Practice

A. Write the topics in an upside-down triangle. Put them in order from the broadest on top to the narrowest at the bottom.

  1. a. chores around a farm   **b.** my first week on a farm
      c. the day I fed the pigs

  2. a. playing on the softball team
      b. winning the championship game   **c.** sports at school

  3. a. the teacher who helped me find my classroom
      b. the first day at my new school
      c. getting lost in the halls

B. Make an upside-down triangle for each of the following topics. Then complete your triangle by limiting each topic twice.

  4. learning to ride a bicycle
  5. a trip to the park
  6. fun in the fourth grade

Narrow Your Topic

APPLY STEP BY STEP

Make an upside-down triangle. Start with the topic you chose. Then narrow it at least twice. Make sure you finish with a topic narrow enough to write about in one paragraph. Save your triangle to help you write your paragraph.

25

Main Ideas and Topic Sentences

Aiko narrowed her topic. Now she is ready to think about exactly what to put in her paragraph. Most paragraphs have one main idea. The **main idea** is the most important idea about the topic. The main idea is usually stated in a sentence called the **topic sentence**. Look at what Aiko wrote.

Topic: a special game

The most important thing about that game is how Aiko changed during it. Here is her main idea.

Main Idea: how I changed from being the worst softball player at camp

The main idea is stated in her topic sentence.

Topic Sentence: I was the worst softball player at camp, but that changed at a special game.

You will use a topic sentence in your personal narrative. It will help you decide which details to include in your paragraph. The topic sentence is usually the first sentence in the paragraph. It should be interesting and exciting enough to make the reader want more.

Here are two possible topic sentences for a personal narrative. Which one do you think is better?

Topic Sentence 1: We had no idea how interesting
our hiking trip would be.
Topic Sentence 2: One day, we decided to go on
a hiking trip.

The first topic sentence is much better. It makes the reader want to find out what was so interesting about the hiking trip.

Practice

A. Read each topic and main idea. Write a topic sentence that states the main idea.

1. Topic: my first ski trip
   Main Idea: fell a lot
2. Topic: the attic in our new house
   Main Idea: filled with old clothes
3. Topic: the school play
   Main Idea: exciting to try acting
4. Topic: my new scouting badge
   Main Idea: a lot of work to get it

How can I make my topic sentence interesting?

B. Read each pair of sentences. Write the one that is a more interesting topic sentence.

5. **a.** I knew something special would happen today.
   b. Here is the story of what happened today.
6. **a.** One day, I took a walk through the park.
   b. An unexpected adventure happened in the park.
7. **a.** Today is my little brother's first birthday.
   b. A year ago today, I got the best present ever.
8. **a.** I'll never forget what happened in school yesterday.
   b. Yesterday was Tuesday, and I was in school all day.

Write Your Topic Sentence

Look at the narrowest topic you chose in the last lesson. Decide what your main idea will be. Then write a topic sentence that states your main idea. Make sure your topic sentence is interesting. Save it for the next lesson.

Using Supporting Details

The topic sentence gives the main idea of the paragraph. **Supporting details** are specific events, feelings, and ideas that tell about the main idea. These details explain the main idea in a clear and interesting way. Supporting details refer directly to the main idea of the paragraph. You should avoid any details that do not support the main idea.

Aiko looked at her topic sentence. To find details to support it, Aiko thought hard about the softball game she had played at camp. She remembered what happened and how she felt. She tried to remember events and feelings very clearly. She wrote a list of the ideas and details that came to mind.

> Topic Sentence: I was the worst softball player at camp, but that changed at a special game.
> played ten games with no hits
> nicknamed Strikeout
> teammates cried when I batted.
> was one of the best swimmers at camp
> pitchers smiled when they saw me
> there were birds chirping in the trees
> finally made a hit

Aiko reread her list of details. She asked herself if all her details were related to her topic sentence. Most of them were, but a few weren't. Aiko crossed out the details that weren't related to her topic sentence. They didn't belong in her paragraph.

Practice

A. Read the topic sentence and the details below. Write the details that tell about the main idea. Do not write the details that do not relate to the main idea.

> Topic Sentence: It was the best class trip I ever had, but they may never let me in the museum again.
> interested in armor in the museum
> didn't notice my class leaving
> too absorbed in my own thoughts
> the museum has five floors of exhibits
> museum lights went out
> shouted "Hello!"—no answer
> there was nobody left
> we learned about mountain lions the next day

B. Write this paragraph. Underline the main idea. Leave out the detail sentences that are not related to the main idea.

> Last year I lost, but this year, my pumpkins were the largest at the fair. There were also some great pies in the Bake Off. In early spring, I planted seeds from the biggest pumpkin I grew last year. When the plants came up, I tended them carefully. These pumpkins aren't very good for pies. I didn't pick my pumpkins until an hour before the fair. I was the last person to enter the contest, but I got first prize!

Do all my details support my main idea?

Write Your Supporting Details

Look at the topic sentence you wrote. Make a list of supporting details. Check that they are all related to your main idea. Save your work for the next lesson.

Writing a First Draft

Read the first draft of Aiko's personal narrative. Remember that it is a first draft so there are probably some mistakes.

I was the worst softball player at camp. but that changed at a special game. In ten games, I hadn't hit the ball once. my nickname wazn't Strikeout for nothing. It was my turn to bat again. The pitcher smiled. The pitcher threw the first ball. He knew I was an eazy out I swung and missed. My teamates groaned. My coach groaned. Keep your eye on the ball Stay calm. I thought of all the suggestions I'd gotten. I hunched down and gripped the bat. I swung with my whole body. Crack! The ball sailed over secont base. The ball rolled into centerfield for a double. Wow, what a hit. Can you believe it. To tell the truth, I couldn't.

Write Your First Draft

Before you begin, you may want to discuss your ideas with your teacher or partner. When you are ready to begin writing, take a sheet of paper and write your topic sentence on the back. Then, turn it over, and begin writing your narrative paragraph. Use your list of supporting details to help you write. Don't worry if your first draft is messy or has mistakes. Just write on every other line of the page so that you'll have room to correct the mistakes later.

Discussing a First Draft

Discussion Strategy

It's always helpful to get another person's ideas about your work. It's especially nice to know someone else likes what you have done. So, always try to make encouraging comments. Aiko told her partner, Joanne, "This story is funny, but I think some of the events are out of time order." This was nicer for Joanne than if Aiko had said "This stupid story is completely out of time order."

Use the Content Checklist to discuss Aiko's first draft with your class.

Content Checklist

- ✔ Does the story tell about an interesting event that involved the writer?
- ✔ Does it tell the writer's feelings about the event?
- ✔ Does it mention the characters, time, and place of the event?
- ✔ Are the parts of the event told in time order?

Revise Your First Draft for Content

To the Reader: Read your partner's first draft. Try to guess the main idea. Then look at the topic sentence on the back of the page. Tell your partner if the idea was easy to guess. Use the Content Checklist to help you judge your partner's work. Remember to use the Discussion Strategy when making comments.

To the Writer: If your main idea was not easy for your partner to guess, try to make it clearer. Take notes on all your partner's comments. Use them to help you revise your first draft.

Combining Sentences

Aiko decided to combine sentences that repeated words. Sometimes she had two sentences with the same subject. Then she could make one sentence if she put *and* between the two predicates, like this.

The dog ran.
The dog barked. > The dog ran and barked.

Sometimes she had two sentences with the same predicate. She could make one sentence if she put *and* between the two subjects, like this.

The parents laughed.
The children laughed. > *The parents and the children laughed.*

Proofreading Marks	
∧	add
⌇	take away
/	small letter

Here is how Aiko combined sentences with repeated words in part of her first draft.

The pitcher smiled. The pitcher ╱ threw the
 and
first ball. He knew I was an eazy out I swung and missed.
My teamates groaned, My coach groaned. Keep your eye on
 and
the ball Stay calm. I thought of all the suggestions I'd
gotten. I hunched down and gripped the bat. I swung with
my whole body. Crack! The ball sailed over secont base.
The ball rolled into centerfield for a double. Wow. what a hit.
 and
Can you believe it. To tell the truth, I couldn't.

32

Practice

Read each pair of sentences. Decide which idea is repeated in each pair. Then, combine the sentences so that the idea is not repeated.

1. My parents wanted a puppy. I wanted a puppy.
2. One day a puppy wandered into our yard. A puppy scratched at our door.
3. The puppy was tiny. The puppy looked helpless.
4. Mom said we could keep it. Dad said we could keep it.
5. My sister liked the name Pip. I liked the name Pip.
6. Pip ate a lot. Pip grew very quickly.
7. Pip outgrew her boxes. Pip barely fit in the bathtub.
8. Dad looked nervous. Dad asked how big she would get.
9. The landlord complained about Pip's barking. The neighbors complained about Pip's barking.
10. Mom said we needed more room. Dad said we needed more room.
11. Dad loves our big new house. I love our big, new house.
12. Mom smiles at Pip. Mom says, "We moved, thanks to this dog."

Revising Checklist
✔ Have I included all of the characteristics of a narrative paragraph? (p. 19)
✔ Have I combined sentences with repeated words to make new sentences?

Revise Your First Draft for Style

Use the Revising Checklist to help you revise your first draft.

Look for sentences that repeat subjects or predicates. Combine these sentences using proofreading marks. Save your revised draft for the next lesson.

Writing Sentences and Paragraphs

Aiko knew that the way she punctuated her sentences would change the way her readers read them. She looked up rules about writing sentences and paragraphs correctly. Next to each rule is an example from her paragraph.

Rule	Example
Begin every sentence with a capital letter.	The pitcher smiled.
Use a period (.) at the end of a declarative sentence.	In ten games, I hadn't hit the ball once.
Use a period (.) at the end of an imperative sentence.	Keep your eye on the ball.
Use a question mark (?) to end an interogative sentence.	Can you believe it?
Use an exclamation mark (!) at the end of an exclamatory sentence.	Wow, what a hit!
Indent the first word of a new paragraph.	→ I was the worst softball player in camp.

Practice

A. Write the sentences. Correct the capitalization and end punctuation.

1. last year I saw the Pacific Ocean for the first time
2. have you ever seen it
3. wow, how beautiful it was
4. go see it when you can
5. it was too cold to swim when I was there
6. obey the lifeguards if you go swimming
7. we saw seals
8. boy, that was fun
9. do you know the difference between seals and otters
10. seals have flippers; otters have paws
11. they are fun to watch

B. Write the paragraph. Add capitalization, end punctuation, and indentation.

last week, I saw snow for the first time have you ever seen snow oh, how pretty it is close your eyes imagine your bedroom covered with snow wow, what a strange idea where would you put the snowman think about it you could build an igloo over your bed

---

Proofreading Checklist
✔ Have I capitalized the first word of each sentence?
✔ Have I used end punctuation correctly?
✔ Is the first word of my paragraph indented?

Proofreading Marks	
∧	add
⌀	take away
¶	indent
≡	capitalize
/	small letter
◯	check spelling
∿	transpose

Proofread Your Paragraph
Use the Proofreading Checklist to help you check your personal narrative. Correct any mistakes you find with proofreading marks. Don't worry if your page looks messy. Keep it to clean up later.

35

Checking Spelling/Writing a Final Copy

Spelling Strategy

Start a spelling log. A spelling log is a notebook that helps you learn spelling. It has one page for each letter of the alphabet. When you don't know how to spell a word, look it up in the dictionary. Then, write the correctly spelled word in your spelling log. Write each word on the page with the first letter of the word.

Read Aiko's final, corrected personal narrative.

I was the worst softball player at camp, but that changed at a special game. In ten games, I hadn't hit the ball once. my nickname *wasn't* Strikeout for nothing. It was my turn to bat again. The pitcher smiled, *and* The pitcher threw the first ball. He knew I was an *easy* out. I swung and missed. My *teammates* groaned, *and* My coach groaned. Keep your eye on the ball, Stay calm. I thought of all the suggestions I'd gotten. I hunched down and gripped the bat. I swung with my whole body. Crack! The ball sailed over *second* base. The ball *and* rolled into centerfield for a double. Wow, what a hit! Can you believe it? To tell the truth, I couldn't.

Check for Spelling

Use proofreading marks to correct any spelling errors. Put any words you had to correct in your spelling log.

Write a Final Copy

Write a final copy of your personal narrative. When you're finished, read both copies to be sure you haven't missed anything.

PRESENTING
Sharing Your Personal Narrative

Speaking/Listening Strategy

When you are speaking, be sure to speak loudly enough for everyone in the audience to hear you. If you are listening, don't talk or move around. Sit quietly, and listen carefully to the speaker.

Choosing a Way to Share

Here are some ways to share your personal narrative.

Reading Aloud   When you read, try to make your voice sound interesting. Imagine you are a radio announcer entertaining an audience.

Presenting a Sketch   Have friends in your class be the characters in your story. As you read the story, they can act out the actions. Prepare costumes or props your friends might need before you begin.

Making a Book   Put your whole class's personal narratives together into a book. Call the book *Our Class*. Display your book in your classroom or in your school library.

Share Your Personal Narrative

Use one of the ideas above to share your narrative with your class, or use an idea of your own. It's your choice!

Begin Your Learning Log

Answer these questions in your learning log.

- What did I like best about my personal narrative?
- Did I learn anything about myself while writing my personal narrative?
- What things will I change the next time I write a personal narrative?

The Literature Connection: Sentences

Think of all the different ways you can communicate with others. You may draw pictures about something you saw or imagined. You might also use gestures or other sign language to express your ideas. The most common means of communication, however, is words. Words can tell other people exactly what you are thinking.

When words express a complete thought, they form a **sentence**. Writers of poems and stories use sentences for many different purposes. Sometimes sentences contain a serious message. Other times they contain messages that are lighthearted and funny.

Sentences may be written on any topic. Some topics are realistic; they tell about actual people in actual situations. Other sentences describe imaginary ideas; they tell about make-believe people, times, and places.

The events in the poem aren't real. Even so, the poem shows how sentences can be used in a funny way.

The Ceiling
by
Theodore Roethke

Suppose the ceiling went outside
And then caught cold and up and died?
The only thing we'd have for proof
That he was gone, would be the roof;
I think it would be most revealing
To find out how the ceiling's feeling.

Discussion

1. What things can you find in the poem that probably couldn't happen?
2. What things really could happen to a ceiling in a house?
3. Have you ever imagined that a thing or an animal could talk? Describe some of the things you think it would say.

The Writing Connection:
Sentences

Be as creative as you want in your writing. Your sentences may express the most unusual or fanciful ideas. On the other page, the poet imagined a ceiling that went away. Here are other imaginary changes you could write about in sentences.

Suppose the floor went on vacation.
We would have to dance on the walls.

Suppose the windows closed their eyes.
We would have to stare out the keyhole.

Activity

Now pretend that you live in a fantastic house. Write sentences that tell about your imaginary house. Use the picture to give you ideas. Finish each sentence below.

◆ Suppose the chairs _____.
  We would have to sit _____.
◆ Suppose the carpet _____.
  We would have to walk _____.
◆ Suppose the table _____.
  We would have to eat _____.
◆ Suppose the _____.
  We would have to _____.

What Is a Sentence?

A **sentence** is a group of words that tells a complete thought.

A. A sentence must always tell a complete thought. It must make sense to the reader.

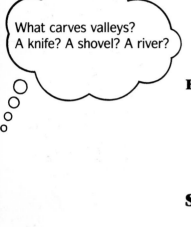

What carves valleys?
A knife? A shovel? A river?

not a complete thought	complete thought
The flat land.	The flat land changes slowly.
Carves valleys.	The river carves valleys.

B. A sentence must start with a capital letter and end with an end mark.

The book tells about the Grand Canyon.
The Colorado River cuts a path through the rocks.

Strategy

After you write a sentence, check to be sure that the meaning is clear.

♦ Read it aloud. Does it make sense?
♦ Give it to someone else to read. Does the reader understand what you mean?

Check Your Understanding

A. Write the letter that tells whether each group of words is a sentence or not a sentence.

1. Splashes against rocks.
    a. sentence   **b.** not a sentence
2. The river runs over rocks and soil.
    a. sentence   **b.** not a sentence

B. Write the letter that tells whether each group of words is a correct sentence.

3. Winds blow against the rocks.
    a. yes   **b.** no
4. the wind carries sand and dust
    a. yes   **b.** no

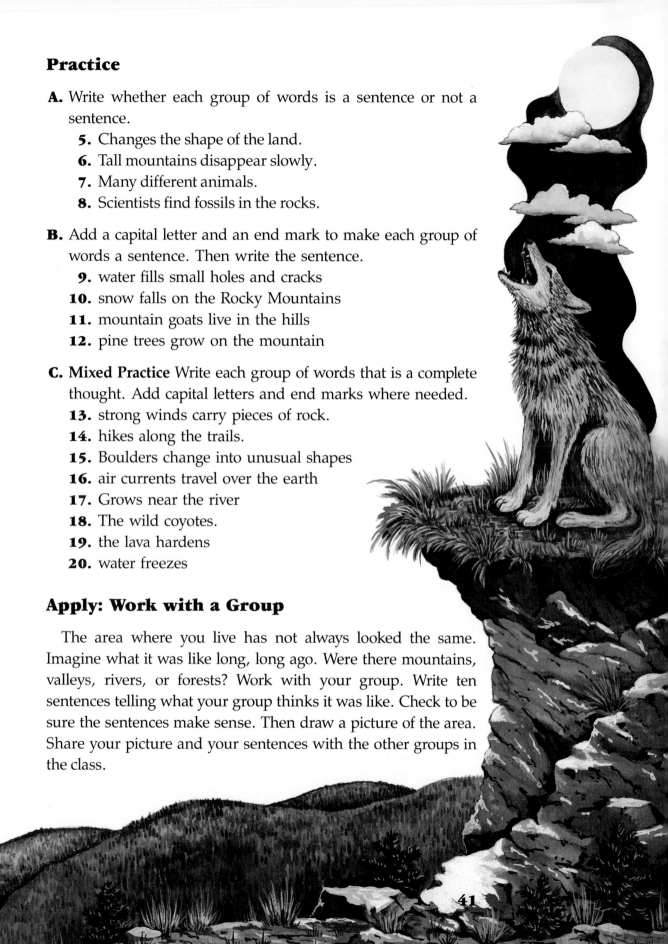

Practice

A. Write whether each group of words is a sentence or not a sentence.

    5. Changes the shape of the land.

    6. Tall mountains disappear slowly.

    7. Many different animals.

    8. Scientists find fossils in the rocks.

B. Add a capital letter and an end mark to make each group of words a sentence. Then write the sentence.

    9. water fills small holes and cracks

   10. snow falls on the Rocky Mountains

   11. mountain goats live in the hills

   12. pine trees grow on the mountain

C. Mixed Practice Write each group of words that is a complete thought. Add capital letters and end marks where needed.

   13. strong winds carry pieces of rock.

   14. hikes along the trails.

   15. Boulders change into unusual shapes

   16. air currents travel over the earth

   17. Grows near the river

   18. The wild coyotes.

   19. the lava hardens

   20. water freezes

Apply: Work with a Group

The area where you live has not always looked the same. Imagine what it was like long, long ago. Were there mountains, valleys, rivers, or forests? Work with your group. Write ten sentences telling what your group thinks it was like. Check to be sure the sentences make sense. Then draw a picture of the area. Share your picture and your sentences with the other groups in the class.

Kinds of Sentences

There are four kinds of sentences.

A. Statements and questions are two kinds of sentences. Study the chart below.

Kind	Use	End Mark	Example
Statement	Tells something	Period	Caterpillars change once a year.
Question	Asks something	Question mark	Did you catch a butterfly?

B. Commands and exclamations are the other two kinds of sentences. Study the chart below.

Kind	Use	End Mark	Example
Command	Orders	Period	Tell me about caterpillars. Please speak slowly.
Exclamation	Shows strong feeling	Exclamation mark	How pretty the butterfly looks! I like the colors!

Strategy

Some sentences can be either exclamations or statements. It is the writer's choice. When you write a sentence, decide whether you want to express strong feeling or surprise. If so, use an exclamation mark.

Check Your Understanding

A. Write the letter of the word that correctly describes each kind of sentence.

    1. Butterflies fly during the day.

        a. statement   **b.** question

    2. Did you watch the moth?

        a. statement   **b.** question

B. Follow the directions for Check Your Understanding A.

   3. Show me the book about insects.
      a. command   **b.** exclamation
   4. Wow, the butterfly moves so quickly!
      a. command   **b.** exclamation

Practice

A. Write each sentence. Tell if it is a *statement* or a *question*.

   5. Some butterflies travel south in winter.
   6. Can you see the moth?
   7. The butterfly landed on the leaf.
   8. Have you read about caterpillars?

B. Write each sentence. Tell if it is a *command* or an *exclamation*.

   9. The caterpillar moves so slowly!
   10. Look at those colorful wings.
   11. How the class liked my butterfly!
   12. Please read the book about caterpillars.

C. Mixed Practice Write each sentence. Use the correct end mark. Then write if it is a *statement, question, command,* or *exclamation*.

   13. The caterpillar eats the leaves on the trees
   14. What kind of butterfly did you see
   15. Tell me about your favorite butterfly
   16. The moth flies near the light
   17. Please write a report about caterpillars
   18. How did the wings flutter
   19. How the wings did flutter
   20. The caterpillar has six eyes

Apply: Test a Partner

Write two riddles. Make each riddle a question. Give the riddles to a friend. Have your friend write statements that answer each riddle. Check to see if each answer is a correct sentence.

Complete Subjects

A sentence has two main parts. They are called the **complete subject** and the **complete predicate**. In this lesson you will learn about complete subjects.

The **complete subject** of a sentence tells who or what the sentence is about.

A. Sometimes the complete subject is one word. The complete subject of each sentence below is shown in red.

> Potters bake clay in an oven.

> Artists make clay objects.

> Mae-Ling reads a book about pottery.

B. Sometimes the complete subject is a group of several words. All these words tell who or what the sentence is about. The complete subject of each sentence below is shown in red.

> Most potters use many types of clay.

> The new potters mix the clay.

> The hot clay shrinks.

Strategy

Look at the beginning of each sentence when searching for the complete subject. Most complete subjects are found at the start of a sentence, *before* the action word.

Check Your Understanding

A. Write the letter of the complete subject in each sentence.
  1. Potters shape the soft clay.
   a. Potters   **b.** shape   **c.** the soft clay
  2. Haruko molds a vase.
   a. Haruko molds   **b.** Haruko   **c.** vase

B. Write the letter of the complete subject in each sentence.

   3. The damp vase bakes in an oven.
   a. The damp vase   **b.** bakes   **c.** in an oven
   4. Strong hands shape the clay.
   a. Strong   **b.** shape the clay   **c.** Strong hands

Practice

A. Write each sentence. Draw one line under the complete subject.

   5. Rex uses many special pottery tools.
   6. Potters mix clay with water.
   7. Clay dries very slowly.
   8. Marie molds two bowls.

B. Follow the directions for Practice A.

   9. Some potters work with special paints.
   10. A special oven bakes the pieces.
   11. The colored pottery turns shiny and hard.
   12. Two friends mix the clay.

C. Mixed Practice Write each sentence. Draw one line under the complete subject.

   13. Students turn the pottery wheel.
   14. Most potters use seven types of clay.
   15. The large dish spins on a wheel.
   16. Sandy creates a bowl without a wheel.
   17. The busy potters baked the clay twice.
   18. Latasha makes a pitcher from different pieces.
   19. The tall, narrow vase holds flowers.
   20. Melba and Agnes mold a large pot.

Apply: Work with a Partner

Draw a sketch of the pottery you would make if you could. Exchange your drawing with a partner. Write four sentences describing your partner's drawing. Underline each complete subject.

Complete Predicates

The **complete predicate** of a sentence tells what the subject is or what it does.

A. Sometimes the complete predicate is one word. The complete predicate of each sentence below is shown in blue.

A cool breeze blows.

Orange and yellow leaves fall.

B. Usually, however, the complete predicate is a group of words. All the words in the complete predicate tell what the subject is or does. The complete predicate of each sentence below is shown in blue.

A new season comes every few months.

The autumn days grow shorter and cooler.

Squirrels gather nuts for the long winter.

Strategy

When looking for the complete predicate, first find the complete subject. Most complete predicates come after the complete subject. Remember that a complete predicate is often more than one word.

Check Your Understanding

A. Write the letter of the complete predicate for each sentence.
1. The autumn moon glows.
   a. The autumn   **b.** moon glows   **c.** glows
2. The dry leaves rustle.
   a. dry leaves   **b.** rustle   **c.** leaves rustle

B. Write the letter of the complete predicate for each sentence below.

    3. Many people enjoy cool weather.
        a. Many people   **b.** people enjoy
        c. enjoy cool weather
    4. The children catch bright leaves.
        a. The children   **b.** catch bright leaves
        c. catch bright

Practice

A. Write each sentence. Underline the complete predicate.
    5. The winter sun sets.
    6. Large groups of birds migrate.
    7. The fur of most animals grows.
    8. The mountain lake freezes.

B. Write each sentence. Underline the complete predicate.
    9. An early snow covers the ground.
    10. Some animals sleep all winter long.
    11. Some people roast chestnuts.
    12. Children wear warm clothes.

C. Mixed Practice Write each sentence. Underline the complete predicate.
    13. Leaves float to the ground.
    14. The schools open.
    15. Workers pick apples from the trees.
    16. The farmer seeds the soil for new crops.
    17. The pumpkins grow.
    18. Many football players practice.
    19. Little birds chirp and fly south.
    20. The winter snow falls and covers the sea.

Apply: Work with a Partner

Write five incomplete sentences about one of your favorite seasons. Leave out either the complete subject or the complete predicate in each. Trade papers and have your partner complete each sentence by adding the missing part.

Dictionary Skills: Finding Words

A. Words in a dictionary are listed in alphabetical order. When words begin with the same letter, they are arranged by their second letter. When the first two letters are the same, the dictionary uses the third letter and so on.

2nd letter:	3rd letter:	4th letter:
adjust, after	aboard, absolute	addition, address

B. Guide words help you find entry words easily.

Guide words are pairs of words at the top of each dictionary page. They show the first and last entry words on the page.

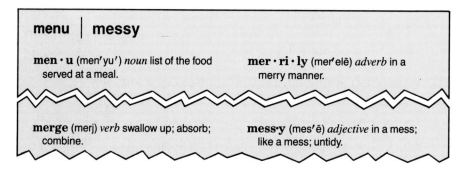

menu | messy

men·u (men′yu′) *noun* list of the food served at a meal.

mer·ri·ly (mer′elē) *adverb* in a merry manner.

merge (merj) *verb* swallow up; absorb; combine.

mess·y (mes′ē) *adjective* in a mess; like a mess; untidy.

On this page, *menu* is the first word, and *messy* is the last. Other words on the page come between the guide words in alphabetical order. Can you explain why *method* does not appear on this page?

Strategy

To find a word in the dictionary, use guide words to spot the page where the word appears.

Check Your Understanding

A. Write the letter of the group of words that is in alphabetical order.

1. **a.** advance, nursery, crumb **b.** plump, pod, product
   c. deer, damage, dove **d.** son, same, tub
2. **a.** hard, harmony, hare **b.** plus, play, please
   c. slap, slip, slow **d.** bend, bench, beneath

B. Use the sample dictionary page. Write the letter of the correct answer.

    3. Which two words would appear on the sample page?

        a. merchant, merit   **b.** merry, meter

        c. many, motion

    4. Which two words would not appear on the sample page?

        a. meow, messy   **b.** merry, mesh   **c.** meek, melt

Practice

A. Write each group of words in alphabetical order.

5. study	**6.** lecture	**7.** arrange	**8.** fleet
tablet	legend	around	flea
stew	learn	arrive	flavor

B. Write the word that would be included on a dictionary page with each pair of guide words below.

    9. jar/joke   joy jacket jewel

  10. point/poodle   poor poke popcorn

  11. adventure/after   afraid accept again

  12. tape/tassel   tall taste target

C. Mixed Practice   Write each group of words in alphabetical order. Underline the word that would appear on a dictionary page with the guide words shown.

  13. moment/moonlight   mole moist monster

  14. grow/guilty   grouse grumpy gulf

  15. force/forgive   foreign forbid forgiveness

  16. band/banner   banana ban banjo barber

  17. golden/gone   gold gong goldfish good

  18. trickle/trolley   trick tribe trombone troll

  19. remark/remote   remain remove remind rename

  20. decline/defend   declare deck defeat defense

Apply: Work with a Partner

Write six words that fall between the guide words **pack/pupil**. Work with your partner to arrange all the words in alphabetical order.

Dictionary Skills: Entry Words

> **earth · quake** (erth′kwak′) *noun*
> shaking or trembling of the ground.
> **earth · worm** (earth′werm′) *noun*
> round worm that lives in the soil.
> **ea · sel** (ē′zel) *noun* stand for holding a
> picture or blackboard: *The artist painted
> at an easel.*
>
> **eas · y** (ē′zē) *adjective* **1** not hard to do:
> *an easy job.* **2** free from pain or worry;
> peaceful: *an easy life.* **3** not strict or
> harsh: *an easy winter.*
> **eat** (ēt) *verb* **1** chew and swallow. **2** destroy
> as if by eating: *Acid can eat away metal.*
> **3** have a meal: *We always eat together.*

A. The words listed alphabetically in a dictionary are called **entry words**. Some entry words are divided into parts called **syllables**. The first two entry words on the dictionary page above are *earthquake* and *earthworm*. Each of these words has two syllables.

The meaning of each entry word is called a **definition**. What is the definition of *easel*? There may also be an **example sentence** or **phrase** to show how the entry word is used. What is the example sentence for *easel*?

B. Many words have more than one meaning. Each meaning is numbered. How many meanings does the word *easy* have? Which meaning fits each of these sentences?

The geography test was easy.
Life was easy on the peaceful island.

Strategy

If you are not sure of the meaning of a word you find while reading, look it up in a dictionary. Read all the meanings and choose the one that makes sense.

Check Your Understanding

A. Use the sample dictionary page to complete these sentences.
  1. An entry word that means a kind of animal is ____.
    a. easel   **b.** easy   **c.** earthworm   **d.** earthquake
  2. "An easy job" is a(n) ____ for the word *easy*.
    a. definition   **b.** example phrase   **c.** entry word

B. Follow the directions for Check Your Understanding A.

    3. The entry word *eat* has ＿＿ meanings.

        a. one   **b.** two   **c.** three   **d.** four

    4. The ＿＿ meaning of *eat* is "to have a meal."

        a. first   **b.** second   **c.** third

Practice

A. Use the sample dictionary page to answer the questions.

    5. How many entry words are shown on the sample page?

    6. Which entry words have two syllables?

    7. Which entry words have example sentences?

    8. What is the definition of the entry word *easel*?

B. Write each sentence. Then write the dictionary definition of the underlined word.

    9. Mr. Williams had an easy visit at the hospital.

    10. The Garcia family always eats at six o'clock.

    11. The puzzle was easy.

    12. Rust often eats at the outside of cars.

C. Mixed Practice   Use the dictionary page to answer these questions.

    13. Which entry word follows *easy*?

    14. How many meanings does the entry word *easy* have?

    15. What is the definition of the entry word *earthquake*?

    16. Which meaning of *eat* fits this sentence? Marcos and Sue eat fruit every day.

    17. Where do earthworms live?

    18. Write an example sentence for the word *earthquake*.

    19. Write a sentence using the first meaning of *eat*.

    20. Write a sentence using the first meaning of *easy*.

Apply: Work with a Partner

In the dictionary, find an entry word with at least three meanings. Write the word and its meanings on a sheet of paper. Exchange papers with a partner. Write three sentences using the different meanings of the word.

Dictionary Skills: Pronunciation

A. If you are not sure how to pronounce a word, the dictionary can help. It uses symbols to show how words sound. A **pronunciation key** tells what the symbols sound like. Study the pronunciation key below. Notice that one letter can have several different pronunciations.

a back	**i** it	**oi** coin	**ch** child	a in about
ā cage	**ī** ice	**ou** out	**ng** sing	e in taken
ä far	**o** dot	**u** cup	**sh** she **ə** =	i in pencil
e let	**ō** open	**u̇** put	**th** thin	o in lemon
ē equal	**ô** order	**ü** rule	**ŦH** that	u in circus
ėr term			**zh** measure	

B. Entry words are followed by their pronunciations. Study this word and its pronunciation.

cat•er•pil•lar   (kat′ ər pil′ ər)

To pronounce *caterpillar* correctly, you must first look at the pronunciation symbols. Then use the pronunciation key to learn the sound of each symbol. All the symbols together tell how the word sounds.

The **accent marks** in the pronunciation (′) (′) tell you which syllables to say loudly. One accent is darker than the other. The syllable with this accent is said the loudest. How do you pronounce the word *caterpillar* correctly? Use the pronunciation key to pronounce these words correctly:

gov • ern • ment (guv′ ərn mənt)
boil (boil)   drop (dräp)

Strategy

Not all dictionaries have the same pronunciation key. Always check the pronunciation key of the dictionary you're using.

Check Your Understanding

A. Use the pronunciation key to write the letter of the correct answer.

   1. Which symbol shows the sound of the *o* in *order*?

      a. o   **b.** ō   **c.** ô   **d.** oi

   2. Which symbol shows the sound of the *e* in *equal*?

      a. e   **b.** ē   **c.** ėr   **d.** ə

B. Follow the directions for Check Your Understanding A.

   3. Which is the correct pronunciation for *city*?

      a. (sit′ē)   **b.** (sīt′ē)   **c.** (sītē′)   **d.** (sīt′ė)

   4. Which syllable is said the loudest in *butterfly*? (but′ ər flī′)?

      a. first   **b.** second   **c.** third

Practice

A. Write each word. Use the pronunciation key to write the symbol for the underlined letter in each word.

5. price	**7.** star	**9.** worm
6. knot	**8.** stage	**10.** soot

B. Write each pronunciation. Then write the entry word that matches the pronunciation.

11. (fāt) fat, fate	**13.** (nēl) kneel, nail
12. (sėr′ kəs) circle, circus	**14.** (kan′ dl) candle, kindle

C. Mixed Practice   Write each pronunciation. Then write the word it stands for. Use the pronunciation key.

15. (bə nan′ ə)	**18.** (lôn)
16. (nā′ bər)	**19.** (hyü′ mər)
17. (skärf)	**20.** (kou′ boi)

Apply: Test a Partner

Choose five one-syllable words from the dictionary. Write the pronunciation of each word. Trade papers with your partner. Write the word that each pronunciation stands for. Check your partner's work.

LANGUAGE IN ACTION

Using the Telephone

You are reading in your room on a Sunday afternoon. Your parents aren't home, and the phone rings. What do you do?

That is one question you might have about using the phone. The phone is important in daily life. Everybody uses it. However, not everybody uses it well. Here's what you should do.

- Never tell a stranger your number.
- Identify yourself. You might say, "Hello, Ramirez residence, Lisa speaking." (Of course, you would use your own name.) You might wait until you know who the other person is before you say your name. Talk to your parents about this.
- Never say that your parents aren't home or that you are alone. Say that they can't come to the phone.
- If the call is not for you, take a message. Write down the caller's name and phone number. Also, write the name of the person the message is for.
- Be polite. Always say *please* and *thank you*. Speak in a pleasant voice.

Practice

On a separate piece of paper, write the three things that are wrong with this phone conversation.

> Kim: Hello?
> Lou: Put Tai on the phone.
> Kim: Who's calling, please?
> Lou: Just get Tai.
> Kim: I'm sorry, he can't come to the phone. May I take a message?
> Lou: Never mind.

Apply

Work with a partner. Pretend your partner is calling you. Be polite. Offer to take a message. Then, pretend to call your partner.

HISTORY OF LANGUAGE

Names of States

You know that there are 50 states in the United States. Each state has a name, and each name has a story.

Many states have Native American names. The Chippewa Indian word for "great lake" is *michigama*. A variation of that word became the name of the only state that touches four great lakes, Michigan. Other states are named for the Native Americans who lived there. The Alibamu were a tribe who lived in what is now the state of Alabama.

Some states are named for people. Maryland is named for Queen Henrietta Maria of England. Washington is named for our first president.

A few states are named for how they look. In French, *vert* means "green" and *mont* means "mount", or "big hill." The green mountains impressed French settlers in what is now Vermont.

Activities

A. Find out how your state got its name. Use an encyclopedia or your history book for help.

B. Write each sentence, and fill in the blank with the correct state name from the box.

Alaska	Arizona	Florida	Kansas	Pennsylvania	Rhode Island

1. ____ is named for Sir William Penn.
2. ____ is famous for its flowers. Its name comes from the Spanish word *florido*, which means "flowery."
3. The Sioux word *kana* means "people of the south wind." It is the origin of the name of the state of ____.
4. ____ was described by an explorer as being about the size of the Greek island Rhodes.
5. Our largest state, ____, comes from the Aleutian word *Ala-a-ska*. It means "great land."

55

UNIT REVIEW

Personal Narratives   *(pages 19-23)*

1. Write three features that make the paragraph below a personal narrative.

   I took a nice canoe trip with my mother. It was the same week as my cousin's wedding. Every day, we went about 10 miles. One time, our canoe tipped over. Luckily, we were wearing life jackets, and our gear was in plastic bags.

Topic Sentence and Supporting Details   *(pages 26-29)*

Answer the questions about the paragraph above.

2. Write the topic sentence of the paragraph.

3. Rewrite the topic sentence to make it more interesting. Make sure it still makes sense in the paragraph.

4. Write the sentence that doesn't support the topic sentence.

Combining Sentences and Writing Sentences and Paragraphs   *(pages 32-35)*

Combine each pair of sentences below into one sentence. Then, write your new sentence.

5. Mom took me to the store. Dad took me to the store.

6. I looked in the window. I saw the perfect pet for me.

7. A rabbit wiggled its nose. A rabbit hopped in its cage.

8. My sister will love it. My brother will love it.

9. Correct the capitalization, end punctuation, and indentation in this paragraph.

   do you know what I did this weekend. I learned to ski Boy, was it fun I never liked winter before? now, it's my favorite season

What Is a Sentence?   *(pages 40-41)*

Write each group of words that is a complete thought. Add capital letters and end marks where they are needed.

10. some birds move fast

11. flies in the air

12. hawks soar in circles

13. large colorful birds

14. chases other small birds

15. many birds peck wood

16. other birds swim

17. hummingbirds fly backwards

Kinds of Sentences *(pages 42-43)*

Write whether each sentence is a *statement, question, command,* or *exclamation.*

18. What a good book Ty found!
19. Please bring the book to class.
20. Will you share the book?
21. The students like the pictures.
22. How tall the giraffe stands!
23. The crocodile swims nearby.
24. Look at that large animal!
25. Which picture do you like best?

Complete Subjects and Predicates *(pages 44-47)*

Write each sentence. Underline the complete subject.

26. Weavers make cloth from yarn.
27. Marie winds yarn on a large wooden loom.
28. One person dyes her own yarn.
29. Dark blue wool boils in a big pot.

Write each sentence. Underline the complete predicate.

30. The students measure the flour.
31. The teacher puts everything in the bowl.
32. Alice punches the dough.
33. The brown bread bakes.

Dictionary Skills *(pages 48-53)*

Write each group of words in alphabetical order. Underline the word that would appear on a dictionary page with the guide words shown.

34. north/note   nothing   nose   noon
35. cost/count   counter   cough   course
36. library/lift   lie   light   liar

Write the letter of the word that correctly completes each sentence.

37. Syllables are _____ of a word.
    a. parts   **b.** meanings   **c.** endings
38. The meaning of a word is the _____.
    a. example   **b.** definition   **c.** entry
39. A word with the same sound as the *u* in *cup* is _____.
    a. moon   **b.** pup   **c.** rule
40. A word with the same sound as the *ou* in *out* is _____.
    a. tour   **b.** famous   **c.** hour
41. A word with the same sound as the *i* in *ice* is _____.
    a. bite   **b.** sleigh   **c.** machine

UNIT 2

Writing Directions

◆

Nouns

What Do You Know?

"Where am I?"

Have you ever gotten lost because you had bad directions? When you go to a new place or visit a new friend, it's easy to get lost. When you get lost, you have a few choices. You can keep looking and hope that you'll find where you're going. You can look at a map if you have one, or you can ask someone for directions.

The root word for directions is *direct*. One meaning of *direct* is "show the way." Another meaning is "clear." To be useful, a set of directions must show the way clearly.

Thinking About Directions

Directions for getting from one place to another should have these features:

- They begin with the **starting point** and include the **destination**. The destination is the place where the person is going.
- They are divided into simple steps.
- The steps are arranged in the order in which they will be followed.
- Whenever possible, they include **landmarks** to make them easy to follow. A landmark is something familiar or easy to see, such as a red house or a flagpole.

Are good directions important? For the answer, take a quick look at American history. Columbus's voyage would have been easier if he had had clear directions to follow! Lewis and Clark found the first trail from the Midwest to the Pacific Ocean with the help of their guide, Sacajawea. She had directions from the elders in her tribe. Lewis and Clark then wrote good directions for others to follow.

Discussion

1. When have you followed directions to get someplace?
2. In what way did the directions help or confuse you?
3. What directions have you given to someone?

59

Reading Directions

Read this story about the Muldies, a pioneer family in Kansas. They have to spend their first winter in a dugout, a home dug into the ground. Then their father goes away to find a better home. He sends directions for his sons to follow.

Wagon Wheels
by
Barbara Brenner

Winter came. And that Kansas winter was mean. It snowed day after day. We could not hunt or fish. We had no more rabbit stew. No more fish fresh from the river. All we had was cornmeal mush to eat.

Then one day there was no more cornmeal. There was not a lick of food in the whole town of Nicodemus. And nothing left to burn for firewood.

Little Brother cried all the time—he was so cold and hungry. Daddy wrapped blankets around him.

"Hush, baby son," he said to him. "Try to sleep. Supply train will be coming soon."

But the supply train did not come. Not that day or the next.

On the third day we heard the sound of horses. Daddy looked out to see who it was. "Oh Lord!" he said. "Indians!"

We were so scared. We had all heard stories about Indians.

I tried to be brave. "I will get my gun, Daddy," I said.

But Daddy said, "Hold on, Johnny. Wait and see what they do."

We watched from the dugout. Everyone in Nicodemus was watching the Indians. First they made a circle. Then each Indian took something from his saddlebag and dropped it on the ground. The Indians turned and rode straight toward the dugouts. "Now they are coming for us!" Willie cried.

We raised our guns. But the Indians rode right past us and kept on going. We waited a long time to be sure they were gone. Then everyone ran out into the snow to see what the Indians had left.

It was FOOD!

Everyone talked at once.

"Look!"

"Fresh deer meat!"

"Dried beans and squash!"

"And bundles of sticks to keep our fires burning."

There was a feast in Nicodemus that night. But before we ate, Daddy said to us, "Johnny, Willie, Little Brother. I want you to remember this day. When someone says bad things about Indians, tell them the Osage Indians saved our lives in Nicodemus."

April went by. Then May and June. We hunted and fished and waited for a letter from Daddy.

Nothing came.

Then in July the post rider came with a letter for us. It said:

Dear Boys,

I have found fine free land near Solomon City. There is wood here to build a house, and good black dirt for growing corn and beans.

There is a map with this letter. The map shows where I am and where you are. Follow the map. Stay close to the Solomon River. Go through the woods. After the forest, keep going until you come to the deer trail. Turn left here. The trail goes uphill. On your right, halfway up the hill is our house.

You will find me. I know you can do it because you are my fine big boys.

Love to you all,
Daddy

The starting point and destination are given. The directions are divided into simple steps. The steps are in order.

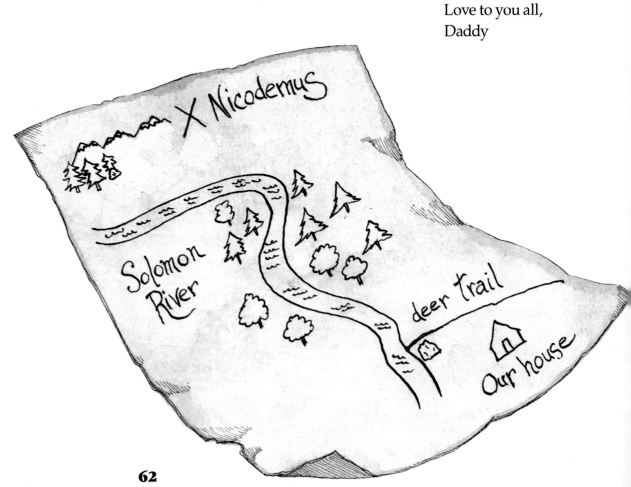

Understanding What You've Read

Answer the questions on a separate sheet of paper.

1. How did the Osage Indians save the lives of the settlers in Nicodemus, Kansas?
2. According to the directions, what should the boys do when they come to the end of the forest?
3. What are the steps in the directions Mr. Muldie sent?
4. What else could he have included to make them clearer?
5. What problems might the boys experience on the way to their new home?

Unit Assignment

Imagine there is a new person in your class. Your new classmate asks you for directions from school to somewhere in town. You will write directions to help your classmates. You will also see how another student writes directions.

Your **audience** is a classmate. Your **purpose** is to help your classmate get to where he or she wants to go.

Choose a Destination

You can write directions to the public library, the swimming pool, or anywhere else. It's your choice. Just make sure it's somewhere you can walk to from your school.

Observing and Taking Notes

Some children who are new to Mindy's school have asked her where the public library is. Mindy wants to give her new friends clear directions to the public library. To make sure she will give good directions, Mindy walks the path herself. She takes notes about where she turns and what landmarks she passes. Here are her notes.

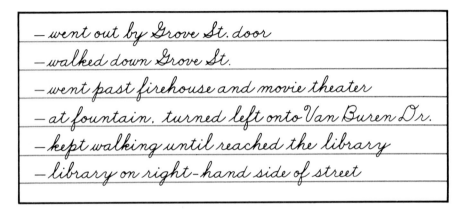

—went out by Grove St. door
—walked down Grove St.
—went past firehouse and movie theater
—at fountain, turned left onto Van Buren Dr.
—kept walking until reached the library
—library on right-hand side of street

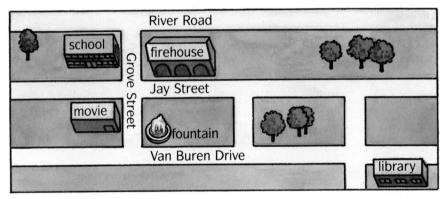

When you walk your path, taking notes, imagine that you are seeing it for the first time. Not everyone knows the places that are familiar to you. What do you need to know to get to where you want to go? Look carefully at the points where you need to make a decision. At these decision points you must note if you turn left or right. Which landmarks help you know how far to go? How far must you go before you reach the next landmark or turn? Write these details down in your notes. Later, the decision points on your path will become the steps in your directions.

Practice

A. The notes below tell about getting from Chad's house to the zoo, as shown on the map. Rewrite the notes so that they are correct. Add any decision points that are missing, and change any incorrect details.

—walked along Amber Ave. as far as the shoe store
—made a right turn onto Ellis St.
—at the radio tower, turned left onto First St.
—walked along First St. to zoo

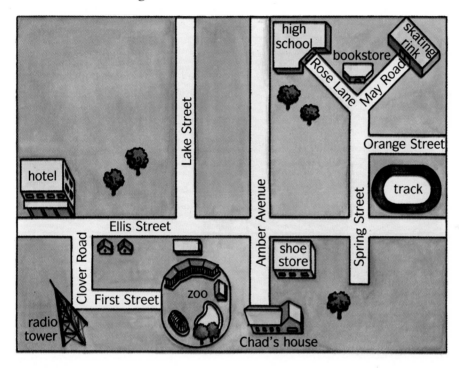

B. Use the map to take notes about getting from Chad's house to the skating rink.

Take Notes on Your Path

Walk from school to the destination you chose. Take notes on your decision points and on the landmarks you see. You do not have to use complete sentences. Be sure to include all information needed to make the directions clear. Save your notes to help you later.

Using Sequence Words

Mindy knows that the steps in directions should always be given in the order in which they are to be followed. **Sequence words** show order, or sequence. Mindy can use them to make the order easy to understand. *First* and *last* are sequence words. So are *next, then, after,* and *finally.*

Mindy wanted to see if order and sequence words really made a difference in giving directions. She gave her friend Kimi these directions.

> Turn left at the second stop sign.
> Leave school by the front door.
> Walk one block to the tennis court.
> Go right on Jay St.

Kimi was confused when she read them. So Mindy gave her this copy.

> Leave school by the front door.
> Go right on Jay St.
> Turn left at the second stop sign.
> Walk one block to the tennis court.

The directions made more sense once the steps were in order. Then, Mindy decided to make them even easier to read.

> First, leave school by the front door.
> Then, go right on Jay St.
> Next, turn left at the second stop sign.
> Finally walk one block to the tenns court.

Adding sequence words made these directions easier for Kimi to read and to follow.

Practice

A. Juana wrote these directions for getting from the library to her house. Underline the sequence words. Use the sequence words and logic to rewrite the directions in order.

    1. Next, go down Cook Lane until it crosses High St. near the park.

    2. Finally, go around to the back door at my house, 679 High St.

    3. First, turn left on Pueblo St. when you leave the library.

    4. Then, make a left onto High St. and walk uphill.

    5. Then, stay on Pueblo St. a few blocks until you reach Cook Lane.

B. Read the following directions. Fill in the blanks with correct sequence words, then read them again. Decide which way the directions are easier to understand.

    6. _____, turn right leaving my house, and walk two blocks.

    7. _____, turn left on Wyllis Ave.

    8. _____, go down Wyllis Ave. until you reach Vine St.

    9. _____, turn left on Vine St.

    10. _____, enter the green house on the left.

Put Your Notes in Order

Make sure the notes you took are in order. Add sequence words to make the order easier to understand. Save your notes to help you write your directions.

Writing a First Draft

Look at the map and the directions Mindy made to help her new friends find the library. Look for the mistakes she made.

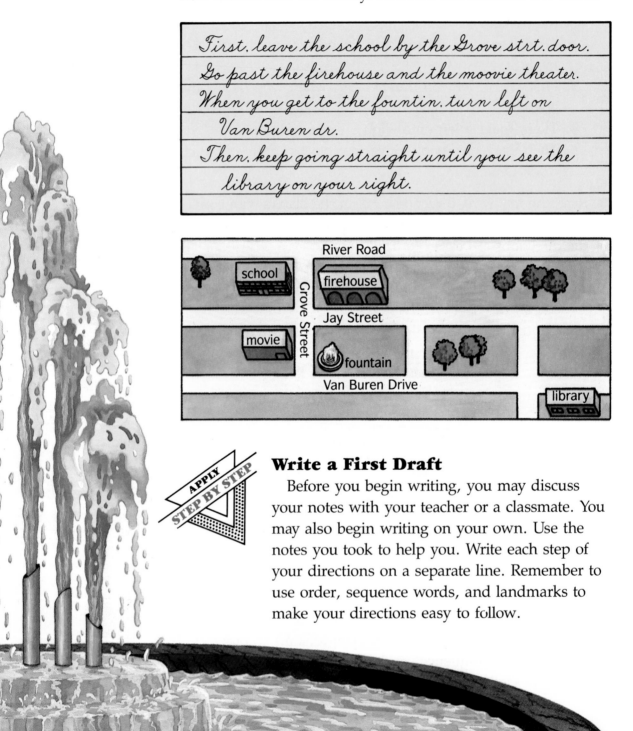

> First. leave the school by the Grove strt. door.
> Go past the firehouse and the moovie theater.
> When you get to the fountin. turn left on
>   Van Buren dr.
> Then. keep going straight until you see the
>   library on your right.

Map:
- River Road
- school
- firehouse
- Grove Street
- Jay Street
- movie
- fountain
- Van Buren Drive
- library

APPLY STEP BY STEP

Write a First Draft

Before you begin writing, you may discuss your notes with your teacher or a classmate. You may also begin writing on your own. Use the notes you took to help you. Write each step of your directions on a separate line. Remember to use order, sequence words, and landmarks to make your directions easy to follow.

Discussing a First Draft

When you finish your first draft, try to improve it. One way to find ideas is to discuss your work with a partner.

Discussion Strategy

When you are discussing your first draft, listen closely to your partner's ideas. For example, Mindy told her partner, Carmen, that she should include landmarks in her directions. Because Carmen listened closely to what Mindy said, she could correct a problem she hadn't noticed on her own.

Use the Content Checklist to discuss Mindy's directions with your class.

Content Checklist
- ✔ Do the directions begin with the starting point and end with the destination?
- ✔ Are the directions divided into simple steps?
- ✔ Are the steps arranged in the order in which they should be followed?
- ✔ Do the directions include landmarks that will make them easy to follow?

Discuss and Revise Your First Draft

To the Reader: Trade papers with a classmate. Imagine you are trying to follow the directions as you read them. Use the Content Checklist and the Discussion Strategy to discuss your partner's directions.

To the Writer: Listen closely to your partner's suggestions. Make any changes that will make your directions clearer or more complete.

Completeness of Information

In the last lesson, Mindy showed her partner that she left out some important information. Good directions include all the information necessary to get to a destination. Here is a list of what to include in directions.

1. Mention all turns, and say whether they are right or left turns.

> Incomplete: Leave the school and turn on Maple Street.
> Complete: Leave the school and turn left on Maple Street.

2. Mention the distance. Be as exact as possible.

> Incomplete: Stay on Maple Street.
> Complete: Stay on Maple Street for six blocks.

3. If possible, mention a landmark to make the direction clear.

> Incomplete: Go straight down Maple Street.
> Complete: Go straight down Maple Street past the bank.

4. If there is anything difficult about the directions, give a special tip to explain.

> Incomplete: Go into the stadium entrance.
> Complete: Go into the stadium entrance, which is behind the souvenir stand.

Read Mindy's revised draft.

Proofreading Marks
∧ add
⌇ take away

> First, leave the school by the Grove strt. door. *(turn right when you)*
> Go past the firehouse and the moovie theater.
> When you get to the fountin. turn left on Van Buren dr.
> Then, keep going straight until you see the *(for two blocks)* library on your right. The yellow door is the children's room.

Practice

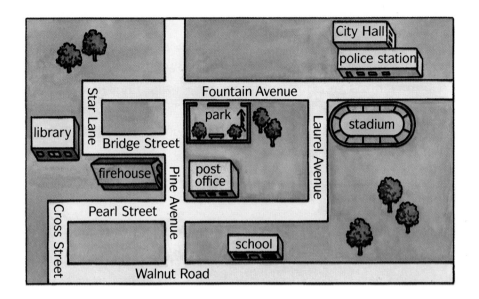

A. Use the map to make the directions complete. Mention if turns are left or right. Mention distance and landmarks. Explain anything that is difficult about the directions.

1. Leave the school and turn onto Walnut Road.

2. Go down Walnut Road and make a right onto Pine Avenue.

3. Go down Pine Avenue to Fountain Avenue.

4. Turn onto Fountain Avenue and go to City Hall.

B. Use the map to write directions from school to the library.

Revising Checklist
- ✔ Have I included all the characteristics of directions? (p. 59)
- ✔ Did I include all necessary information?

Revising Your Directions for Style

Make sure your directions are complete. Use the Revising Checklist to look for changes to make on your draft. Check your notes to be sure you included all necessary information.

71

Using Abbreviations

Are all my abbreviations right?

Mindy made one copy of her directions for each of her new classmates. To save time, she used abbreviations in her writing. Abbreviations are shortened forms of words. They save time and space in notes and directions. They aren't used in writing reports or stories. Always use standard abbreviations so that everyone will understand them.

Look at the rules for abbreviations that Mindy found.

Rule	Example
An abbreviation is a shortened form of a word. It ends with a period.	Sun. Mon. Tues. Wed. Thurs. Fri. Sat.
The abbreviation of a proper noun begins with a capital letter.	Jan. Feb. Mar. Apr. Aug. Sep. Oct. Nov. Dec.
Street names are often abbreviated in addresses and directions.	Main St. Lake Ave. Park Blvd. Ocean Rd.
Abbreviate ordinal numbers like first and second by using the numeral and an ending. Do not use a period.	1st 2nd 3rd 4th 8th 10th 21st 22nd 23rd 34th 39th 50th

BUSINESS HOURS:

Mon. 9:00 AM. to 5:30 P.
Tue. 9:00 AM. to 5:30 P
Wed. 9:00 AM. to 5:30 P
9:00 AM. to 8:00

Oct. 18

MEMOS

Soccer game
Sat., Nov.
10:30 a.

Practice

A. Look at the sentences below. Rewrite them using as many abbreviations as possible.

1. Sunday, February third—I went shopping on Main Street. It's the third block past the statue.
2. Friday, August twenty-first—My whole family is leaving tomorrow on the first flight to Pasadena.
3. Tuesday, August eighth—We went hiking on Bear Mountain, the second exit off the highway.
4. Thursday, November twenty-second—My mother's plane landed at 11:30. It was the first flight from Boston today.
5. Monday, December eighteenth—My parents celebrated their fifteenth anniversary by going to Paris.
6. Wednesday, January twelfth—We went skating at the Center Avenue Rink, near the Wilson Theater.

B. Correct the abbreviations on this list of events.

7. Mo., Sep. 1t—Recycling Day—Emma Lazarus Boule.
8. Tus., Ja. 15st—Flower Planting—Grand Av.
9. Wen., Octo. 9nth—Parade—Shore Ro.
10. Thrs., Ap. 2ond—Block Party—Burns Str.
11. Frid., Febr. 4rth—Fair—Green ST
12. Satur., Agst. 11h—SwimFest—Robert Aven.
13. Su., No. 1th—Costume Ball—Jane BVD

Proofreading Checklist
- ✔ Do all my sentences have correct end punctuation? (p. 34)
- ✔ Have I capitalized the first word in each sentence? (p. 34)
- ✔ Do all my sentences express complete thoughts?
- ✔ Have I used abbreviations correctly?

Proofreading Marks	
∧	add
⌇	take away
¶	indent
≡	capitalize
/	small letter
◯	check spelling
∼	transpose

Proofread Your Directions
Use the Proofreading Checklist to check your directions. Make sure you have used abbreviations correctly. Don't worry if your page is messy. Keep it to make a clean copy later.

Checking Spelling/Writing a Final Copy

Spelling Strategy

If you are unsure how to spell a word, use a dictionary. First, look up the spelling that you think is correct. If it is not listed, try another spelling. Check until you find the correct spelling in the dictionary.

Read Mindy's revised and proofread directions.

> *turn right when you*
> First, leave the school by the Grove ~~strt.~~ *St.* door.
> Go past the firehouse and the ~~moovie~~ *movie* theater.
> When you get to the ~~fountin~~ *fountain* turn left on
> Van Buren ~~dr.~~
> Then, keep going straight until you see the *for two blocks*
> library on your right. The yellow door is the
> children's room.

Check Your Spelling

Look for misspelled words in your directions. Correct them with the Proofreading Marks. Use the Spelling Strategy. Add the words you misspelled to your spelling log.

Write a Final Copy

Write a neat, final copy of your directions. Be sure to proofread your work. Keep your final copy.

APPLY STEP BY STEP

NO. 185
FIRE STATION

PUBLIC LIBRARY
OPEN DAILY

Sharing Your Directions

Speaking/Listening Strategy

When reading aloud, pay attention to your speed. Do not read too fast to be understood or so slowly that it's boring. When listening, you may take notes to remember details.

Choosing a Way to Share

Here are some ways to share your directions with your class.

Reading Aloud   Read your directions aloud to classmates. Read the directions carefully and clearly as if you were giving them to someone who had never been in your town. Do not give the destination. See if your classmates can guess where your directions lead.

Map Activity   Draw a map of your city on the chalkboard. As you read your directions, have a partner trace the route you are describing on the map. See if your partner ends up in the correct destination.

Bulletin Board   Place a map of your town on the bulletin board. Place the directions your classmates have written around the map. Try to follow each other's directions on the map.

Share Your Directions

Choose the way you prefer to share your directions. Present your directions to your class.

Add to Your Learning Log

Answer the questions in your learning log.

◆ How do I feel about the directions I wrote?
◆ What was the most fun about writing directions?
◆ Next time I write directions, what will I do differently?

The Literature Connection: Nouns

Writing often reflects the changes that take place over a period of time. A description of your town fifty years ago would be different from a description of your town today. People and places change; old buildings come down and new ones take their place. New roads and highways are paved. Some people move into town and others leave.

To show how things stay the same or change, writers may use nouns. **Nouns** are words that name persons, places, or things.

Sometimes, people or animals change their ways or live differently than others. One way to tell how they are different is to compare their lives.

The poem below compares a city mouse with a garden mouse. Although they may look the same, these creatures are very different. The poem shows their differences by comparing where they live and what they do.

The City Mouse
by
Christina Rossetti

The city mouse lives in a house;
    The garden mouse lives in a bower,
He's friendly with the frogs and toads,
    And sees the pretty plants in flower.

The city mouse eats bread and cheese;
    The garden mouse eats what he can;
We will not grudge him seeds and stalks.
    Poor little timid furry man.

Discussion

1. What nouns in the poem tell where the city mouse lives and where the garden mouse lives?
2. What nouns in the poem help tell about things that the city mouse and the garden mouse do?
3. Would you rather be a city mouse or a garden mouse? Tell why.

The Writing Connection: Nouns

Do you live in the city or the country? You can use many different nouns to write about where you live. In the poem, nouns show how the city mouse and the garden mouse are different. In the sentences below, nouns show some of the differences between life in the city and life in the country.

City people live in tall buildings.
Country people live in houses with one or two floors.

Where do you live?

Activity

Carlos lives in the city. Suzanne lives in the country. Look at the pictures above and think about where you live. Then write the sentences below. Use nouns to help you complete each sentence.

Carlos rides ____.
Suzanne rides ____.
I ride ____.
Carlos plays ____.
Suzanne plays ____.
I play ____.
Carlos buys food ____.
Suzanne grows food ____.
I get my food ____.

Nouns

A **noun** is a word that names a person, place, or thing.

A. Nouns give you names of all the people, places, and things around you. Many nouns name things you can see or touch.

Person	Place	Thing
worker	park	wheat
teacher	zoo	tools
doctor	town	tractor

B. A sentence can have more than one noun.

The <u>women</u> pick the <u>vegetables</u>.
New <u>machines</u> helped the <u>farmer</u>.
The <u>cows</u> and <u>horses</u> sleep in the <u>barn</u>.

Strategy

How can you be sure that a word is a noun? Ask these two questions. Can I see the thing it names? Can I touch the thing it names? If the answer is *yes*, the word is probably a noun.

Wow, I know a lot of nouns!

Check Your Understanding

A. Write the letter of the noun, or nouns, in each sentence.
1. A tall farmer stands nearby.
   a. A   **b.** tall   **c.** farmer   **d.** stands
2. The vegetables are ripe.
   a. The   **b.** vegetables   **c.** are   **d.** ripe

B. Write the letter of the noun, or nouns, in each sentence.
3. A horse pulls the plow.
   a. A, horse   **b.** horse, pulls   **c.** horse, plow
4. Farmers use many machines.
   a. Farmers, use   **b.** Farmers, machines
   c. many machines

Practice

A. Write each sentence. Underline the noun in each sentence.

    5. Farmers work hard.

    6. The children helped.

    7. Some farms were very large.

    8. The plow was heavy.

B. Write each sentence. Underline the nouns in each sentence.

    9. Horses helped the farmer.

  10. Neighbors traded crops.

  11. Women paid for clothes with vegetables.

  12. Tractors and trucks replaced horses.

C. Write each sentence. Underline the nouns in each sentence.

  13. Many farmers raise animals.

  14. The cows eat hay in the fields.

  15. The vegetables grow slowly.

  16. A tractor is very loud.

  17. Scientists study the soil in a laboratory.

  18. The animals sleep soundly.

  19. Children feed the pigs, horses, and chickens.

  20. The farmers grow fruit and vegetables for the people in the city.

Apply: Exploring Language

Write one sentence about farms. Use one noun that names a person. Use one noun that names a place. Use two nouns that name things. Read your sentence to the class.

Singular and Plural Nouns

A **singular noun** is a word that names one person, place, or thing. A **plural noun** is a word that names more than one person, place, or thing.

A. You can follow rules to make most singular nouns plural. Look at the end letters of the singular noun to decide which rule to use.

Singular Form	Rule	Example
most singular nouns	Add s.	block ⟶ block<u>s</u> bicycle ⟶ bicycle<u>s</u>
nouns ending with <u>s</u>, <u>ss</u>, <u>x</u>, <u>z</u>, <u>ch</u>, <u>sh</u>	Add es.	bo<u>x</u> ⟶ bo<u>xes</u> bu<u>sh</u> ⟶ bu<u>shes</u>
nouns ending with a <u>consonant</u> and <u>y</u>	Change <u>y</u> to <u>i</u> and add <u>es</u>.	famil<u>y</u> ⟶ famil<u>ies</u> cit<u>y</u> ⟶ cit<u>ies</u>
nouns ending with a <u>vowel</u> and <u>y</u>	Add s.	subwa<u>y</u> ⟶ subwa<u>ys</u> ke<u>y</u> ⟶ ke<u>ys</u>

B. Some nouns do not follow any rules for forming the plural. The following nouns have special plural forms.

child ⟶ children	mouse ⟶ mice
foot ⟶ feet	ox ⟶ oxen
goose ⟶ geese	tooth ⟶ teeth
man ⟶ men	woman ⟶ women

Strategy

There are a lot of rules to remember about forming plural nouns. But, there are many more nouns than rules. It's easier to remember the rules than the plural form of every noun you know.

Check Your Understanding

A. Write the letter of the correct plural of each underlined noun.

    1. <u>peach</u>   **a.** peachs   **b.** peachies   **c.** peaches

    2. <u>penny</u>   **a.** pennies   **b.** pennys   **c.** pennyes

B. Follow the directions for Check Your Understanding A.

    3. <u>tooth</u>   **a.** tooths   **b.** teeth   **c.** teeths

    4. <u>goose</u>   **a.** gooses   **b.** goose   **c.** geese

Practice

A. Write the plural form for each singular noun.

    5. tree   **8.** house   **11.** fox

    6. city   **9.** lunch   **12.** wish

    7. monkey   **10.** pencil   **13.** fly

B. Write the plural form for each singular noun.

    14. tooth   **16.** foot   **18.** goose

    15. woman   **17.** mouse   **19.** child

C. Write each sentence. Use the plural form of the noun in parentheses.

    20. The local store sold _____. (dish)

    21. Two _____ walked along the road. (ox)

    22. The farmer picked many _____. (cherry)

    23. The _____ pulled the wagon. (horse)

    24. People ride many _____ in the city. (taxi)

    25. _____ ride the bus to school. (Child)

    26. _____ worked in _____. (Man, factory)

    27. Small _____ grew into large _____. (town, city)

Apply: Learning Log

What part of this lesson did you find most difficult? Which rule will be the hardest to remember? In your learning log, write down a way to help yourself remember how to write the plural forms of nouns.

Common and Proper Nouns

A **common noun** is a word that names any person, place or thing. A **proper noun** is a word that names a particular person, place or thing.

A. A common noun begins with a small letter.

doctor   state   building

B. A proper noun always begins with a capital letter. Some proper nouns have more than one word. Each important word of a proper noun is capitalized. Don't capitalize short words such as *a, an, of,* and *the.*

Type	Common Nouns	Proper Nouns
person	girl	Dolores
	doctor	Doctor Sabin
	captain	Captain Magellan
place	city	New York City
	school	Hallen School
	country	United States of America
thing	ship	*Victoria*
	building	Empire State Building
	river	Hudson River

Strategy

Sometimes it is hard to tell if a noun that names a thing is a proper noun. If you aren't sure, ask yourself if the noun names something famous. If so, the noun is probably a proper noun.

common noun: a blue house
proper noun: The White House

Check Your Understanding

A. Write the letter of the common noun in each sentence.
1. The old ship sailed smoothly.
    a. old   **b.** ship   **c.** sailed   **d.** smoothly
2. The largest ocean was explored.
    a. The   **b.** largest   **c.** ocean   **d.** explored

B. Write the letter of the proper noun in each sentence.

   3. The sailors came from Spain.
       a. the   **b.** sailors   **c.** came   **d.** Spain
   4. King Charles paid for the ships.
       a. King Charles   **b.** paid   **c.** for   **d.** ships

Practice

A. Write each sentence. Underline the common nouns.

   5. Five ships sailed together.
   6. Strong storms came quickly.
   7. The sailors worked very hard.
   8. Dry land seemed far away.

B. Write each sentence. Capitalize the proper nouns.

   9. The ships left spain.
   10. magellan crossed many oceans.
   11. Two ships landed at the philippine islands.
   12. Later the ships sailed to the spice islands.

C. Write each sentence. Underline the common noun. Capitalize the proper nouns.

   13. Every ship had a captain.
   14. doctor oretega cared for the sailors.
   15. The victoria carried many sails.
   16. The san antonia sailed into the harbor.
   17. The men traveled across the indian ocean.
   18. magellan steered the ships very carefully.
   19. ferdinand magellan saw the shores of south america.
   20. The tip of africa is called the cape of good hope.

Apply: Work with a Group

Imagine that you and your group have written a play about exploring an unknown island. Your group needs to plan each scene of the play. Fill in the lists below to help you. Remember to capitalize all proper nouns.

Characters   **Place**   **Items Needed**

Possessives

A **possessive** is a word that tells who or what owns or has something.

A. Many nouns can be changed into possessives. Look at the underlined nouns in the chart below. Notice the possessive form for each.

Owner	What Is Owned	Possessive	What Is Owned
The girl	owns a bicycle.	the girl's	bicycle
The airplane	has wings.	the airplane's	wings
The park	has trees.	the park's	trees

B. Add 's to make most singular nouns possessive. (The ' mark is an apostrophe.)

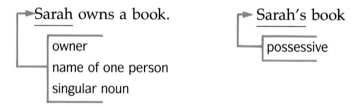

Sarah owns a book.
- owner
- name of one person
- singular noun

Sarah's book
- possessive

The pilot has a uniform.   the pilot's uniform
The building has windows.   the building's windows

Strategy

We use possessives all the time. When we talk, we don't have to worry about the apostrophe. But when we write, we must remember the apostrophe.

one owner + 's = possessive

Check Your Understanding

A. Write the letter of the correct possessive form.
  1. The man owns a boat.
    a. the boat's man   **b.** the man's boat
  2. The car has tires.
    a. the car's tires   **b.** the tires' car

B. Write the letter of the possessive for the noun in parentheses.

    3. The (pioneer) horses pulled the wagons.

        a. pioneers'   **b.** pioneer'   **c.** pioneeres   **d.** pioneer's

    4. (Fulton) steamboat sailed quickly.

        a. Fulton'   **b.** Fultons'   **c.** Fulton's   **d.** Fultons

Practice

A. Read each sentence. Write who or what is the owner and what is owned.

    5. The Eskimo has sleds.

    6. The emperor owns a chariot.

    7. The horse has a saddle.

    8. The man owns camels.

B. Write each sentence. Write the noun in parentheses as a possessive.

    9. The pioneers emptied the (wagon) cargo.

    10. (Starley) model changed bicycles.

    11. The (plane) engines needed fuel.

    12. The women fixed the (truck) roof.

C. Write the noun that names who or what owns or has something. Then write that word as a possessive.

    13. The sailor has a cabin. the _____ cabin

    14. The airport has runways. the _____ runways

    15. A boat has a compass. a _____ compass

    16. The girl has luggage. the _____ luggage

    17. A spaceship has computers. a _____ computers

    18. The conductor has keys. the _____ keys

    19. The passengers of the ship enjoyed the food. the _____ passengers

    20. People travel faster and farther with each new invention of a scientist. a _____ invention

Apply: Work with a Partner

    Invent your own machine for traveling. Draw a picture of your invention. Use five possessives to describe it. Here's an example: The machine's doors are round. Share your work with the class.

More About Possessives

A. A **plural possessive** shows that more than one person, place, or thing has or owns something.

Owner	What Is Owned	Possessive	What Is Owned
The <u>stores</u>	had telegraphs.	the <u>stores</u>'	telegraphs
The <u>girls</u>	own a telephone.	the <u>girls</u>'	telephone

If a plural noun ends in *s*, add an apostrophe (') to form the possessive.

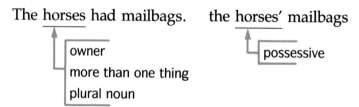

If a plural noun does *not* end in *s*, add *'s* to form the possessive.

The <u>children</u> own books.   the <u>children</u>'s books
the <u>men</u> have letters   the <u>men</u>'s letters

B. Remember to add *'s* to form the possessive of all singular nouns.

<u>Janice</u> owns a computer.   <u>Janice</u>'s computer
The <u>television</u> has wires.   the <u>television</u>'s wires

Strategy

People often get confused about when to add *'s* and when to add just an apostrophe (') to form the possessive. Always remember to add an *'s*, except for plural nouns that end in *s*.

Check Your Understanding

A. Write the letter of the correct possessive.
    1. The (pioneers) letters traveled by pony.
        a. pioneers   **b.** pioneer's   **c.** pioneers'

2. The (women) telegram arrived early.

    a. women's   **b.** women'   **c.** womens'

B. Write the letter of the correct possessive.

    3. (Tammy) typewriter prints clearly.

        a. Tammys'   **b.** Tammy's   **c.** Tammy'

    4. Students type on the (school) computers.

        a. school's   **b.** schools'   **c.** schools

Practice

A. Write the correct possessive for each item.

    5. The kings had messengers.

    6. The messengers owned horses.

    7. The men have a message.

    8. The cities have mailmen.

B. Write the correct possessive for each item.

    9. The telegraph has needles.

   10. Nina owns a radio.

   11. The letter has a stamp.

   12. The student owns a pen.

C. Write the noun in parentheses as a possessive.

   13. The cavemen painted on the (cave) walls.

   14. Few people understood the (men) drawings.

   15. The (train) mailbags hung on the hook.

   16. Scientists called (Marconi) radio a wireless.

   17. The (women) telephones rang constantly.

   18. The (children) computer plays many games.

   19. Many people still use (Samuel Morse) code.

   20. Today, different machines send (people) messages all over the world.

Apply: Test a Partner

Solve this riddle: My brothers' mother went to my father's father's house. Who went where? Write a riddle using possessives. Have a friend solve it.

Abbreviations

An **abbreviation** is a shortened form of a word. Many abbreviations begin with a capital letter and end with a period.

A. The chart below shows some common abbreviations.

Titles			
Mr. a married or unmarried man Ms. a married or unmarried woman		Mrs. a married woman Miss an unmarried woman Dr. a doctor	

Addresses		Time	
St. Street Blvd. Boulevard Ave. Avenue Rd. Road		a.m. midnight to noon (before noon) p.m. noon to midnight (after noon)	

DAYS						
Sun.	Mon.	Tues.	Wed.	Thurs.	Fri.	Sat.

MONTHS							
Jan. Feb. Mar. Apr. Aug. Sept. Oct. Nov. Dec. May, June, and July have no abbreviations.							

B. Here are some examples of how you would use abbreviations.

Titles	Dates	Addresses
Mr. Luis Garcia	Sat., Nov. 11	23 Highland Ave.
Dr. Julia Rand	Mon., Feb. 24	9 Saw Mill Rd.

Strategy

You may use abbreviations for days, months, and addresses for taking notes, labeling maps and charts, and addressing envelopes. You should *not* use these abbreviations when writing complete sentences in letters, reports, and stories. Abbreviations for titles and time are always used in writing.

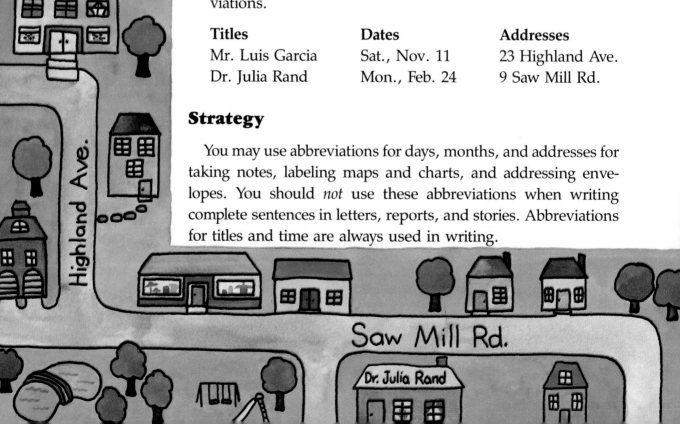

Check Your Understanding

A. Write the letter of the correct abbreviation.

   1. Doctor   **a.** dr.   **b.** Dr.   **c.** dr

   2. Boulevard   **a.** Boul.   **b.** Blvrd.   **c.** Blvd.

B. Write the letter of the correct abbreviation.

   3. a married or unmarried man

   a. mr. Samuels   **b.** Mr. Samuels   **c.** MR. Samuels

   4. Wednesday, August 31

   a. Wed., Aug. 31   **b.** Wed, Aug. 31

   c. Wed., Augt. 31

Practice

A. Write the abbreviated form of each item.

   5. noon to midnight   **8.** Avenue

   6. Sunday   **9.** Street

   7. September   **10.** midnight to noon

B. Write the abbreviated form of each item.

   11. Tuesday, October 12

   12. (a married woman) Ellen Thomas

   13. Hollow Road

   14. (a married or unmarried woman) Denise Sacks

C. Rewrite each item below in full or in abbreviated form.

Full Word	Abbreviated Form
Tuesday, December 16	_____
_____	Balsam Ave.
_____	Dr. Susan Sands
1:30 in the afternoon	_____
_____	Thurs., July 10
Monday, May 9	_____

Apply: Journal

   Keep a daily journal for one week. Write about something you did each day. Be sure to write the date. You may use abbreviations if you want to.

Compound Words

A **compound word** is a word made up of two smaller words.

A. Read the sentences below. Look at the underlined compound words. What two smaller words make up each compound word?

> The seeds grow into a blackberry bush.
> Flowers bloom in the sunlight.

B. You can figure out the meaning of a compound word if you know the meaning of the words that form it.

> A blackberry is a berry that is black.
> Sunlight is light from the sun.

What do you think these words mean?

> haystack   fishbowl   overflow

Strategy

If you aren't sure how to spell a compound word, think of the two smaller words that form it. Then, spell each smaller word. If you still aren't sure, look up the word in a dictionary.

Check Your Understanding

A. Write the letter of the compound word.
  1. Some plants grow with a lot of rainfall.
    a. some   **b.** plants   **c.** grow   **d.** rainfall
  2. A watermelon grows best in hot weather.
    a. watermelon   **b.** grows   **c.** hot   **d.** weather

B. Write the letter of the word that completes the sentence correctly.

    3. A flowerpot is a pot for _____.

        a. tulips   **b.** seeds   **c.** flowers   **d.** dirt

    4. A rainstorm is a storm with _____.

        a. thunder   **b.** rain   **c.** lightning   **d.** snow

Practice

A. Match each word with a word from the box below to form a compound word. Write the new word.

board	house	side	bush

    5. rose   **7.** green

    6. hill   **8.** chalk

B. Write each sentence. Write the word that completes the sentence.

    9. A bookstore is a _____ that sells books.

   10. Moonlight is _____ that comes from the moon.

   11. A farmhouse is a _____ on a farm.

   12. A horseshoe is a _____ for a horse.

C. Mixed Practice Write each sentence. Write the compound word that completes the sentence.

   13. A field full of corn is a _____.

   14. The ground where children play is called a _____.

   15. A berry that is blue is a _____.

   16. The time when people go to bed is called _____.

   17. A shell from the sea is called a _____.

   18. Work done at home is called _____.

   19. Corn that is popped is called _____.

   20. A tree that stays green forever is called an _____.

Apply: Work with a Partner

Write five compound words. Then, rewrite the words by mixing the smaller words to create "nonsense words." Trade papers with your partner. Unscramble the nonsense words to write the original compound words.

LANGUAGE IN ACTION

Taking Messages

You are home reading and the phone rings. You answer it. Identify yourself and speak politely. The person wants to speak to your father, but he's busy. Can you take a message correctly?

It's important to take complete messages. Everybody wants to get useful messages. Here's a good way to take a message.

- Listen carefully. You need to hear everything the person says. If you don't hear something, ask the caller to say it again.
- Read your message back to the caller to make sure you wrote down everything correctly.
- Be sure to write the following information:
    - the caller's name.
    - the name of the person the message is for.
    - the complete message.
    - the time of the call.
    - the caller's phone number.
    - who took the message.
- Write neatly. If a message can't be read, no one can use it.

Practice

On a separate piece of paper, write two things that are wrong with each of the following messages.

1. Dad —
   Mr. Okitsu called at 6:15. He called about the car.
2. LaToya called for Debbie. If you get in soon, call her, Tim.
3. David Olvado called. Call him back at 260-3784, Sue.

Apply

Work with a partner. Pretend to call your partner. Leave a message. Trade roles and take a message from your partner.

TEST TAKING

Studying for a Test

How you study for a test is as important as how you take it. With good study habits, you will find test-taking easier. Here are some ways to help you study better.

- First, know what the test will cover and the type of test it will be. When your teacher talks about the test, listen for special reminders and take notes.
- When you are ready to study, be sure you have all the books, notes, worksheets, and old tests that you will need to review for the test.
- Find a quiet place to work. Study at a desk or table. Be sure the area is well lit.
- Set aside a block of time when there won't be any interruptions. Allow yourself enough time to study. Don't wait until the last minute to study.
- Set up a good study system for yourself. Here are several different ways you can study:

  Reread the things that are being tested.
  Outline the main ideas as you study.
  Think of possible test questions and answers.

Practice

Answer the questions below.
1. What should you do when your teacher assigns a test?
2. What things do you need to study for a test?
3. Where should you study for a test?
4. When is the best time to study?

Apply

Learning Log   Decide what things from this lesson you found helpful. Write them in your learning log.

UNIT REVIEW

Writing Directions *(pages 59-63)*

1. Write three features of directions.

Using Sequence Words *(pages 66-67)*

2. Use the sequence words and logic to write these directions in order.

    a. Then, go down Maple Ave. three blocks until you see the post office.

    b. Finally, walk up Bank St. two blocks; the circus is on your left.

    c. First, leave the library and turn left on Maple Ave.

    d. Next, after you pass the post office, turn right on Bank St.

Completeness of Information and Using Abbreviations
(pages 70-73)

3. Use the map to complete the directions from Ray's house to the pool.

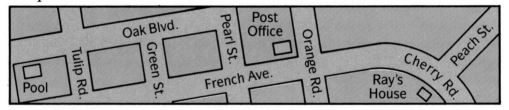

    First, take Cherry Rd. to French Ave. Turn off French Ave. and walk up to Oak Blvd. The pool is on the corner of Tulip Rd.

    Write each note below, using as many abbreviations as possible.

4. Monday, February sixteenth—No school, today is President's Day.

5. Friday, October thirty-first—I got a pumpkin on Robin Road.

6. Thursday, November twenty-second—parade on Fifth Avenue.

Nouns *(pages 78-79)*

Write each sentence. Underline the nouns in each sentence.

7. Scientists study the different wolves.

8. Some wolves live in forests.

9. These animals look like dogs.

10. Small pups live in a den.

11. The beautiful fur grows very thick.

12. Wolves hunt other animals for food.

Singular and Plural Nouns *(pages 80-81)*
Write the plural form for each singular noun.

13. man
14. ox
15. fin
16. valley
17. donkey
18. pony
19. ax
20. ash
21. child
22. goose
23. telephone
24. bus
25. glass
26. house
27. mouse
28. wrench

Common and Proper Nouns *(pages 82-83)*
Write each sentence. Underline the common nouns. Capitalize the proper nouns.

29. robert frost wrote many poems.
30. frost won a prize for poetry.
31. The poet studied at harvard college in massachusetts.
32. Today, students still read many of his poems.
33. Once, frost read a poem to honor president kennedy.
34. frost worked as a teacher in new england.

Possessives *(pages 84-87)*
Write each noun in parentheses as a possessive.

35. In 1867, people called Alaska (Seward) Icebox.
36. People find (bears) dens near the Arctic coast of Alaska.
37. Workers check the sled dogs on the (women) sleds at a big race.
38. The (student) family lives in Fairbanks.
39. A (penguin) wings paddle quickly through the water.
40. The (farmers) crops grow in Matanuska Valley.

Abbreviations *(pages 88-89)*
Write the abbreviated form of each item.

41. Doctor Leona Williams
42. Marigold Avenue
43. (a married woman) Luana Petrillo
44. Monday, December 12
45. (a married or unmarried man) José Diaz

Compound Words *(pages 90-91)*
Write each sentence and supply the missing compound word.

46. The yard in back of a house is called a _____.
47. A book used in school is called a _____.
48. The light we see during the day is called _____.
49. A flower that looks like the sun is called a _____.

MAKING ALL THE
CONNECTIONS

You and several classmates will now write a news article together. Use what you have learned about sequence to help you in your writing.

You will do the following in your news article:

♦ Tell about an interesting event.
♦ Answer *who*, *what*, *when*, *where*, *why*, and *how*.
♦ State the main idea of the paragraph in a topic sentence.
♦ Use detail sentences to tell about the event in order.

Reading a News Article

Read the following news article about how car racing changed in 1908. Notice the side notes that point out the features of a news article. After reading, discuss the article with your classmates. Then you will all write a news article together.

The topic sentence tells the main idea of the paragraph.
Details tell *who*, *what*, *when*, and *where* about the subject.

Details tell *why* and *how*.

In 1908 history was made when an American driver in an American car won the Vanderbilt Cup auto race for the first time. The winner of the race, held yearly on Long Island near New York City, was George Robertson. He drove a huge 120-horsepower Locomobile. Thousands of people watched the exciting contest. For over four hours Robertson led the other cars, averaging 64 miles an hour. Near the end he developed tire trouble and had to stop for repairs. Even so, he crossed the finish line first, reaching a speed of 102 miles an hour.

Speaking and Listening

Your teacher will assign you to a group. Choose a group leader. Talk about these questions.

1. In the news article you read on page 96, what information is given in the topic sentence?
2. What important details about the race did you learn from reading the article? Include details that tell *who, what, when, where, why,* and *how.*
3. What details about the race did you learn from the picture at the top of this page?
4. What part of the news article interested you most? Tell why.

Thinking

Brainstorming

Choose one person from your group to be a note taker. Have the person take notes as you discuss these questions. Save your notes.

1. What exciting school event, such as a race or game, have you watched? Give details that tell *who, what, when, where, why,* or *how* about the event.
2. What made the event so exciting to see?
3. If you could draw one picture of the event, exactly what would it show?

Organizing

When you gather information for a news article, it helps to put your details in a chart. Study the chart below. It shows details that were used to write the news article about the Vanderbilt Cup race.

Who	What	When
George Robertson	won the Vanderbilt Cup auto race	1908

Where	Why	How
Long Island, near New York City	stopped because of tire trouble	won by speeding to 102 mph.

With the rest of your group, discuss an exciting game or contest you once watched. Be sure to tell *who, what, when, where, why,* and *how.* Have one group member take notes and write them in a chart such as the one above.

Writing a News Article

Imagine that the members of your group were reporters at a school game or contest. The editor has asked for a news article about the event. You will use the chart of details you made to help write the news article together.

Planning

- Review the chart you made as a group. Add any new details you may think of now.
- Talk about the main idea of your paragraph.
- Then, talk about details you wish to include. Make sure they tell *who, what, when, where, why,* and *how.* Also make sure they tell about the event in a logical sequence.
- Organize your information in an outline. First write your main idea. Below it, list all your details in order.

Composing

♦ Work with your group to write your news article. Choose one member to write down the first draft. Everyone should suggest ideas.
♦ Decide exactly how to word the topic sentence of the paragraph.
♦ Next, decide exactly how to word each detail sentence.

Revising

♦ As a group, read over your news article sentence by sentence. Think of ways to improve the content.
♦ Check that your topic sentence states the main idea. Also check that your details are in a logical sequence.

Proofreading

With other members of your group, proofread your news article. Choose one group member to make the changes on your draft. Answer these questions:

♦ Does every sentence have a subject and a predicate?
♦ Does each sentence end with the correct punctuation?
♦ Are proper nouns capitalized correctly?
♦ Are all words spelled correctly?

Presenting

♦ Choose one group member to write a clean, final copy of your news article.
♦ Display your group's article on the bulletin board.

Cumulative Review

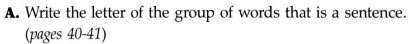

A. Write the letter of the group of words that is a sentence.
(*pages 40-41*)

1. **a.** Meg collects coins.
   b. Many old coins.
   c. Holds an 1865 coin.
2. **a.** Chinese coins.
   b. The Greeks made coins.
   c. The coins of China.
3. **a.** Meg visited a coin show.
   b. Displayed many rare coins.
   c. One very old coin.
4. **a.** Other kinds of metals.
   b. Discovered an old penny.
   c. The coin fell on the floor.

B. Write the letter of the word that names each kind of sentence.
(*pages 42-43*)

5. Put this record on the record player.
   a. exclamation **b.** statement **c.** command **d.** question
6. Did Mom take the records from the rack?
   a. exclamation **b.** statement **c.** command **d.** question
7. The record skips at that spot.
   a. exclamation **b.** statement **c.** command **d.** question

C. Write the letter of the sentence that has one line under the complete subject and two lines under the complete predicate. (*pages 44-47*)

8. **a.** Mars orbits the sun.
   b. The moon rises slowly.
   c. The ship passes Mars.
9. **a.** Two moons circle Mars.
   b. The rocket lands on Venus.
   c. Spaceships travel to the moon.

D. Write the letter of the group of words that is in alphabetical order.
(*pages 48-49*)

10. **a.** length, lemon, lend
    b. cabbage, cabin, cable
    c. couple, course, counter
11. **a.** dandelion, danger, dark
    b. titanic, title, tight
    c. statue, state, station

E. Write the letter of the word that would appear on a dictionary page with the guide words shown. (*pages 50-51*)

12. **elbow/elegant** **a.** elect **b.** eighty **c.** elevator
13. **racket/radio** **a.** radish **b.** radiator **c.** raccoon

F. Write the letter of the words that are nouns. (*pages 78-79*)

14. The fish swam quickly in the tank.

    a. the, fish   **b.** fish, quickly   **c.** fish, tank

15. Many small sea animals live in seashells.

    a. small, animals   **b.** animals, live   **c.** animals, seashells

16. Seaweed floated on top of the ocean.

    a. seaweed, ocean   **b.** seaweed, floated   **c.** floated, ocean

G. Write the letter of the correct plural noun. (*pages 80-81*)

17. The ____ in class 4A went on a picnic. (child)

    a. childs   **b.** childes   **c.** children

18. Rob brought apples, plums, and ____. (cherry)

    a. cherries   **b.** cherrys   **c.** cherryes

19. Trees and ____ grew in the picnic ground. (bush)

    a. bushs   **b.** bushies   **c.** bushes

20. Mrs. Mendez forgot the car ____. (key)

    a. keies   **b.** keys   **c.** keyes

H. Write the letter of the proper noun that is written correctly. (*pages 82-83*)

21. a. north Carolina   **b.** Miss stone   **c.** Pacific Ocean

22. a. Princess Anne   **b.** captain Smith   **c.** lake Erie

23. a. nile river   **b.** Doctor Rivera   **c.** Mary lee Burke

I. Write the letter of the correct possessive of each noun in parentheses. (*pages 84-87*)

24. The ____ trip to the desert began today. (men)

    a. man's   **b.** mens'   **c.** men's

25. Al followed the ____ footprints to a big rock. (lizards)

    a. lizard's   **b.** lizards's   **c.** lizards'

26. Lee mailed ____ photographs by mistake. (Greg)

    a. Greg's   **b.** Gregs'   **c.** Gregs

J. Write the letter of the abbreviation that is written correctly. (*pages 88-89*)

27. a. Dr Tony Sato   **b.** Mister. Al Vos   **c.** Miss Hall

28. a. 61 Beech Str.   **b.** 45 Rose Blvrd.   **c.** 693 Pine Ave.

29. a. Tues., Oct. 9   **b.** Thu., Mar. 7   **c.** Fri, Dec. 10

PART TWO

Solutions

For every problem under the sun
There is a remedy or there is none.
If there is one, go out and find it,
If there is none, then never mind it.

Traditional English Rhyme

◆

Some problems are easier to solve than others. Some solutions require special skills or abilities. In the next two units, think about how people—including yourself—solve the problems they face.

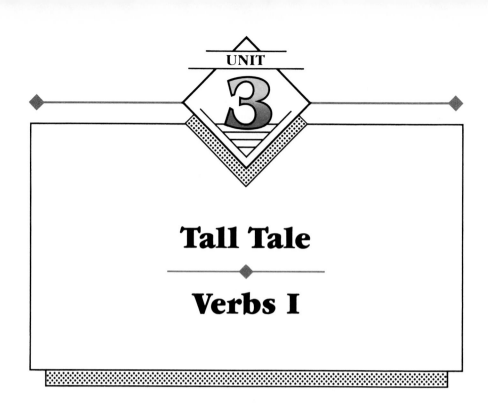

UNIT 3

Tall Tale

◆

Verbs I

What Do You Know?

Do you have any heroes? Who are they? What did they do to become heroes? Throughout history, people have written and told stories about their heroes. Some stories are about real heroes, such as Annie Oakley. Other stories are about make-believe heroes, such as King Arthur. Are your heroes real or make-believe?

A tall tale is a special kind of hero story. The heroes of tall tales are "larger than life." This means that they are bigger or stronger than real people. They solve problems in ways that are hard to believe or impossible. This makes tall tales fun to read. Perhaps you have heard or read tall tales about Pecos Bill, the cowboy, or John Henry, the railroad worker.

104

Thinking About Tall Tales

What is a Tall Tale?

A **tall tale** is a story that has these features:

♦ A larger-than-life, or superhuman, main character with a specific job.
♦ A problem that is solved in a funny way.
♦ Exaggerated details that describe things as greater than they are or could be.
♦ The characters use everyday language.

In America, tall tales were first told by settlers who made their homes in the American wilderness. In those days, before TV and movies, people depended on storytelling for entertainment. After a long day's work, people gathered to tell each other funny tales.

Different groups of workers—cowboys, loggers, railroad and steel workers—each had its own tall-tale hero. Having a superhuman hero with the same job somehow made their lives easier. Perhaps it gave them strength or courage to do their difficult and dangerous work.

Discussion

1. Name some stories you have read about real heroes.
2. Identify some stories with make-believe heroes.
3. In what stories did a larger-than-life hero do something impossible?

Reading a Tall Tale

Read this tall tale about Paul Bunyan, the lumberjack.

The Story of Paul Bunyan
by
Barbara Emberley

When this country was young most of it was one great forest stretching from the Atlantic to the Pacific. At that time, there lived mighty men who were twice as big and twice as strong as any men who have lived before or since. It was their job to cut down huge trees, chop them into logs, and send them down the river to be cut up into lumber. These men were called loggers, or lumberjacks.

As I said, the loggers were mighty men. But the mightiest, the biggest, and the strongest of them all was Paul Bunyan. A man so big, he used to comb his beard with an old pine tree he yanked right out of the ground.

Paul was strong. And you won't forget it when I tell you that he could squeeze water out of a boulder and drive stumps into the ground with his bare fists. It's a good thing that Paul was kind and gentle and would only pick on someone his own size. Paul used most of his strength for logging—like the time he dug himself a river to help move his logs.

Paul was cutting trees one morning up in Minnesota. He had to get them to the sawmill which was in New

Orleans. He decided the best way to do it would be by river—but there was no river. So Paul had a light lunch of: 19 pounds of sausage, 6 hams, 8 loaves of bread, and 231 flapjacks, and each flapjack was slathered with a pound of butter and a quart of maple syrup. It was a skimpy lunch for Paul but he figured on eating a hearty supper to make up for it. Paul dug his river that afternoon. He called it the Mississippi, which as far as I know, is what it is called to this day. Once it looked like Paul was going to be too *strong* for his own good. But it was being *smart* that saved him, and a good thing, too! Paul was clearing the state of Iowa for the farmers and he wanted to get done in time for them to plant their first crop of corn. But every time he would try to make his ax cut more than six or seven trees, the handle would break. So he wove a handle of tough swamp grass. It worked so well and cleared Iowa so quickly that he had time to clear Kansas, too. I think the farmers planted wheat in Kansas.

You'd think a man as big as Paul would be slow on his feet. Well, he wasn't. Why, even when he was an old man he could outrun his shadow in a fair race over flat ground, although he didn't give his shadow a head start as he did when he was in his prime.

Of course, Paul wasn't always so big. I've been told that when the twelve storks brought baby Paul to his mother in Kennebunkport, Maine, he didn't weigh more than 104 or 105 pounds. Forty-six pounds of that was his black curly beard.

Exaggerated detail

The main character is larger than life and has a specific job.

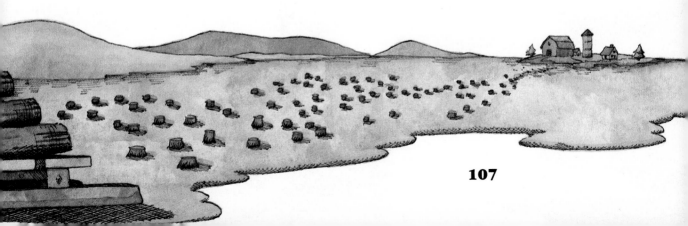

107

A problem is solved in a funny way.

Paul was a happy baby, but restless. Before he was more than a few weeks old he had flattened several acres of trees and a few barns with his playful kicking. So the folks around Kennebunkport built him a huge log cradle. Then they anchored him a few miles off shore. This delighted Paul, but his bouncing around caused such high waves that one of the biggest towns in Maine at that time, Boston, was washed out to sea. It floated down to Massachusetts, where it still is to this day.

When Paul was older he got hold of all the books that had ever been written. He took them up to a cave in Canada and read them. He had just finished the last book (it was about swamp grass and how tough it was)—when a snowflake blew into his cave and it was the most brilliant *blue* he had ever seen.

It snowed, and snowed, and snowed, covering everything with a blanket of blue. When it stopped snowing, Paul decided to take a walk. He was down by Niagara Falls when he noticed a big blue oxtail sticking out of the snow. And what should he find on the other end of the big blue oxtail but a big blue ox! The snow had turned that ox *blue* from head to toe.

108

Some folks say that when the blue snow melted it turned into those real blue lakes that we sometimes see—but then you can't believe everything you hear.

Paul carried the ox back to his cave to warm up and to give him some food. Paul called his ox Bébé, which is French-Canadian for *Baby*. "Babe" grew to be so big that he measured 42 ax-handles from brass-tipped horn to brass-tipped horn. Babe grew so heavy that he left hoof marks in solid rock. Babe and Paul became great friends.

Now that Paul had a great Blue Ox to help him, it was natural that he should decide to go logging. It was also natural that he had some of the biggest men who walked the woods working for him. Even the chore boy was twelve feet tall. Everyone picked on him because he was too little to fight back.

109

Paul's crew slept in a bunkhouse that was so tall it had a hinged chimney to let the sun go by. There was a chow hall so long that the waiters had to ride on horseback to get around. The flapjack griddle was so big, it took three sharp-eyed men four days to look across it. It took six men three days skating around it, with hog fat strapped to their shoes, to get it greased.

Paul put all these buildings on runners, hitched them up to Babe. They went back and forth across this great country clearing the land. They cleared the West so the cattle could graze. They cleared Kansas for wheat and Iowa for corn—just to mention a few states they worked in. They did such a good job of ridding this country of the Saugus, the Hodags, the Wampus, and the man-eating jackrabbits that you hardly ever hear of these anymore.

When Paul and Babe had finished their work, they went deep into the woods to take a good, long rest. And as far as anyone knows they are resting still.

Understanding What You've Read

Answer these questions about the story of Paul Bunyan.

1. How long did it take Paul to dig the Mississippi River?
2. Where does the story say Boston used to be?
3. How did Paul move the bunkhouse and other buildings?
4. What are some of the most exaggerated parts of the story?
5. What are some humorous solutions to problems in this tale?
6. Where are there samples of everyday language?
7. Explain how Paul Bunyan might have created the Grand Canyon.

Writing Assignment

Imagine that one day, when you get to school, everyone in your class is frowning. You are the only person who can still smile. It's up to you to teach the others to smile again. The only way you can do this is by telling a three-paragraph tall tale with exaggerated details. Your **audience** is your classmates, and your **purpose** is to make them laugh.

Choose a Main Character

Your **main character**, or hero, can be a well-known tall-tale hero or one you have made up. It's your choice!

Make one list of words that describe the hero you have chosen, and another about the hero's job. Save your work for the next lesson.

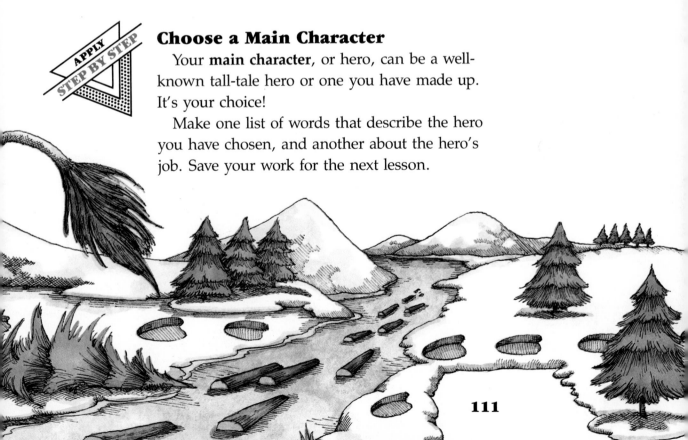

Making a Plot Outline

A student named Carlos decided to make up a character for his tall tale. The hero's name is Super Sally the firefighter. Now, Carlos has to make a plot outline for his story. A **plot outline** is a good way to plan what a story will be about. It shows the introduction, the problem, and the solution of the tale. There are different ways to make a plot outline.

Cartoon

Carlos used a cartoon to outline his plot. Each picture of his cartoon shows what will be in one paragraph of his tall tale.

Introduction **Problem** **Solution**

Plot List

Instead of a cartoon, Carlos could have made a plot list. His plot list might have looked like this.

Should I use a cartoon or a plot list to outline my tall tale?

Introduction: Sally is a little girl who dreams of fighting fires. She grows up to be Super Sally.
Problem: A building is on fire. There's no water in the hydrants.
Solution: The smoke makes Super Sally's eyes water. That puts the fire out.

Practice

Below are the plot outlines for three different tall tales. One part of each plot outline is missing. Supply the missing part of each outline. Draw a picture or write a sentence for your answer.

1. Introduction: (You supply this part).
        Problem: The gate opens and 20 cows escape.
        Solution: The cowboy lassoes all 20 cows at once with a gigantic rope.

2.

Introduction

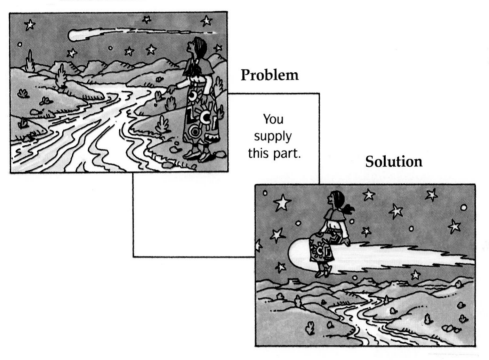

Problem

You supply this part.

Solution

3. Introduction: A family is riding in a covered wagon.
        Problem: The road is blocked by a giant, fallen tree.
        Solution: (You supply this part).

Make a Plot Outline

It will help you keep track of what will happen in each paragraph of your tall tale. Show the introduction, the problem, and the solution. Use a cartoon or a plot list. It's your choice! Keep it to help you later.

Using Exaggerated Language

Carlos chose a main character and outlined the plot of his tall tale. He knows that his tall tale also needs exaggerated language. *Exaggerated language* makes something sound bigger or greater than it actually is.

Carlos planned the details he would exaggerate in his story. He wanted to exaggerate the description of his main character, Super Sally. He also wanted to exaggerate her actions.

Carlos began by making an exaggeration triangle. The triangle started with a simple statement. Then the statement became more exaggerated each time he rewrote it.

1. Super Sally was very tall.
2. Super Sally was over **50** feet tall.
3. Super Sally was so tall she danced with the Statue of Liberty.
4. Super Sally was so tall she hung her hat on the moon.

Practice

A. Read each pair of statements. Write the statement that is more exaggerated.

   1. a. Paul Bunyan was a very powerful man.
   b. Paul Bunyan pulled up trees like carrots.
   2. a. Paul used a mountain for a pillow.
   b. Paul's head was very big.
   3. a. Paul could jump very far.
   b. Paul could jump across wide rivers.
   4. a. Paul's laughter could wake up people a mile away.
   b. Paul's laughter was louder than anybody else's.

B. Form an exaggeration triangle. Use this sentence as the first statement: *Paul's blue ox Babe was very heavy.* Then add two or more sentences that exaggerate Babe's weight in a colorful way. You may want to start your sentences like this:

   Babe was so heavy _____.

Make Two Exaggeration Triangles

Look at the lists of words you wrote to describe your hero and your hero's job. (p. 111) Use one word from each list in a sentence. Examples: *Strong—Super Sally was strong. Extinguish— She extinguished many fires.* Complete your triangles by exaggerating each sentence twice.

Writing a First Draft

Read Carlos's first draft. Look for his mistakes.

Super Sally Fights a Fire

Sally wanted to be a fire fighter. Everyone laughed because she was too small and week for such a hard job. Then Sally started to grow. She didn't stop until she was a hundred feet tall. Now, people called her Super Sally.

One day Super Sally visited the Statue of Liberty. She liked to visit her freind, the statue because she was the only hundred-foot person Sally knew. "Do you smell smoke" the statue asked. Super Sally said "something's burning" and ran to where the fire was. The firefighters were their. They had hooked up there hoses, but the hydrants were dry.

Smoke billowed from the fire. It made Super Sally's eyes water. At first, a trickle came from her eyes. The trickle turned into a stream that put out the fire.

Write Your First Draft
Use your description lists and exaggeration triangles to help you write your first draft. Include some conversation, and save your work.

REVISING
Discussing a First Draft

◆

Discussion Strategy

Before you point out something you *don't* like in your partner's work, first mention something that you *do* like. For example, Carlos's partner, Yoko, said, "I think that the way Super Sally put out the fire without even trying is very funny." Then she said, "I don't understand why the fire hydrants were dry. That part is sort of confusing." Carlos was much happier to listen to Yoko's suggestion once he knew that she liked parts of his work.

Use the Content Checklist to discuss Carlos's first draft with your class.

◆————————————————————————————————◆

Content Checklist

✔ Who is the hero, and what is the hero's job?
✔ What are the problem and solution in this tall tale?
✔ What examples of exaggeration and humor are given?

◆————————————————————————————————◆

Revise Your First Draft for Content

To the Reader: When you comment on your partner's work, remember to use the Discussion Strategy. Use the Content Checklist above to examine your partner's work.

To the Writer: Take notes on what your partner says so that you will be sure to remember everything. Remember that these are your partner's suggestions. You don't *have* to use them, but you should think about them carefully.

117

Adding Describing Words

In tall tales, the characters do things that are hard to believe. As a writer, you want to help your readers picture everything clearly. You can do this with **describing words**. There are two kinds of describing words. One kind tells about the people, places, or things in a story.

Read these sentences. Picture the scene in your mind.

> The worker swung his ax.
> The giant worker swung his ax.

How does the describing word help you to picture the scene? You may add several describing words to one sentence.

> The giant, friendly worker swung his sharp, shiny, ax.

Giant, friendly, sharp, and *shiny* are words that describe people or things. They come before the noun they describe.

Other describing words tell about actions. You can put them in different places in a sentence. Read these sentences.

> The oak tree fell.
> The oak tree fell suddenly. Suddenly, the oak tree fell.

You may add more than one word to describe an action.

> The oak tree fell suddenly, swiftly, and silently.

Suddenly, swiftly, and *silently* give readers a clear picture of what is happening.

Here is how Carlos revised the end of his tall tale.

Proofreading Marks	
∧	add
⸌	take away
/	small letter

Thick, black
Smoke billowed from the fire. It made
Super Sally's eyes water. At first, a tiny trickle
came slowly from her eyes. The trickle turned gradually
into a tremendous stream that put out the fire.

Practice

A. Add one or more describing words to tell more about each underlined word. Write your new sentence.

   1. This is a <u>story</u> about Pecos Bill.
   2. The <u>state</u> of Texas suffered from a lack of rain.
   3. The <u>people</u> needed water immediately.
   4. They told Pecos Bill about their <u>problem</u>.
   5. Soon, Pecos Bill came up with an <u>idea</u>.

B. Add one or more describing words to each underlined word. Write your new sentence.

   6. Bill <u>took</u> a long rope from his shack.
   7. He <u>lassoed</u> a hurricane near Mexico.
   8. Bill <u>pulled</u> the storm back to Texas.
   9. Pecos Bill <u>squeezed</u> the powerful hurricane.
   10. Rain <u>poured</u>, and the drought <u>ended</u>.

Revising Checklist
✔ Have I included all the characteristics of a tall tale? (p. 105)
✔ Can I combine like subjects or like predicates from two sentences into one sentence? (p. 32)
✔ Have I used describing words?

Revise Your Tall Tale for Style

Add describing words to tell more about the people, places, things, and actions in your tall tale. Use the Revising Checklist and the Proofreading Marks to make changes on your first draft. Save it to work with later.

Where can I add describing words?

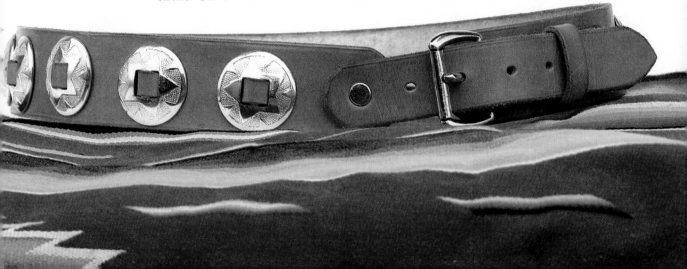

Punctuating Conversation

Carlos wasn't sure he wrote the conversation correctly in his tall tale. He found these rules for writing conversation. Next to each rule is an example from Carlos's revision.

Is the conversation in my tall tale written correctly?

Rule	Example
Use quotation marks around a speaker's exact words. Capitalize the first word of the quote.	Super Sally said, "Something's burning,"
Use a comma to separate the speaker's words from other words in the sentence.	Super Sally said, "Something's burning," and ran to where the fire was.
If the quotation is a question or an exclamation, use a question mark or exclamation mark instead of a comma at the end of a quote.	"Do you smell smoke?" the statue asked. "Hooray!" Super Sally has saved City Hall.
Put the period inside the quotation marks when the quote is a the end of the sentence.	Everyone said, "Thank you, Super Sally."
Indent to show that a different person is speaking.	"Do you smell smoke?" the statue asked. ⟶ Super Sally said, "Something's burning," and ran to where the fire was.

Practice

Write each sentence below. Add the correct capitalization and punctuation.

1. The loggers said look how many logs we've cut down
2. What are you going to do with them Paul Bunyan asked
3. We are in Minnesota, but the sawmill is 1,000 miles away in New Orleans he explained
4. The loggers said how foolish of us realizing the mistake
5. Can you help us get our logs to the mill they asked
6. Paul replied get me my shovel, please getting ready to dig
7. Look at Paul dig the loggers shouted excitedly
8. He's halfway to New Orleans already someone yelled
9. My ditch is all finished now said Paul that night
10. He added I think I'll call it the Mississippi River

Proofreading Checklist

✔ Have I capitalized the first word of each sentence? (p. 34)
✔ Have I used quotation marks and punctuation in quotes correctly?
✔ Have I spelled all plural nouns correctly?

Proofread Your Tall Tale

If your tall tale has no conversation, add some to make your characters seem more real. Then revise your tall tale using the Proofreading Checklist above. Don't worry if your page is messy right now. Keep it to work on later.

Proofreading Marks	
∧	add
⌀	take away
¶	indent
≡	capitalize
/	small letter
◯	check spelling
∼	transpose

Checking Spelling/Writing a Final Copy

Spelling Strategy

There are three ways to learn spelling. Find the way that works best for you.

- *Look* at the word. Picture the letters in your mind.
- *Say* the word aloud. Listen to the sounds.
- *Write* the word.

Read the last part of Carlos's revised and proofread tall tale.

Super Sally Fights a Fire

One day Super Sally visited the Statue of Liberty. She liked to visit her ~~freind~~ *friend*, the statue because she was the only hundred-foot person Sally knew. "Do you smell smoke," the statue asked. Super Sally said "something's burning" and ran to where the fire was. The firefighters were ~~their~~ *there* (SP). They had hooked up ~~there~~ *their* (SP) hoses, but the hydrants were dry.

Thick, black Smoke billowed from the fire. It made Super Sally's eyes water. At first, a *tiny* trickle came *slowly* from her eyes. The trickle turned into a *Tremendous* stream that put out the fire.

Check Your Spelling

Reread your first draft carefully, looking for spelling mistakes. Correct any spelling mistakes you find. Then, write a neat, final copy of your tall tale. Include your corrections.

Sharing Your Tall Tale

Listening/Speaking Strategy

Even if your story has imaginary events, read it as if everything were true. If you are part of the audience, close your eyes and imagine that you are listening to a radio program. Picture the characters and their activities in your mind.

Choosing a Way To Share

Here are ideas for ways to share your tall tale.

Reading Aloud   Read your tall tale to the class. Try to make them smile with your funny solution. As you read, you may use sound effects, such as a knock on the door or the wind blowing.

Presenting a News Show   Perform your tall tale as part of a TV news program. Read the story the way a news announcer would. Have other students act out the events while you "report" them.

Making a Class Reader   Collect other students' tall tales and arrange them in a book titled *The Tall Tale Reader*.

Share Your Tall Tale

Use the method above that is best for you. It's your choice!

Add to Your Learning Log

Answer these questions in your learning log.

♦ What am I most proud of about my tall tale?

♦ What did I like best about writing my tall tale?

♦ If I write another tall tale, how will I do it differently?

123

The Literature Connection: Verbs

How do you solve the problems you face? You may think about the problem by yourself, or you may discuss it with another person. Either way, you can share your solution with others by writing about it.

The solution to almost any problem usually involves some sort of action. If a stream of water is flooding the sidewalk, you may have to *leap* over the water or *step* around it to stay dry. Your solution involves an action you must take.

When writers want to describe action, they use verbs. **Verbs** are action words. They tell what someone or something does.

Without verbs, our writing would be stiff. It would be almost frozen. Nothing would move or change. Verbs give writers the ability to make things happen in poems and stories.

In the poem below, Fernando has a funny way of doing things. What is his solution to not having a basket for his ball? As you read, notice how the writer uses verbs to make Fernando's world seem real. You can almost hear the ball bounce!

Fernando
by
Marci Ridlon

Fernando has a basketball.
He tap, tap, taps it down the hall,
then leaps up high and shoots with care.
The fact a basket isn't there,
he totally dismisses.
He says he never misses.
My crazy friend Fernando.

Discussion

1. Which verbs name Fernando's actions in the poem?
2. What other verbs name actions you might do with a basketball?
3. Think of some verbs that tell how you would use another kind of ball, such as a basebell or soccer ball.

124

The Writing Connection: Verbs

In your own writing, you are in charge. You can choose verbs to tell about imaginary actions or real ones. Much of the action in the poem "Fernando" takes place inside Fernando's imagination. Here are other sentences that use verbs to describe a *real* basketball game.

> One player <u>races</u> across the court.
> Suddenly, another player <u>passes</u> the ball.

In your own writing, use verbs to describe actions that are real or imaginary.

Activity

The pictures above show Fernando playing in a real basketball game. Use the pictures to describe what is happening in the game. Complete the sentences below. The first sentence is provided as an example for you.

First, <u>the other player passes the ball.</u>

Then, Fernando ____.

Next, he ____.

After that, he ____.

The ball ____.

The crowd ____.

Action Verbs

An **action verb** is a word that tells what someone or something does.

A. Every sentence has a verb. Some action verbs are easy to find. They tell about actions we can see or do.

> Men <u>pour</u> the concrete.
> Workers <u>stacked</u> the bricks.

B. Some action verbs tell about actions we cannot see. They tell about who or what owns or has something.

> Builders <u>own</u> many tools.
> Workers <u>have</u> machines today.
> The women <u>had</u> bags of sand.

Strategy

When looking for an action verb, remember that some verbs tell about actions that cannot be seen.

Check Your Understanding

A. Write the letter of the action verb.
    1. Men used a wedge.
        a. men **b.** used **c.** a **d.** wedge
    2. Some workers dragged stones.
        a. Some **b.** workers **c.** dragged **d.** stones

B. Write the letter of the action verb.
    3. Builders had hard jobs long ago.
        a. Builders **b.** had **c.** hard **d.** jobs
    4. Today builders have many machines.
        a. Today **b.** builders **c.** have **d.** machines

Practice

A. Write each sentence. Underline the action verb.

5. Workers lifted heavy rocks.
6. Today machines dig large holes.
7. Bulldozers scrape the ground.
8. Trucks carry the dirt away quickly.

B. Write each sentence. Underline the action verb.

9. Workers have strong arms.
10. Each builder owns a hard hat.
11. A wheelbarrow has three wheels.
12. Builders own many kinds of shovels.

C. Mixed Practice   Write each sentence. Underline the action verb.

13. Workers carried bricks up a building.
14. A crane lifts heavy loads of bricks.
15. Builders had many problems before machines.
16. Steam shovels have large engines.
17. Women pull the levers in the machines.
18. A worker owns boots.
19. Workers like the new tools.
20. People want new buildings.

Apply: Test a Partner

Write all the action verbs you can think of in two minutes. Trade papers with a partner. How many verbs did your partner write? Are all of them action verbs?

127

Linking Verbs

A **linking verb** joins the subject of the sentence with a word or words in the predicate. A linking verb usually tells what the subject *is* or *is like*.

A. Read each sentence. See how the underlined linking verb joins the subject with the word in the predicate.

Children were sick. (*Were* joins *children* with *sick*.)

Medicine is helpful. (*Is* joins *medicine* with *helpful*.)

Most linking verbs are forms of the verb *be*. The chart shows when to use each form.

Main word of the subject	Form of *be*
I	am and was
singular noun, she, he, it	is and was
plural noun, you, we, they	are and were

B. Action verbs tell what the subject does. Linking verbs tell who or what the subject is or is like.

Scientists write about new cures.

action verb

They are hopeful.

linking verb

Hopeful describes *they;* so I know that *are* is a linking verb.

Strategy

Sometimes it is hard to tell if a verb is a linking verb. To be sure, look at the words in the predicate. If they *describe* the subject, the verb is probably a linking verb.

Check Your Understanding

A. Write the letter of the linking verb.
1. The hospitals were small long ago.
   a. The   **b.** hospitals   **c.** were   **d.** small
2. A cure is important.
   a. A   **b.** cure   **c.** is   **d.** important

B. Write the letter that names the underlined word.

3. Some diseases <u>are</u> dangerous.
   a. action verb   **b.** linking verb
4. Doctors <u>give</u> people medicine.
   a. action verb   **b.** linking verb

Practice

A. Write each sentence. Underline the linking verb.

5. Doctors' offices were small.
6. New machines were necessary.
7. The machines are very expensive.
8. A germ is invisible without a microscope.

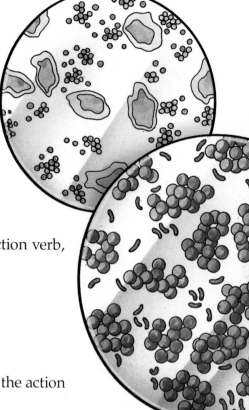

B. Write each sentence. If the underlined verb is an action verb, write *AV*. If the verb is a linking verb, write *LV*.

9. People <u>build</u> new hospitals.
10. Hospitals <u>are</u> important.
11. Computers <u>show</u> a person's heartbeat.
12. One hospital in Paris <u>is</u> very old.

C. Mixed Practice   Write each sentence. Underline the action verbs once and the linking verbs twice.

13. I am happy about the new hospital.
14. Few people went to the hospitals.
15. A doctor visited the people at home.
16. New hospitals are large.
17. An ambulance is loud.
18. Some doctors operate in the office.
19. Many doctors work and sleep in the hospital.
20. A nurse's job will be more difficult.

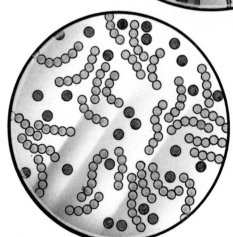

Apply: Work with a Group

Make a list of ten nouns. Make another list of ten words that can describe nouns. Work together and write ten sentences using a linking verb that links a noun with a word that describes it. Read your group's sentences to the class.

Present, Past, and Future Tenses

The **tense** of a verb tells when something happens.

A. A verb in the *present tense* tells about something that is happening now.

> The women <u>walk</u> to the boat.
> The boat <u>sails</u> across the river.

A verb in the *past tense* tells about something that already happened. Past tense verbs often end in *ed*.

> The women <u>walked</u> to the boat.
> The boat <u>sailed</u> across the river yesterday.

B. A verb in the *future tense* tells about something that will happen in the future. The word *will* is part of each future tense verb.

> The women <u>will walk</u> to the boat.
> The boat <u>will sail</u> across the river tomorrow.

Strategy

Look for clue words in a sentence to help you determine the tense of a verb. Words such as *today*, *yesterday*, and *tomorrow* tell you when something is happening.

Check Your Understanding

A. Write the letter of the tense of the underlined verb.
   1. Sailors <u>watched</u> the stars long ago.
      a. present   **b.** past
   2. A sailor <u>uses</u> a compass today.
      a. present   **b.** past

B. Write the letter of the tense of the underlined verb.
   3. The sailor <u>will fix</u> the compass.
      a. present   **b.** past   **c.** future
   4. The men <u>will take</u> the equipment on the trip tomorrow.
      a. present   **b.** past   **c.** future

Practice

A. Write each sentence. If the underlined verb is in the present tense, write *present*. If the verb is in the past tense, write *past*.

   5. Sailors <u>dropped</u> the anchors into the water.
   6. A machine <u>pulls</u> the anchor into the ship.
   7. A captain <u>talks</u> to people on land with a radio.
   8. Sailors <u>mapped</u> the ships' routes.

B. Write each sentence. Underline the verb. Write *present*, *past*, or *future* to tell the tense of the verb.

   9. Sailors will use better compasses next year.
   10. Shipbuilders will place radar equipment in ships.
   11. The needle on the compass will point north.
   12. Scientists will build new equipment for navigation.

C. Mixed Practice   Underline the verb. Write *present*, *past*, or *future* to tell the tense of the verb.

   13. Nathaniel Bowditch explained navigation methods.
   14. Matthew Maury charted the direction of winds long ago.
   15. A sailor sends radio signals to other ships.
   16. Computers will steer the ships.
   17. Scientists will experiment with new inventions.
   18. People used compasses with magnets long ago.
   19. Men attached a piece of metal to a straw in compasses.
   20. A computer receives and prints messages from other ships.

Apply: Journal

   Keep a daily journal for a week. Write about the things you do each day. Write about things you will do the next day. Remember to use the present, past, and future tenses when you write.

Making Subjects and Verbs Agree

The subject and the verb in the present tense must work together in a sentence. When they work together, they **agree**.

A. Notice how the verb works with a singular noun, and with *he, she, it*. Look at the chart.

Type of subject	Rule for verb	Example
singular noun and he, she, it	ends with s or es	The woman fixes the car. He rides the bus.

B. Notice how the verb works with a plural noun, and with *I, you, we, they*. Look at the chart.

Type of subject	Rule for verb	Example
plural noun and I, you, we, they	does not end with s or es	The women fix the car. They ride the bus.

Strategy

Sometimes it's hard to decide which form of the present tense verb is correct. Remember to look at the subject of the sentence. Is it a singular noun? Add *s* or *es* to the verb. Is it a plural noun? Don't add anything.

Check Your Understanding

A. Write the letter of the correct form of the verb.

1. An engineer ____ in oil fields.
   a. dig   **b.** digs
2. She ____ the water off.
   a. turns   **b.** turn

B. Write the letter of the correct form of the verb.

   3. We ____ the light bulbs.

     a. change   **b.** changes

   4. Store owners ____ the heat to low.

     a. switches   **b.** switch

Practice

A. Write each sentence, using the correct form of the verb.

   5. The Alaskan pipeline ____ oil. (carry, carries)

   6. A scientist ____ with energy. (experiments, experiment)

   7. She ____ about the results. (writes, write)

   8. A car ____ on gasoline. (run, runs)

B. Write each sentence, using the correct form of the verb.

   9. Children ____ about energy. (read, reads)

  10. Large machines ____ oil. (pump, pumps)

  11. They ____ a dam. (builds, build)

  12. Steam engines ____ coal. (burns, burn)

C. Mixed Practice   Write each sentence, using the correct form of the verb.

  13. Sunlight ____ many houses. (heats, heat)

  14. Machines ____ sunlight to energy. (change, changes)

  15. A mirror ____ the rays of the sun. (traps, trap)

  16. A windmill ____ the wind for energy. (catch, catches)

  17. Chemists ____ coal into gas. (turns, turn)

  18. We ____ wood for fire. (cuts, cut)

  19. Scientists ____ and ____ new types of energy. (research, researches); (study, studies)

  20. People ____ a lot of energy. (uses, use)

Apply: Work with a Partner

Write five incomplete sentences. Leave out the subject and use a verb in the present tense. Trade papers with a partner. Rewrite each sentence with a subject. Be sure the subject works with the verb.

Spelling Verbs

A. Many verbs in the **present tense** end with *s* or *es*. You can follow these rules to form the present tense of most verbs.

Present Tense

Type of Verb	Rule	Example
most verbs	add s	walk ⟶ walks
verbs ending with s, ss, ch, sh, x or z	add és	rush ⟶ rushes mix ⟶ mixes
verbs ending with y	change y to i and add es	carry ⟶ carries

B. Many verbs in the **past tense** end with *ed*. You can follow these rules to form the past tense of most verbs.

Past Tense

Type of Verb	Rule	Example
most verbs	add ed	walk ⟶ walked
verbs ending with e	drop the final e and add ed	use ⟶ used
verbs ending with a consonant + y	change y to i and add ed	carry ⟶ carried
verbs with one syllable; ending with consonant + vowel + consonant	double the final consonant; add ed	drop ⟶ dropped

Strategy

The rules to follow when adding *s* or *es* endings to verbs are like the rules for forming noun plurals. For example, you add *es* to nouns and verbs that end in *ch*. (bench⟶benches)

Check Your Understanding

A. Write the letter of the correctly spelled verb in the present tense.

   1. The child (watch) the railroad workers.

      a. watchess   **b.** watches   **c.** watchs

   2. A worker (carry) the iron and steel.

      a. carries   **b.** carrys   **c.** carryes

B. Write the letter of the correctly spelled verb in the past tense.

    3. Before the railroad, people (cross) the wilderness in wagons.

        a. crossd   **b.** crossed   **c.** crosed

    4. Men (use) the early railroads in coal mines.

        a. used   **b.** useed   **c.** usied

Practice

A. Write each sentence, using the correct form of the verb in the present tense.

    5. The passenger (hurry) to the train.

    6. A girl (push) the luggage.

    7. The conductor (toot) the horn.

    8. The government (supply) land.

B. Write each sentence, using the correct form of the verb in the past tense.

    9. People (chop) many trees for the tracks.

   10. Workers (arrive) from China.

   11. The men (chip) through the rocks.

   12. Dynamite (blast) the rocks.

C. Mixed Practice   Write each sentence. Write the underlined verb using the tense in parentheses.

   13. The workers map the train's routes. (past)

   14. A train carry many people. (present)

   15. Snow often bury the tracks. (present)

   16. An engineer fix the engine. (past)

   17. The conductor rush to the train. (present)

   18. The officials pound the Golden Spike. (past)

   19. Many people stop and watch the special event. (past)

   20. The girls play and ride on the train. (present)

Apply: Learning Log

What part of this lesson did you find most difficult? Which rule will be the hardest to remember? Think of a way to help yourself remember how to write the present and past tenses of verbs. Write your idea in your learning log.

Synonyms and Antonyms

A. Read the sentences below.

Ed examines the results. Ed studies the results.

Both sentences mean almost the same thing. The words *examines* and *studies* are synonyms.

Synonyms are words with the same or similar meanings.

Look at these pairs of synonyms.

little, small   observed, watched   windy, breezy

B. Read the sentences below.

She lost the book. She found the book.

The words *lost* and *found* are antonyms.

Antonyms are words with opposite meanings.

Look at these pairs of antonyms.

create, destroy   huge, tiny   all, none

Strategy

When you write, try not to use the same word over and over. Synonyms help make your writing more interesting. One synonym may give more information than another.

She was a good scientist. She was a skillful scientist.

Skillful is more exact than *good*. It tells us more about the scientist.

Check Your Understanding

A. Write the letter of the synonym for the underlined word.
1. Benjamin Banneker watched the tides and stars.
   a. observed   **b.** drew   **c.** ignored
2. He built a clock out of wood.
   a. saw   **b.** made   **c.** broke

136

B. Write the letter of the antonym of the underlined word.

   3. Luther Burbank worked with many different plants.
       a. same   **b.** new   **c.** strange

   4. He was always interested in plants.
       a. sometimes   **b.** once   **c.** never

Practice

A. Write each sentence using a synonym for the underlined word. Choose from the words in parentheses.

   5. Marie Curie looked for radium. (searched, found)
   6. The Nobel Committee picked Curie. (chose, gave)
   7. She won one of the first prizes. (oldest, earliest)
   8. Curie received two prizes. (awarded, got)

B. Write each sentence using an antonym for the underlined word. Choose from the words in parentheses.

   9. Edison's inventions made him rich. (old, poor)
   10. He often worked very long hours. (never, once)
   11. Morse invented the first telegraph. (last, new)
   12. His code is famous today. (welcome, unknown)

C. Mixed Practice Write the sentences. Write *synonym* or *antonym* to name each pair of underlined words.

   13. Some experiments are successes. Others are failures.
   14. All inventors and scientists make mistakes.
   15. Edison invented a light bulb. He created a phonograph.
   16. Charles Drew did experiments with blood. He conducted many experiments.
   17. Most puzzles and problems have solutions.
   18. We need cures for both common and rare diseases.
   19. Some scientists study illness. Their cures bring people back to health.
   20. Scientists look for explanations, solutions, and answers.

Apply: Exploring Language

Think of three synonyms. Write a sentence with one of the words. Then, write the sentence replacing the word with each synonym. Is the meaning of the sentence the same?

LANGUAGE IN ACTION

Holding a Conversation

People have conversations for many reasons. They might want to find out information. They might try to convince someone of something. They might just want the pleasure of talking to a friend. Here are some tips for holding a conversation.

- Listen. Pay attention to what the other person is saying. Think about what the person said.
- Don't interrupt. You wouldn't want someone to interrupt you, would you?
- Keep the conversation moving. Don't just repeat what someone else said. Don't suddenly change the subject.
- Ask questions. Questions show that you are interested in what the other person is saying. They also help you find out information. A good way to start a conversation is by asking a question.
- Give everyone a chance to speak. What you have to say may be interesting. Other people have interesting things to say, too.

Practice

On a separate piece of paper, answer the following questions.

1. What are some reasons for a conversation?
2. What is a good way to start a conversation?
3. What should you do while someone else is speaking?
4. Is it OK to interrupt someone if you have something interesting to say?
5. Should you ask questions during a conversation?

Apply

For this activity, you will work in groups of three. Have a conversation with your partners. You may pretend to be someone else, or you may speak as yourself.

HISTORY OF LANGUAGE

Braille

Reading a good book is something that we all enjoy. Most of us can see the words on the page. Blind people read by feeling the words. They use braille, a reading system of raised dots.

Braille was invented by a fifteen-year-old, blind, French boy named Louis Braille. He based his system on a code that French soldiers used to send secret messages.

Braille letters are punched onto a page. To read each letter, a person runs his or her fingers over the raised dots. Today, there are machines that print books, newspapers, and magazines in braille. Wristwatches, elevator buttons, and other things we use every day are made with braille numbers. Some blind musicians have special machines that write music in braille.

Here is the braille alphabet.

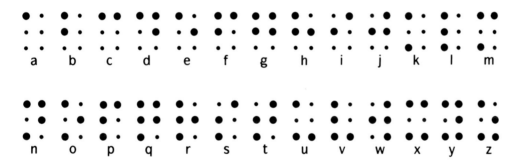

Activity

Use the braille alphabet above to translate the braille words into English and the English words into braille.

1. **2.** **3.**

4. ball   **5.** fruit   **6.** shoe

UNIT REVIEW

Tall Tale   *(pages 105-111)*

1. Read this story. Write three features that make it a tall tale.

   Golden Gus was the best miner in San Francisco. The people there wanted a golden bridge for their beautiful city, but there wasn't enough gold. One day, Golden Gus dug so deep that he came out in China. He sailed home in a ship made of the gold from his mine. With the leftover gold, he built the Golden Gate Bridge.

Using Exaggerated Language   *(pages 114-115)*

Make three exaggeration triangles. Exaggerate each sentence twice.

2. The sun was very hot.

3. Golden Gus dug very fast.

4. Farmer Fran's corn was taller than anybody's.

Adding Describing Words and Punctuating Conversation
(pages 118-121)

Add a word to describe each underlined word. Write your new sentences.

5. Golden Gus was a <u>miner</u>.   **7.** Farmer Fran raised <u>cattle</u>.

6. He dug a <u>tunnel</u> to China.   **8.** She <u>worked</u> on her farm every day.

Rewrite the conversation below. Add correct capitalization and punctuation.

9. Farmer Fran said "a big storm is coming.

10. "Can you do anything, Farmer Fran " the neighbors asked.

11. I don't know, but I can try" Farmer Fran answered.

12. Everyone said, "thank you, Farmer Fran, when she brushed the storm away.

Action Verbs and Linking Verbs   *(pages 126-129)*

Write each sentence. Underline the verb. Then write *action verb* or *linking verb* to name each verb.

13. Llamas work as pack animals in South America.

14. Llamas were pack animals hundreds of years ago.

15. A llama is very strong.

16. The animal carries heavy loads through the mountains.

Present, Past, and Future Tenses   *(pages 130-131)*

Write the sentences. Underline the verbs. Write *present*, *past*, or *future* to tell the tense of each verb.

17. Alice reads *Little House on the Prairie.*

18. The class will read the *Little House* books next week.

19. The books tell of the pioneer childhood of Laura Ingalls Wilder.

20. Laura's family moved west over 100 years ago.

21. The family started new farms in several places.

22. The books will teach the class many things about pioneers.

Making Subjects and Verbs Agree   *(pages 132-133)*

Write each sentence, using the correct form of the verb.

23. Meg ____ a movie. (watch, watches)

24. The next day some friends ____ about it. (ask, asks)

25. Meg never ____ the name of the movie. (say, says)

26. Instead, Meg ____ the story of the movie. (tell, tells)

27. Stephen ____ the name of the movie first. (guess, guesses)

28. The next day, all the children ____ the movie. (see, sees)

29. Meg ____ it again with the others. (enjoy, enjoys)

Spelling Verbs   *(pages 134-135)*

Write each sentence. Write the underlined verb, using the tense in parentheses.

30. The children paint pictures in class. (present)

31. Ms. Ky teach the class something new every day. (present)

32. Yesterday the class try a new kind of paint. (past)

33. Alan use just two colors in the picture. (past)

34. Ms. Ky step over to his painting. (past)

35. Now the painting hang on the classroom wall. (present)

Synonyms and Antonyms   *(pages 136-137)*

Write the sentences. Write *synonym* or *antonym* to name each pair of underlined words.

36. Life is not easy on a farm. Everyone does hard work.

37. Farm families must finish many chores and duties each day.

38. Farmers use machines frequently. Machines often make work easier.

39. Many farmers harvest grain in the fall. Others gather fruits.

40. Farmers of the future will learn from farm life of the past.

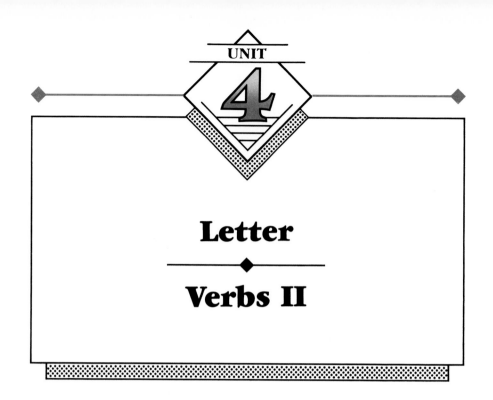

UNIT 4

Letter

◆

Verbs II

What Do You Know?

"Is there any mail for me?"

Do you often wonder about that when you look in the mailbox? Why is it that getting cards, letters, and postcards is so much fun? An exchange of letters, called a correspondence, can be like a written conversation between friends.

Letters help you keep in touch with friends and relatives. With a pen pal, letters can even help you make a new friend. Friendly letters are a good way to share thoughts and events, or just to say *Hi*. Letters can help solve the problem of homesickness for someone away from home.

142

Thinking About Letters

What Is a Letter?

A friendly letter has these features:

◆ It contains news and helps you stay in touch with a friend or relative.
◆ It can respond to news or questions the other person sent you.
◆ It is written in everyday language.
◆ It has five parts: a heading, a greeting, a body, a closing, and a signature.

Ever since people learned how to write, they have written letters to each other. Before telephones and telegraphs, letters were the only way to share information with people far away. Before there were post offices, people counted on travelers or messengers to carry mail. The Pony Express was a famous American mail service. Its riders carried mail on horseback from Missouri to California, changing horses every 10 miles.

Today, letter writing is still very important. Unlike a phone call, a letter is permanent. You can keep it and reread it to check information. Sending a letter is less expensive than making a long-distance phone call. Sometimes, when you make a phone call, nobody's home. A letter will wait for someone to come home.

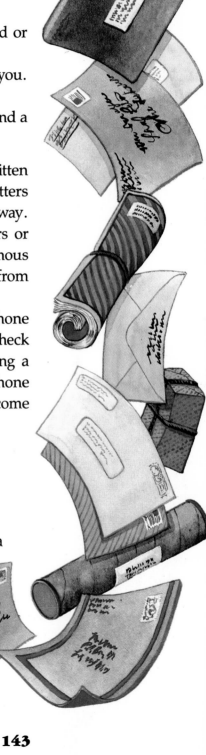

Discussion

1. What kind of mail have you gotten recently?
2. What letters have you sent?
3. When would it be better to send a letter than to make a phone call?

Reading a Letter

Read this letter a girl named Abby wrote to her parents from summer camp.

Summer Challenge
by
Jane O'Connor

The heading is only the date. Abby's parents know her address.

August 15

Greeting

Dear Ma and Daddy,

The writer shares news with her relatives.

Body

The letter is written in everyday language.

Guess what? You'll never guess!

I dived (dove? who cares!) All I know is I did it!

For almost the whole period I was jumping in, just like always. Then one time I was standing on the end of the board, trying really hard to get up the nerve to dive. Roberta kept yelling good luck and telling me how I shouldn't be scared. I turned around to tell her to shut up. That's when I lost my balance. All I remember is crouching my head down cause I was afraid I was going to hurt myself.

The next thing, Roberta is jumping up and down on the dock and Laurel is giving me the V for victory sign. It was all an accident! But once I did one dive, I could do it again and again. Keep your fingers crossed that I pass.

Closing

Love,

Signature

Abby

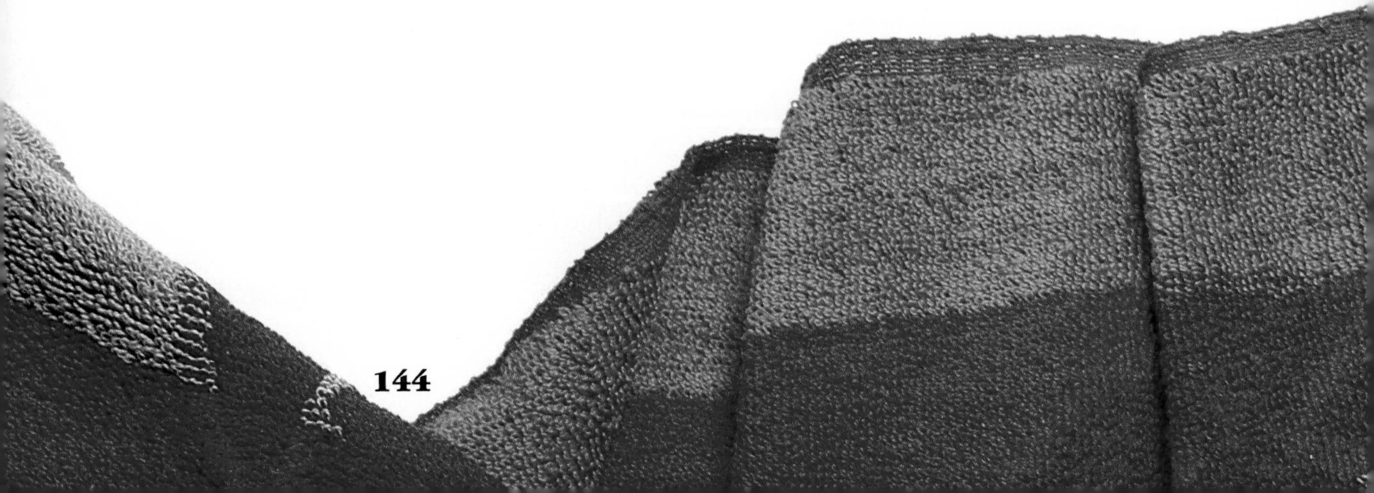

Understanding What You've Read

Answer the questions about Abby's letter.

1. Whom did Abby write to?
2. Who told Abby that she shouldn't be scared?
3. What is the news in Abby's letter?
4. What is unusual about her news?
5. Give at least two examples of everyday language.
6. Do you think Abby is having a good time at summer camp? Explain why you think so.

Writing Assignment

Someone opens the mailbox every day and says, "I hope there's something for me!" In this unit, you'll write a friendly letter and make that wish come true. You will also see how Thomas, another student, writes a letter.

Your **purpose** for writing will be to share news. Your **audience** will be a friend, a pen pal, or a relative.

Choose an Audience

You can write to a friend, a relative, or a pen pal. It's your choice. Make sure you spell the person's name and address correctly. If you don't know the address, look it up. Write down the name and address of the person to whom you are writing. Save this information for later.

Planning a Friendly Letter

Read this friendly letter that Thomas got from his friend Clayton. Notice the different parts of the letter, what they contain, and where they appear. Also notice the use of everyday language in the letter.

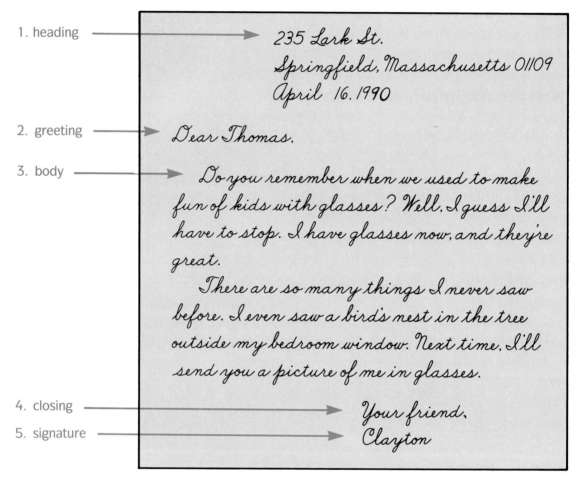

1. heading

2. greeting

3. body

4. closing

5. signature

235 Lark St.
Springfield, Massachusetts 01109
April 16, 1990

Dear Thomas,

    Do you remember when we used to make fun of kids with glasses? Well, I guess I'll have to stop. I have glasses now, and they're great.
    There are so many things I never saw before. I even saw a bird's nest in the tree outside my bedroom window. Next time, I'll send you a picture of me in glasses.

Your friend,
Clayton

1. The **heading** usually includes the writer's address, and always includes the date the letter was written.
2. The **greeting** is the word *Dear* and the name of the person receiving the letter. It ends with a comma.
3. The **body** includes all of the information the writer wants to send, including any replies to a letter the writer received.
4. The **closing** finishes the letter and ends with a comma.
5. The **signature** is the writer's written or typed name.

Practice

A. Rewrite the letter, putting the parts in the correct order.

1. Dear Masako,
2. 1212 Green Street
   Boulder, Colorado 80111
   April 27, 1989
3. Love,
4.   It was great to hear from you after almost a year. Thanks for sending me your new address. I promise to try to write more often. Will you be at camp this year?
5. Ana

B. Read this letter. Answer the questions below.

> 910 River Road
> Cusick, Washington 99119

Ana,

   What a fast answer! I'm not going to camp this year, but my parents said you can stay with us. Ask your parents if it's okay. It's so much fun here. We have apple and cherry trees right in the backyard. I never picked fruit straight from the tree before. Write back soon.

> Love,

6. What else should be in the heading?
7. What is wrong with the greeting?
8. What is missing at the end of the letter?

Plan Your Letter

   Decide what news to put in your letter. Your journal is a good place to look for ideas. Write about things that will interest the other person. Take notes about what you want to say, and keep them with your notes from the last lesson. Think about your closing. Will you use *Love, Your friend*, or something else? It's your choice.

Addressing an Envelope

The envelope is an important part of sending a letter. It must be addressed correctly. Otherwise, your letter will not reach its destination. The correct way to write an address is on three lines. Line 1 is the person's full name. Line 2 is the street address, which may include an apartment number. Line 3 is the city, the state or postal abbreviation, and the Zip code.

Here is the envelope of the letter that Thomas will send to Clayton. Both addresses on it are on three lines.

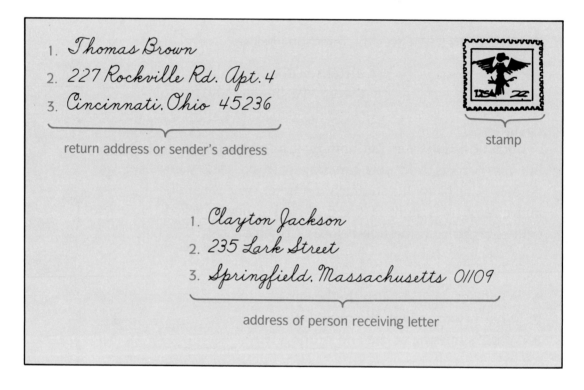

1. Thomas Brown
2. 227 Rockville Rd. Apt. 4
3. Cincinnati, Ohio 45236

return address or sender's address

stamp

1. Clayton Jackson
2. 235 Lark Street
3. Springfield, Massachusetts 01109

address of person receiving letter

Clayton's name and address are in the center of the envelope. Thomas wrote his own name and address in the upper left hand corner. This is called the return address. It tells the post office where to return the letter if it cannot be delivered. Notice that both addresses have Zip codes. Zip codes are very important in helping the post office deliver the letter. Of course, Thomas put a stamp in the upper right-hand corner of his envelope.

The full list of state postal abbreviations is on the next page.

148

Practice

A. Before Dawn Lawson mails a letter to her cousin Charlene Davis, she double-checks the envelope. Answer the questions below about Dawn's envelope.

Dawn Lawson
Smithtown, NY 11787

         Charlene Davis
         654 West Street
         La Crosse, Wisconsin

1. What is missing from Dawn's return address?
2. What is missing from Charlene's address?

B. Draw an envelope for the letter described below.
   Jaime Velez sent a letter to his friend Karen Taylor. Karen lives at 3411 Central Avenue, Akron, Ohio, 44313. Jaime's address is 245 Grant Street, San Francisco, California, 94120.

States

Alabama. . . . . . AL	Idaho . . . . ID	Missouri. . . . . . MO	Pennsylvania . . PA
Alaska . . . . AK	Illinois IL	Montana . . . . . MT	Rhode Island . . RI
Arizona . . . . . . AZ	Indiana. . . . . . IN	Nebraska . . . . . NE	South Carolina . SC
Arkansas . . . . . AR	Iowa. . . . . IA	Nevada . . . . . . NV	South Dakota . . SD
California . . . . CA	Kansas. . . . . . . KS	New Hampshire NH	Tennessee . . . . TN
Colorado . . . . CO	Kentucky . . . . KY	New Jersey . . . NJ	Texas . . . . TX
Connecticut . . . CT	Louisiana . . . . . LA	New Mexico. . . NM	Utah. . . . . UT
Delaware . . . . . DE	Maine . . . . ME	New York . . . . . NY	Vermont. . . . . . VT
District of	Maryland . . . . . MD	North Carolina . NC	Virginia. . . . . . . VA
Columbia . . . . DC	Massachusetts . MA	North Dakota. . ND	Washington . . . WA
Florida . . . . FL	Michigan . . . . . MI	Ohio. . . . . OH	West Virginia . . WV
Georgia . . . . . . GA	Minnesota . . . . MN	Oklahoma . . . . OK	Wisconsin. . . . . WI
Hawaii . . . . HI	Mississippi . . . . MS	Oregon . . . . . . OR	Wyoming . . . . . WY

Address Your Envelope
   Get an envelope. Put the address of the person you're writing to in the middle. Put your address in the top, left corner. Put a stamp in the top, right corner. Use the list on this page for state abbreviations. Don't lose this envelope. You'll need it to mail your letter.

Writing a First Draft

Here is the first draft of Thomas's answer to Clayton's letter. Remember it's only a first draft. It probably has some mistakes.

---

227 Rockville Rd. Apt. 4
Cincinnati Ohio 45236

Dear Clayton,

   This is amazing. I can't beleeve you just got new glasses. So did I!
   My glasses help when I play softball. They make reading easier, too. My glasses change the way I see the world. There's just one bad thing about waring glasses. Now I can see what a mess my room is.
   I can't wate to get your picture. I'll try to send you one, too.

               your friend
               Thomas

Write Your First Draft

♦ Start with the heading. Include your full address and the date.
♦ Then write the greeting.
♦ Now write the body. Use everyday language to express your news or greetings.
♦ Finish with *Love,* or *Your friend,* or whatever closing you wish.
♦ Sign your name a few lines below the closing.

Discussing a First Draft

Discussion Strategy

When you have a comment about your partner's work, try to phrase it as a question. That way your partner won't be insulted. For example, Thomas's partner asked, "Did you forget to put the date in your heading?" rather than saying, "You forgot the date, dummy!"

Discuss Thomas's first draft with your class using the Content Checklist.

Content Checklist

- ✔ Does the heading have both the writer's address and the date?
- ✔ Does the letter have a greeting, a body, a closing, and a signature?
- ✔ Is the main idea in the body to give news or to stay in touch?
- ✔ Is the letter written in everyday language?

Revise Your First Draft for Content

To the Reader: Use the Content Checklist to help you think about your partner's letter. Remember to try to use the Discussion Strategy.

To the Writer: Write down all of your partner's comments. Keep your notes as reminders for revising your first draft.

Varying Your Sentences

Thomas wanted to improve his letter. He saw that three sentences in his second paragraph began with the subject, *My glasses*, or *They*. When people write quickly, they often use too many sentences that have the same pattern. Their sentences almost always begin with the subject. It is more interesting to read a letter, or any text, with sentence beginnings that are varied.

There are two ways to vary sentence beginnings. One is to change the order of the words in a sentence that begins with the subject. Look at these examples.

> I had a great idea on the way to school.
> On the way to school, I had a great idea.

> My face lit up like a light bulb.
> Like a light bulb, my face lit up.

Another way to vary sentence beginnings is to insert a word or phrase in front of the subject, like this.

> The solution was obvious.
> *Suddenly*, the solution was obvious.

> They published my idea in the school paper.
> *On Tuesday*, they published my idea in the school paper.

Here is how Thomas revised his second paragraph to vary his sentence beginnings.

Proofreading Marks	
∧	add
⅄	take away
≡	capitalize
/	small letter
∿	transpose

Luckily, My glasses help when I play softball. They make reading easier, too. *When I wear them,* My glasses change the way I see the world. There's just one bad thing about waring glasses. Now I can see what a mess my room is.

Practice

A. Change the word order in each sentence so that it does not begin with the name *Andrea* or the word *She*.

1. Andrea stared at the water for almost a minute.

2. She began her dive suddenly.

3. She sliced through the air like an arrow.

4. Andrea proudly accepted first prize later that day.

B. Use the words and phrases in the box to change each sentence so that it does not begin with *Larry* or *He*.

> Every day
> Finally
> For the whole soccer season
> Immediately
> On his first shot

5. Larry had sat on the bench.

6. Larry practiced for hours.

7. Larry was put in a game.

8. He kicked the ball hard.

9. Larry had scored a goal.

Revising Checklist
✔ Have I included all the characteristics of a letter?
✔ Can I combine sentences with like subjects or predicates? (p. 32)
✔ Is all my information complete? (p. 70)
✔ Where can I add describing words? (p. 118)
✔ Where can I vary sentence beginnings?

Revise Your First Draft for Style
Use the Revising Checklist to help you improve your letter. To vary sentence beginnings, either change the word order in a sentence, or add a word or phrase at the beginning. It's your choice. Save your changes for your final copy.

Do many of my sentences begin the same way?

153

Punctuation in Letters

Thomas knew that capitalization and punctuation were used in special ways in letters. He looked up the rules in a grammar book. Here are the rules that Thomas found. Next to each rule is an example from his letter.

Rule	Example
There is always a comma between the city and the state. This is true for both the envelope and the address in the letter heading. Remember to capitalize proper nouns.	Cincinnati, Ohio
A comma always goes between the day and the year in the date. If you use an abbreviation for the month, remember to use a period.	January 27, 1988 Jan. 30, 1988
There is a comma after the last word in the greeting. Every word in the greeting starts with a capital letter, except the word *and*.	Dear Clayton,
A comma also follows the last word in the closing. Only the first word in the closing starts with a capital letter.	Your friend,

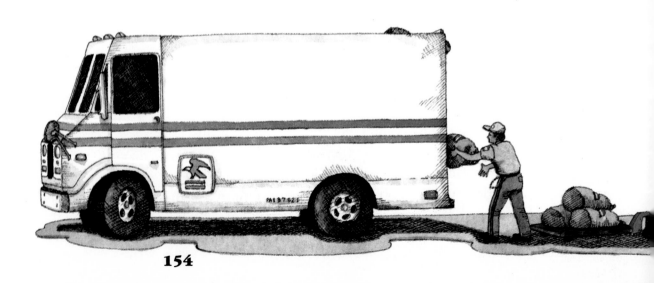

Practice

Rewrite these letter parts using correct capitalization and punctuation. Use separate lines where necessary. Then label each letter part.

1. 89 Jefferson Street Mapleton Iowa 51034 November 9 1990
2. your friend Malcolm
3. Winnebago Indian Reservation Route 1 Winnebago Nebraska 68071 June 1 1990 Dear Uncle Logan
4. dear, uncle fred
5. sincerely yours Mateo Gomez
6. 365 Lexington Avenue New York New York 10016 May 1 1990
7. dear Al and Betty
8. best regards Julio
9. 1211 Blue Ridge Road Charlottesville Virginia 22903 December 12 1990
10. 122 Bluebell Avenue Baker Oregon 97814 July 14 1990

Proofreading Checklist
✔ Are all my paragraphs indented? (p. 34)
✔ Do all my sentences end with proper end punctuation? (p. 34)
✔ Do all my abbreviations have correct capitalization and punctuation? (p. 72)
✔ Did I capitalize and punctuate all letter parts correctly?
✔ Did I use verbs correctly?

Proofread Your Letter

Check that you have used commas correctly in your letter. Then use the checklist to proofread your letter. Don't worry if it is messy. Save it for the next lesson.

Proofreading Marks
∧ add
⌇ take away
¶ indent
≡ capitalize
/ small letter
◯ check spelling
∼ transpose

155

Checking Spelling/Writing a Final Copy

Spelling Strategy

Some words share the same letter pattern. Knowing a letter pattern can help you spell many words.

These words contain the *-all* letter pattern:

ball, call, tall, fall

Thomas made a final check for spelling. Read his letter.

---

227 Rockville Rd. Apt. 4
Cincinnati, Ohio 45236
April 30, 1990

Dear Clayton,

    This is amazing. I can't ~~beleeve~~ *believe* you just got new glasses. So did I!

Luckily My glasses help when I play softball. *When I wear them* They make reading easier, too. My glasses change the way I see the world. There's just one bad thing about ~~waring~~ *wearing* glasses. Now I can see what a mess my room is.

    I can't ~~wate~~ *wait* to get your picture. I'll try to send you one, too.

            your friend
            Thomas

Check Your Spelling

    Reread your work carefully. Look up in the dictionary any words you're not sure you spelled correctly. Then, write your final copy. Proofread it and neatly fix any errors.

Sharing Your Letter

Speaking/Listening Strategy

To the Speaker: When you read aloud, make your voice interesting. Vary your tone and loudness. Pretend you are speaking directly to one person.

To the Listener: As you listen, imagine the speaker is speaking directly to you. Pay attention to all the details, and keep your eyes on the speaker.

Choosing a Way to Share

Here are some ideas for sharing your letter.

Reading Aloud Tell the class that you are not going to read the greeting. When you are finished reading your letter, ask them to guess to whom you wrote the letter.

Acting Out Your Letter Your letter may tell about something that happened to you. Have classmates mime the events as you read the letter aloud.

Where Will Our Letters Go? Place a map of the United States on the bulletin board. Tack the letters around the map. Put a piece of yarn leading from each letter to the place it will be sent.

APPLY STEP BY STEP

Share Your Letter

Mail your letter, but first, make a copy to share with your class. Use one of the ways to share explained on this page. It's your choice.

Add to Your Learning Log

Answer these questions in your Learning Log.
- What part of my letter am I most pleased with?
- Am I satisfied with the changes in my letter?
- What things might I change in my next letter?

The Literature Connection: Verbs

In stories and poems, action is very important. Action describes what happens. Action words describe how characters solve their problems. They tell us what characters do and how they think.

Writers describe different types of action with verbs. **Verbs** are action words, such as *run*, *hit*, and *play*. Each verb tells the exact action someone takes. A person looking at something may *gaze*, *stare*, or *peek*. A person walking down the street may *stroll*, *march*, or *tiptoe*. A verb can describe the specific action someone has to take to solve a problem.

In the poem below, the author has a problem: How can everyone on the trapeze keep from falling off? His solution to the problem is clever, and also funny. As you read the poem, try to "see" the picture that each action verb describes.

The Acrobats
by
Shel Silverstein

I'll swing
By my ankles,
She'll cling
To your knees
As you hang
By your nose
From a high-up
Trapeze.
But just one thing, please,
As we float through the breeze—
Don't sneeze.

Discussion

1. List three verbs from the poem.
2. How many people are flying on this trapeze?
3. Suppose the trapeze were only two feet off the ground. How would this change the verbs the author might use to describe hanging from the trapeze?

The Writing Connection: Verbs

On the previous page, verbs were used to describe people flying on a trapeze. In your writing, you can use verbs to describe any activity you want. Here are some examples of activities you could write about.

If I were an acrobat, I could <u>walk</u> on my hands.

If I were an acrobat, I could <u>leap</u> through a hoop.

Activity

Imagine you are in a circus. Write five things you would do. Use the picture above and your imagination to get ideas. An example is provided for you.

If I were in the circus, I would ride elephants.

Main Verbs and Helping Verbs

The verb part of a sentence can have more than one verb. A **main verb** is the most important verb in the sentence. A **helping verb** helps the main verb tell about an action.

A. Look at the underlined verb in the following sentence. It is made up of a main verb and a helping verb.

Hurricanes <u>have</u> <u>smashed</u> all the houses.
　　　　　　↑　　　↑
　　　helping verb main verb

Most helping verbs are forms of the verb *be* or *have*.

Forms of *be*	Forms of *have*
am, is, are, was, were	have, has, had

The hurricane <u>is</u> <u>moving</u> fast. It <u>has</u> <u>arrived</u> quickly.

B. A main verb usually ends in *ing* or *ed*. Study the chart below to see how the main verb is formed.

Helping verb	Main verb	Example
am, is, are, was, were	ends with <u>ing</u>	She <u>is reading</u> about hurricanes.
have, has, had	ends with <u>ed</u>	Scientists <u>had watched</u> the storm.

Strategy

Watch for the verbs *am, is, are, was,* and *were*. When one is used alone in a sentence, it is a linking verb, not a helping verb. When one is used before another verb, it is a helping verb.

Check Your Understanding

A. Write the letter of the helping verb in each sentence.
  1. Scientists are mapping the path of the hurricane.
    a. are　**b.** mapping　**c.** path　**d.** hurricane
  2. It has moved close to the city.
    a. It　**b.** has　**c.** moved　**d.** city

160

B. Write the letter of the correct helping verb.

    3. They ___ bringing people food.
        a. have   **b.** are

    4. She ___ escaped from the hurricane.
        a. has   **b.** is

Practice

A. Write each sentence. Underline the helping verb once. Underline the main verb twice.

    5. Airplanes are flying over the ocean.
    6. A plane is carrying radar equipment.
    7. The pilot has spotted the hurricane.
    8. They had followed the storm.

B. Write each sentence, using the correct form of the main verb.

    9. He had ___ the photographs. (studied, studying)
    10. I am ___ to the weather report. (listened, listening)
    11. She is ___ the doors. (locked, locking)
    12. They have ___ the people. (warned, warning)

C. Mixed Practice Write each sentence, using the correct helping verb or main verb in parentheses.

    13. He ___ sending an emergency message. (was, had)
    14. The girls are ___ the pets indoors. (put, putting)
    15. Tall waves had ___ the boat. (destroyed, destroying)
    16. We were ___ in the basement. (stayed, staying)
    17. A powerful wind ___ howling. (was, had)
    18. It had ___ through the roof. (crashed, crashing)
    19. They ___ not covered the windows. (were, had)
    20. The storm has ___ and has ___ on. (passed, passing) (going, gone)

Apply: Work with a Group

Work with several classmates to write a report about the weather in your area. In each sentence of your report, use one of the helping verbs in this lesson.

Irregular Verbs

◆

Irregular verbs do not form the past tense by adding *ed*.

A. To form the past tense of most verbs, you must add *ed*. Irregular verbs do not follow this rule. Study the irregular verbs in the chart below.

Present	Past	Present	Past
begin	began	run	ran
come	came	ride	rode
do	did	see	saw
go	went		

B. Irregular verbs that are used with *have, has,* or *had* do not end in *ed*. Look at the chart below.

Present	Past with *have, has,* or *had*	
begin	(have, has, or had)	begun
come	(have, has, or had)	come
do	(have, has, or had)	done
go	(have, has, or had)	gone
run	(have, has, or had)	run
ride	(have, has, or had)	ridden
see	(have, has, or had)	seen

Strategy

Irregular verbs are difficult to learn. Use the chart to help you remember the past tense of the irregular verbs in this lesson. Watch for irregular verbs when you write.

Check Your Understanding

A. Write the letter of the correct form of the verb in the past tense.
  1. News ＿＿ slowly from distant places long ago.
    a. come   **b.** came
  2. People ＿＿ to the general store for messages.
    a. went   **b.** go

B. Follow the directions for Check Your Understanding A.

    3. Weeks had ____ by without any letters.

        a. went   **b.** gone

    4. People had ____ to the next town for news.

        a. ridden   **b.** rode

Practice

A. Write each sentence, using the correct past tense form of the verb in parentheses.

    5. Alexander Graham Bell ____ work in 1874. (begin)

    6. Bell ____ to Boston. (go)

    7. There he ____ the telegraph. (see)

    8. Bell ____ home with a new idea. (ride)

B. Follow the directions for Practice A.

    9. Bell and Thomas Watson have ____ much work. (do)

    10. The first telephone message has ____. (come)

    11. Watson has ____ into the room in excitement. (run)

    12. News about the telephone has ____ everywhere. (go)

C. Mixed Practice Write each sentence, using the correct past tense form of the verb in parentheses.

    13. Messengers had ____ across country. (ride)

    14. Bell's invention ____ a new age. (begin)

    15. Guglielmo Marconi had ____ work on radio. (do)

    16. Messages ____ all around the world. (run)

    17. Now signals have ____ through space. (go)

    18. People have ____ great progress. (see)

    19. Have you ____ the news? (hear)

    20. Television ____ popular in the 1950s. (become)

Apply: Test a Partner

Make up a quiz for your partner. Write five present tense verbs from this lesson. Trade papers with your partner. Rewrite each verb in the past tense and then write it with the helping verbs *have*, *has*, or *had*. Check each other's work. Did you write the correct forms?

More Irregular Verbs

A. You have already learned that irregular verbs do not form the past tense by adding *ed*. Here are seven other irregular verbs you use often. Study the chart below.

Present	Past	Present	Past
bring	brought	take	took
fly	flew	throw	threw
grow	grew	write	wrote
say	said		

B. Remember that when the past tense of an irregular verb is used with *have, has,* or *had,* it does not end in *ed*. Study the chart below.

Present		Past
bring	(have, has, or had)	brought
fly	(have, has, or had)	flown
grow	(have, has, or had)	grown
say	(have, has, or had)	said
take	(have, has, or had)	taken
throw	(have, has, or had)	thrown
write	(have, has, or had)	written

Do I write have took or have taken?

Strategy

There aren't any rules for forming the past tense of irregular verbs. You may not always know which form to use. If you're not sure, look up the verb in the dictionary. It will tell you the correct past tense form of the verb.

Check Your Understanding

A. Write the letter of the correct form of the verb in the past tense.

1. People _____ about space travel long ago.
   a. write   **b.** wrote
2. In one story a slingshot _____ a ship into space.
   a. threw   **b.** throw

164

B. Follow the directions for Check Your Understanding A.

    3. Balloons had _____ people into the air.

        a. took   **b.** taken

    4. No one had _____ before the Wright brothers.

        a. flew   **b.** flown

Practice

A. Write each sentence with the correct past tense form of the verb in parentheses.

    5. The first airplane _____ in 1903. (fly)

    6. A rocket _____ astronauts to the moon in 1969. (bring)

    7. Neil Armstrong _____ the first step on the moon. (take)

    8. He _____ several words over television. (say)

B. Follow the directions for Practice A.

    9. The astronauts had _____ oxygen. (take)

    10. They had _____ special food, too. (bring)

    11. People have _____ many books about the flight. (write)

    12. Interest in space travel has _____. (grow)

C. Mixed Practice Write each sentence, using the correct past tense form of the verb in parentheses.

    13. Women _____ on the space shuttle. (fly)

    14. They have _____ new ideas to science. (bring)

    15. Rockets have _____ very powerful. (grow)

    16. Spacecrafts have _____ to other planets. (fly)

    17. Special cameras _____ many pictures in space. (take)

    18. The moon _____ a shadow across the earth. (throw)

    19. What has the President _____ about space? (say)

    20. We have _____ research on space colonies. (begin)

Apply: Learning Log

Think about both lessons on irregular verbs. Which part was the most difficult for you? Think of a way to remember the irregular verbs. Write your method in your learning log. Then practice your skills.

Contractions with *Not*

A **contraction** is a shortened form of two words. An apostrophe (') takes the place of the missing letters.

A. Some verbs can be combined with the word *not* to form contractions. Read the following sentences:

> We <u>could not</u> see the star without a telescope.
> We <u>couldn't</u> see the star without a telescope.

Both sentences mean the same thing. In the second sentence, the words *could* and *not* are joined to form the contraction *couldn't*. The apostrophe takes the place of the *o* in *not*.

Look at the contractions in the chart below.

is + not —→ isn't	do + not —→ don't	has + not —→ hasn't
are + not —→ aren't	does + not —→ doesn't	had + not —→ hadn't
was + not —→ wasn't	did + not —→ didn't	could + not —→ couldn't
were + not —→ weren't	have + not —→ haven't	should + not —→ shouldn't
		would + not —→ wouldn't

B. To form these contractions, combine the verb and the word *not*. Drop the *o* in *not* and replace it with an apostrophe.

> is not ——→ isnⱥt ——→ isn't

Strategy

Remember that a contraction is one word made from two words. Always replace the missing letter or letters with an apostrophe.

Check Your Understanding

A. Write the letter of the two words that form the contractions.

1. Scientists <u>didn't</u> have telescopes long ago.
   a. did not   **b.** does not   **c.** had not   **d.** do not
2. The telescope <u>wasn't</u> invented until 1608.
   a. were not   **b.** is not   **c.** was not   **d.** would not

B. Write the letter of the contraction for each pair of underlined words.

    3. Many stars <u>are not</u> visible without a telescope.

      a. ar'not   **b.** are n't   **c.** are'nt   **d.** aren't

    4. I <u>have not</u> looked through a telescope.

      a. haven't   **b.** hav'nt   **c.** have'nt   **d.** have n't

Practice

A. Write the two words from which each contraction is made.

5. haven't	**9.** aren't	**13.** hadn't
6. doesn't	**10.** hasn't	**14.** couldn't
7. isn't	**11.** shouldn't	**15.** wasn't
8. wouldn't	**12.** don't	**16.** weren't

B. Write the contraction for each pair of words.

17. could not	**21.** did not	**25.** have not
18. should not	**22.** are not	**26.** do not
19. is not	**23.** were not	**27.** has not
20. was not	**24.** had not	**28.** does not

C. Mixed Practice Write each sentence using a contraction for the underlined words.

    29. We <u>could not</u> see the craters on the moon.

    30. People <u>would not</u> know much without telescopes.

    31. Scientists <u>had not</u> seen the rings of Saturn.

    32. A spacecraft <u>has not</u> traveled to the planet Pluto.

    33. The stars <u>were not</u> very bright.

    34. A telescope <u>does not</u> show all the stars.

    35. Scientists <u>have not</u> learned all about the stars.

    36. They <u>are not</u> sure what causes gravity.

    37. Astronauts <u>cannot</u> travel to other planets yet.

    38. <u>Is</u> space travel <u>not</u> important?

Apply: Journal

What are some things you have not done but would like to do? Write about them in your journal. Use as many of the contractions in this lesson as you can.

Homophones

Homophones are words that sound the same but have different spellings and different meanings.

A. Read each pair of sentences below. Notice the underlined words.

> We studied for an hour. Our test was about science.
> The two scientists work hard. He works hard, too.

The underlined words in each sentence are homophones. They sound the same but are spelled differently and have different meanings.

B. To decide which homophone to use in a sentence, you must look at the meaning of each word. Which word belongs in each sentence below?

> George Carver _____ about farms.   *new* or *knew*
> He studied _____ types of food.

> Lola digs a _____ for the seeds.   *hole* or *whole*
> She planted the _____ garden.

Strategy

Homophones can be confusing when you write. If you aren't sure of the correct spelling of a word, look up the word in the dictionary.

Check Your Understanding

A. Write the letter of the homophone for the underlined word.
1. Carver thought <u>through</u> many new ideas.
   a. in   **b.** inside   **c.** threw   **d.** about
2. The scientist <u>rode</u> the train to the laboratory.
   a. road   **b.** took   **c.** ran   **d.** walked

B. Write the letter of the word that completes the sentence.

   3. Scientists _____ about the experiments.
      a. write   **b.** right
   4. People _____ the results.
      a. sea   **b.** see

Practice

A. Write each sentence. Underline the two homophones.

   5. No scientist can know all the answers.
   6. The pale girl carried the pail of water.
   7. The farmer's son worked in the hot sun.
   8. She blew out the blue flame.

B. Write each sentence using the correct homophone.

   9. George Washington Carver Day is in the first _____ of January. (weak, week)
   10. Carver _____ the Spingarn Medal. (won, one)
   11. He made _____ from sweet potatoes. (flower, flour)
   12. Many people _____ the new product. (ate, eight)

C. Mixed Practice Write each sentence using each homophone in the correct place.

   13. _____ bushels were _____ the experiments. (for, four)
   14. People _____ about the _____ methods. (write, right)
   15. Did you _____ about Carver _____? (here, hear)
   16. They flew the _____ over the _____. (plane, plain)
   17. People soon _____ of the _____ products. (new, knew)
   18. He buried the _____ root in the _____. (hole, whole)
   19. She _____ not burn the _____ near the old barn. (wood, would)
   20. The _____ scientists went _____ the field _____ many times. (too, two, to)

Apply: Work with a Partner

List some homophones that you and your partner know. Then, write two sentences using two pairs of homophones in each sentence.

LANGUAGE IN ACTION

Invitations and Thank-You Notes

Have you ever had a birthday party? How did you invite people? Did people bring gifts? How did you thank them?

Invitations give important information. Here are some tips on invitations:

- Describe the party. Is it a birthday party, a beach party or just a party? Tell people what to expect.
- Include your full name. *John's birthday* is not enough. There are other people named John.
- Tell when and where the party will take place. Give the complete date and your full address.
- Include R.S.V.P. and your phone number. **R.S.V.P.** is an abbreviation of the French phrase, *please answer*.

It's polite to send thank-you notes. Here are some tips on thank-you notes:

- Use the same form you used for writing letters. A thank-you note is simply a special kind of letter.
- Tell why you're writing. Say something specific, such as ''Thank you for the poster.''
- Say something more. Describe your favorite part of the party. Tell how you use the gift.

Practice

On a separate piece of paper, answer the following questions.
1. Why should you give your full name on an invitation?
2. What should you tell about the party?
3. What is the form of a thank-you note?

Apply

Pretend you just had a birthday party. Write a thank-you note thanking someone for the gift he or she gave you.

TEST TAKING

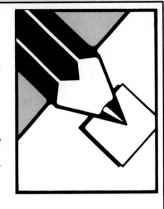

Following Directions

When taking a test, read the directions carefully. Make sure you understand how to answer the questions. If there is a sample, study it closely before you begin.

Study the test directions and samples below.

Directions: Circle the letter of the word that best completes the sentence.
Sample: George Washington was the _____ President.
(a.) first   b. only   c. next

Directions: On the line, write the letter of the year for each event.
Sample: Declaration of Independence ___c___
a. 1930   b. 2001   c. 1776

Directions: Fill in the circle of the correct answer.
Sample: 3 + 5 - 2 = _____   ○ 5   ● 6   ○ 7   ○ 8

Practice

Answer the questions about the sample test.

Directions: Circle the word in each group that does not belong.
Sample: clouds   sky   sun   (house)
  1. goldfish   puppy   ~~toy~~   hamster
  2. blue   paint   green   yellow

1. In what way does the sample follow the directions?
2. What is wrong with the way question 1 is answered?
3. What is wrong with the way question 2 is answered?

Apply

Learning Log   Decide what things from this lesson you found helpful. Write them in your learning log.

UNIT REVIEW

Letters *(pages 143-147)*

1. Read this letter. Then write which letter parts are missing.

Joan, guess what I'm doing during winter recess. My Girl Scout troup is having a newspapers drive. We'll bring old newspapers to the recycling center. It will help save trees and should be fun, too.

Regan

Addressing an Envelope *(pages 148-149)*

2. Use the information below to make an envelope for the letter above.

Regan Albert lives at 59 Balson Avenue, Bridgeport, Connecticut, 06606. Joan Gomez lives at 1010 Waylon Street, Portland, Oregon 97208.

Varying Your Sentences and Punctuating Letters *(pages 152-155)*

Change the word order so that these sentences won't begin with *Koyi*.

3. Koyi had been afraid of water since he was a little boy.

4. Koyi decided to take swimming lessons one day.

5. Koyi learned, after weeks of lessons, to put his face in the water.

6. Koyi wasn't afraid to swim after that.

Correct the capitalization and punctuation in these letter parts.

7. dear duane

8. your friend
    rosa

9. 36 forest ave
    Olney Maryland 20832

10. November 11 1990

Main Verbs and Helping Verbs *(pages 160-161)*

Write each sentence, using the correct helping verb or main verb in parentheses.

11. Maud Powell had (playing, played) the violin.

12. The girl (had, was) lived in Peru, Illinois.

13. Maud was (practicing, practiced) the violin by the age of nine.

14. Maud (was, had) studying the violin with William Lewis.

15. Maud and William Lewis (were, have) performed together.

Irregular Verbs *(pages 162-163)*

Write each sentence using the correct past tense form of the verb in parentheses.

16. Hernán Cortés (go) to Mexico in 1519.

17. The ship had (come) from Spain.

18. Cortés (begin) the journey with 11 ships.

19. Hernán (see) the beauty of the Aztec Empire.

20. Cortés had (go) to Cuba.

21. Cortés had (ride) in Central America.

22. Students have (do) many reports on Cortés.

More About Irregular Verbs *(pages 164-165)*

Write each sentence using the correct past tense form of the verb in parentheses.

23. John Muir (take) many trips outdoors.

24. Muir (write) about the wilderness.

25. Muir's books (say) many wonderful things about nature.

26. Muir had (grow) comfortable in the forest.

27. Wild birds (fly) all around.

28. Muir (bring) new ideas about nature to others.

29. Many people have (write) about nature.

Contractions with *Not* *(pages 166-167)*

Write the contraction for each pair of words.

30. should not

31. does not

32. were not

33. had not

34. do not

35. has not

36. could not

37. did not

38. are not

39. have not

40. would not

41. was not

Homophones *(pages 168-169)*

Write each sentence using each homophone in the correct place.

42. Everyone at school _____ about our _____ boat. (new, knew)

43. A _____ tree grew near the sandy _____. (beach, beech)

44. Do _____ tie that rope into a _____. (not, knot)

45. Dan painted the metal _____ a _____ blue color. (pail, pale)

46. Please _____ that trunk down the long _____. (hall, haul)

CONNECTIONS

You and several classmates will now use what you have learned about letter writing to write a business letter.

You will do the following in your letter:

- ◆ Write to a company or an official.
- ◆ Describe a problem and suggest a solution.
- ◆ Use facts and reasons to support your suggestion.
- ◆ Include all the features of a letter (p. 146).

Reading a Business Letter

Read the following business letter and side notes.

The heading shows the writer's address and the date the letter was written.

The inside address shows where and to whom the letter is being sent.

The greeting is followed by a colon.

The problem is described in the first sentences.

Next the writer suggests a solution.

Facts and reasons help support the suggestion.

The letter ends with the closing and signature.

19 Bell Road
Ames, Iowa 57023
October 3, 1989

Mayor Chen
Town Hall
Ames, Iowa 57023

Dear Mayor Chen:

Many students who walk to school have a problem crossing James Street at Polk Lane. The light turns red before we can get across. Perhaps you could allow more crossing time. The light stays green for only 9 seconds. Changing it to 15 or 20 seconds would make crossing safer. No crossing guard works at that corner, so a longer green light is really needed.

Sincerely,
Ms. Nelson's 4-A Class

Speaking and Listening

Your teacher will assign you to a group. Choose a group leader. Talk about these questions with your group.

1. In the letter you read on page 174, what problem is mentioned in the first two sentences?
2. What solution is offered in the paragraph? Name facts and details that support the suggestion.
3. Look at the picture above. What possible danger or problem can you see, based on what is happening?
4. What other solutions could you think of to solve the problem shown in the picture?

Thinking

Brainstorming

Choose one person from your group to be a note taker. Have the person take notes as you discuss these questions. Save your notes.

1. What problems do you feel exist in your school or town? Explain why the problems need to be solved.
2. What solutions would you suggest to solve the problems?
3. What facts or reasons could you give to support your suggestions?

MAKING ALL THE CONNECTIONS

Organizing

When you prepare to write a business letter, it helps to put your information in a chart. Study the chart below. It shows details that were used to write the letter about the street-crossing problem.

Problem	Solution	Supporting Facts/Reasons
Green light turns red too quickly.	Adjust light so that it stays green longer.	Green light lasts only 9 seconds; no crossing guard works at corner.

With the rest of your group, discuss a serious problem you feel exists in your school or town. Describe the problem clearly. Then talk about a possible solution to the problem. Be sure to give facts and reasons to support your suggestion. Have one group member take notes and write them in a chart such as the one above.

Writing a Business Letter

Imagine that you and other group members were chosen to serve on your school's Improvement Committee. The head of the committee has asked you to write a letter to the town mayor or school principal about a problem you feel must be solved. You will use the chart of details you made to help you write the letter.

Planning

- Review the chart you made as a group. Add any new details you may think of now.
- Talk about the problem that you feel exists.
- Then discuss a solution to the problem. Mention facts and details that help support your solution.
- Organize your information in an outline. First state the problem. Then write your solution using supporting facts and reasons.

176

Composing

- Work with your group to write your business letter. Choose one member to write the first draft as everyone suggests ideas.
- Include your school's address and today's date in the heading. Name the person receiving the letter in the greeting.
- Next, decide exactly how to state the problem in the beginning of the paragraph.
- Then, decide how to state the solution and the supporting facts and reasons in the rest of the paragraph.
- End the letter with a closing and signature. Sign all your names individually, or write one name that identifies your entire group.

Revising

- As a group, read over your letter sentence by sentence. Think of ways to improve the content.
- Check that the information in the heading is correct.
- Check that you have stated the problem and solution clearly.

Proofreading

As a group, proofread your letter. Choose one group member to make the changes on your draft. Answer these questions:

- Do all verbs agree with their subjects?
- Are all irregular verbs written correctly?
- Are all words spelled correctly?
- Is correct punctuation used in the heading, greeting, and closing?

Presenting

- Choose one group member to write a clean final copy of your letter.
- Send the letter to the person to whom it is written.

Cumulative Review

A. Write the letter of the group of words that is a sentence.
(*pages 40-41*)

1. a. Plays the flute.
   b. The two drummers.
   c. Al writes music.

2. a. The first harps.
   b. Long, long ago.
   c. Nina plays the harp.

3. a. Ed meets the music teacher.
   b. Teaches Ed a new song.
   c. The piano.

4. a. The tuba booms loudly.
   b. A very big horn.
   c. The youngest tuba player.

B. Write the letter of the word that names each kind of sentence.
(*pages 42-43*)

5. Did you ride in the balloon?
   a. exclamation   **b.** statement   **c.** command   **d.** question
6. That balloon really flew high!
   a. exclamation   **b.** statement   **c.** command   **d.** question
7. Watch the balloon with red trim on the sides.
   a. exclamation   **b.** statement   **c.** command   **d.** question

C. Write the letter of the sentence with one line under the complete subject and two lines under the complete predicate. (*pages 44-47*)

8. a. Amy hits the ball.
   b. Jim runs quickly.
   c. Ed swings the bat.

9. a. The boy reaches first base.
   b. The ball flies into the air.
   c. The team wins the game.

D. Write the letter of the group of words that is in alphabetical order.
(*pages 48-49*)

10. a. final, finger, film
   b. slide, slim, slither
   c. route, round, routine

11. a. knot, knock, knowledge
   b. terrace, term, territory
   c. crinkle, crisp, critic

E. Write the letter of the word that would appear on a dictionary page with the guide words shown. (*pages 50-51*)

12. trust/tug   **a.** true   **b.** try   **c.** tune
13. daughter/dazzle   **a.** dawn   **b.** date   **c.** dash

F. Write the letter of the words that are nouns. (*pages 78-79*)

14. The goats leaped over the tall rocks.

    a. goats, leaped   **b.** goats, rocks   **c.** tall, rocks

15. Sheep walked on the high cliff.

    a. sheep, walked   **b.** sheep, high   **c.** sheep, cliff

16. The eagle flew over the gray clouds.

    a. eagle, flew   **b.** eagle, clouds   **c.** gray, clouds

G. Write the letter of the correct plural noun. (*pages 80-81*)

17. Three _____ stand in the hall. (box)

    a. boxes   **b.** boxs   **c.** box

18. Three _____ open the flaps. (man)

    a. mans   **b.** men   **c.** mens

19. Three _____ leap from each box. (monkey)

    a. monkeies   **b.** monkeys   **c.** monkeyes

20. The people jump three _____ into the air. (foot)

    a. foots   **b.** feets   **c.** feet

H. Write the letter of the proper noun that is written correctly.
(*pages 82-83*)

21. a. new Hampshire   **b.** Rocky Mountains   **c.** congo river

22. a. red sea   **b.** anna wong   **c.** Harry Benson

23. a. King John   **b.** doctor Chu   **c.** lake placid

I. Write the letter of the correct possessive of each noun in parentheses.
(*pages 84-87*)

24. The _____ sound woke the boys. (wind)

    a. wind's   **b.** winds   **c.** winds'

25. Then _____ voices filled the house. (children)

    a. childrens'   **b.** children's   **c.** childrens'

26. The _____ day began. (boys)

    a. boy's   **b.** boys'   **c.** boys's

J. Write the letter of the abbreviation that is written correctly.
(*pages 88-89*)

27. a. Mr Ed Maas   **b.** Mrs. Ellen Wynn   **c.** MS. Ann Reed

28. a. Tues., Sep. 17   **b.** Wed., Sept. 18   **c.** Sat, Nov 7

29. a. 17 Adams Road.   **b.** 64 Plains Aven.   **c.** 7 Park Blvd.

K. Write the letter of the line of conversation that is written correctly. (*pages 120-121*)

30. **a.** "What is that sound" asked Jo?
    b. Harry said, "someone is ringing the doorbell."
    c. Meg said, "Charles is outside with a box."

31. **a.** "Look in the box!" said Meg.
    b. "Do you like my new gift," asked Charles.
    c. Jo said "It is a wonderful puppy."

L. Write the letter of the word that is an action verb. (*pages 126-127*)

32. Gina walks onto the ice rink.
    a. Gina   **b.** walks   **c.** rink

33. Bill skates in a fast circle.
    a. skates   **b.** fast   **c.** circle

34. One girl spins very quickly to the music.
    a. girl   **b.** quickly   **c.** spins

M. Write the letter of the sentence that contains a linking verb. (*pages 128-129*)

35. **a.** The horse is fast.
    b. The colt walks away.
    c. Mo rides the pony.

36. **a.** Horses eat oats.
    b. Oats grow in fields.
    c. Oats are a grain.

37. **a.** Nate has a horse.
    b. Alice calls to the colt.
    c. Ted is in the barn.

38. **a.** Horses have strong legs.
    b. The horse's ears are soft.
    c. The horse nibbles grass.

N. Write the letter of the correct tense of the verb. (*pages 130-131*)

39. The dog scratched a paw.
    a. present tense   **b.** past tense   **c.** future tense

40. The vet will examine the dog's paw.
    a. present tense   **b.** past tense   **c.** future tense

41. Dr. Wells bandages the paw carefully.
    a. present tense   **b.** past tense   **c.** future tense

O. Write the letter of the correct present-tense verb. (*pages 132-133*)

42. The girls _____ a film.
    a. watch   **b.** watches

43. A cowboy _____ to town.
    a. ride   **b.** rides

44. Bart _____ the gold.
    a. save   **b.** saves

45. The children _____ at the end.
    a. clap   **b.** claps

P. Write the letter of the correct spelling for each underlined verb using the tense in parentheses. (*pages 134-135*)

46. Ben drop a box in the hall. (past)
    a. droped   **b.** dropped   **c.** drop

47. The cat chase the box's ribbon. (past)
    a. chase   **b.** chaseed   **c.** chased

48. Now Ben carry the box more carefully. (present)
    a. carrys   **b.** carryes   **c.** carries

Q. Write the letter of the words that are correctly capitalized and punctuated. (*pages 154-155*)

49. a. Your Friend,   **b.** Your friend   **c.** Your friend,

50. a. Dear Vera,   **b.** Dear vera,   **c.** dear Vera,

R. Write the letter of the correct main or helping verb. (*pages 160-161*)

51. Many inventors _____ worked on new kinds of airplanes.
    a. have   **b.** were   **c.** are

52. Before 1900, people _____ traveling in hot-air balloons.
    a. were   **b.** has   **c.** had

53. The Wright Brothers had _____ the first plane by 1903.
    a. invent   **b.** inventing   **c.** invented

S. Write the letter of the correct past-tense verb. (*pages 162-165*)

54. Amanda _____ many stories.
    a. has wrote   **b.** has writed   **c.** has written

55. Many of Amanda's ideas _____ from folktales.
    a. have come   **b.** have came   **c.** have comed

56. One story _____ at a market.
    a. begin   **b.** began   **c.** begun

57. A boy _____ home some unusual beans.
    a. bringed   **b.** brought   **c.** brung

58. A huge beanstalk _____ from the seeds.
    a. grew   **b.** growed   **c.** grown

T. Write the letter of the correct contraction. (*pages 166-167*)

59. did not   **a.** did'nt   **b.** didn't   **c.** didnt'

60. would not   **a.** wouldn't   **b.** wouln't   **c.** would'nt

61. was not   **a.** was'nt   **b.** wasn't   **c.** wa'snt

PART THREE

Travels

"Chariots of gold," says Timothy.
"Silvery wings," says Elaine.
"A bumpity ride in a wagon of hay for me,"
says Jane.

> from "Bunches of Grapes"
> by Walter de la Mare

◆

    People travel to many places and for many reasons.
Traveling can teach you about new and exciting lands. In
the coming units, think about travels you have taken or
would like to take. Imagine where you would go and what
you would do when you got there.

Descriptive Writing

♦

Pronouns

What Do You Know?

"This postcard can't show how beautiful it is here."

"Did you ever get a postcard that said something like that? People who are traveling often describe details or scenes that a postcard can't show. They can describe how it feels to walk barefoot in the mud or how the wind sounds. They may even tell how food tastes or a flower smells. There are many things that can be described better with words than with pictures.

Descriptive writing is like making a special picture with words. Unlike a regular picture, word pictures can include sounds, smells, tastes, and feelings.

Thinking About Descriptive Writing

What is Descriptive Writing?

Descriptive writing has these features:

- It tells about a particular person, place, or thing.
- It uses sensory words to describe. **Sensory words** tell how something looks, feels, sounds, tastes, or smells.
- It paints a picture with colorful words.

Description is used in many types of writing. A story may describe the hot sand and cool, salty water of a beach. A poem may describe a shiny, new car. Both of these descriptions would help a reader imagine what it would be like to be there—on the beach or in the car. With descriptive writing, you can go anywhere and describe anyone or anything. Other people can see, feel, hear, taste, or smell what you saw, felt, heard, tasted, or smelled.

Discussion

1. Did you ever write or receive a postcard from a place away from home?
2. What books have you read that describe places you've never seen?
3. Name three things that could be described better with words than with pictures.

185

Reading Descriptive Writing

The main character in this story, Wilbur, is a piglet. Wilbur was born very small. At first, Wilbur was cared for like a pet by Fern Arable on her parents' farm. When Wilbur was big enough, Mr. Arable sold him to Fern's uncle, Homer Zuckerman, who had a farm nearby. This way, Fern could still visit Wilbur. Wilbur went to live in Mr. Zuckerman's barn with other animals, including some geese and cows. In the passage below, Wilbur is about to get out and see the world outside the barnyard.

Escape
by
E. B. White

"When I'm out here," he said, "there's no place to go but in. When I'm indoors, there's no place to go but out in the yard."

"That's where you're wrong, my friend, my friend," said a voice.

Wilbur looked through a fence and saw the goose standing there.

"You don't have to stay in that dirty-little dirty-little dirty-little yard," said the goose, who talked rather fast. "One of the boards is loose. Push on it, push-push-push on it, and come on out!"

"What?" said Wilbur. "Say it slower!"

"At-at-at, at the risk of repeating myself," said the goose, "I suggest that you come on out. It's wonderful out here."

"Did you say a board was loose?"

Wilbur walked up to the fence and saw that the goose was right—one board was loose. He put his head down, shut his eyes, and pushed. The board gave way. In a minute he had squeezed through the fence and was standing in the long grass outside his yard. The goose chuckled.

"How does it feel to be free?" she asked.

Here the writer uses the goose's words to describe how the yard looks.

186

"I like it," said Wilbur. "That is, I *guess* I like it."
Actually, Wilbur felt queer to be outside his fence, with
nothing between him and the big world.

"Where do you think I'd better go?"

"Anywhere you like, anywhere you like," said the
goose. "Go down through the orchard, root up the sod!
Go down through the garden, dig up the radishes! Root
up everything! Eat grass! Look for corn! Look for oats!
Run all over! Skip and dance, jump and prance! Go
down through the orchard and stroll in the woods! The
world is a wonderful place when you're young."

"I can see that," replied Wilbur. He gave a jump in
the air, twirled, ran a few steps, stopped, looked all
around, sniffed the smells of afternoon, and then set off
walking down through the orchard. Pausing in the
shade of an apple tree, he put his strong snout into the
ground and began pushing, digging, and rooting. He
felt very happy.

The writer describes
Wilbur's feelings here.

The writer tells what
Wilbur sees, smells, and
feels.

The following poem is also an example of descriptive writing. It describes a season that the writer especially enjoys. Notice how the writer uses sensory details in an unusual way.

Smells
by
Kathryn Worth

The writer describes her feelings.

Through all the frozen winter
My nose has grown most lonely
For lovely, lovely, colored smells
That come in springtime only.

She uses smells to describe spring.

The purple smell of lilacs,
The yellow smell that blows
Across the air of meadows
Where bright forsythia grows.

The writer uses color to describe the smell of flowers.

The tall pink smell of peach trees,
The low white smell of clover,
And everywhere the great green smell
Of grass the whole world over.

Understanding What You've Read

Answer these questions about the story and the poem.

1. What sensory details does the writer of "Escape" use to describe Wilbur's surroundings?
2. How does the writer's description show that Wilbur is in a place that is new to him?
3. Which two senses does the poem describe?
4. What particular thing does the poem describe?
5. Which one paints a clearer word picture for you, the story or the poem?

Writing Assignment

Imagine you write for a travel magazine. You want to tell your readers about a place you have visited. In this unit you will learn to write a descriptive paragraph that is colorful and interesting. You will also learn to use descriptive language in a poem.

Your **audience** will be your teacher and classmates. Your **purpose** will be to have them see, feel, and hear what you saw, felt, and heard.

Choose a Place

Before you begin your description, you must choose a place to describe. Pick an idea from this list or any place you want. It's your choice. Write the place on a piece of paper. Keep the paper for the next lesson.

What do I want to describe?

a place you went on vacation	a field
an unusual building	a house
a playground	a beach
a stream	a farm

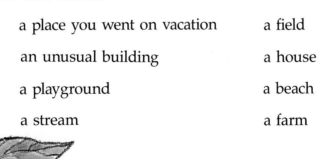

Organizing Sensory Details

Steve decided to tell about the field he saw when he visited his cousin's farm. He wanted the scene to be as clear to his readers as it had been to him. He knew he would have to choose his words and ideas carefully.

Before Steve described the scene, he closed his eyes and imagined it. What could he see, hear, smell, taste, and touch in that place? He organized his details in a cluster map as shown below.

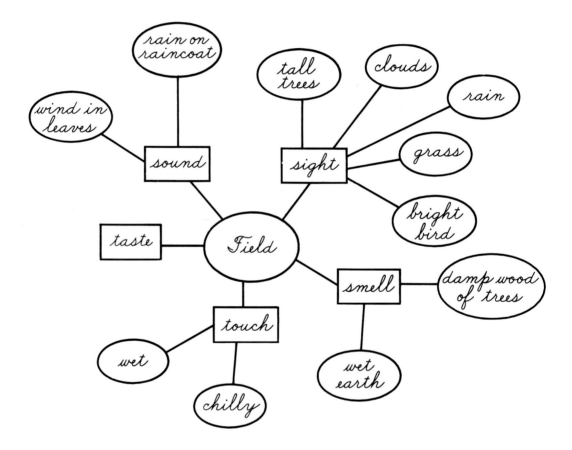

Notice that the topic appears in the center of the map. The five senses are arranged in boxes around the topic. Details about each sense are connected to the box. Notice that Steve did not fill in anything in the *taste* section. Sometimes you may not have a detail for every sense.

190

Practice

A. Copy this cluster map onto your paper. Fill in the blanks to complete the description of the topic in the center.

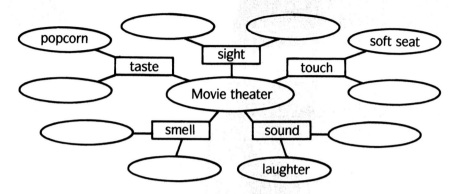

B. Imagine you are standing on a beach one hot summer day. Make a cluster map with the word *beach* in the center. Then list the five senses in boxes around the topic. For each sense, give two details.

Make a Cluster Map

Think about the place you chose. Use all of your senses. Think of words and phrases that describe details from your place. Make a cluster map to organize your details. Save your work for the next lesson. You will also use your cluster map for the poem you will write later.

Using Precise Details

Steve remembered seeing a bright bird in the field he was describing. He wanted his readers to see the bird as clearly as he had. Steve knew he should give precise details to make a clear picture.

He looked in a book about birds for a picture of the bird he saw. He found these four birds. They are similar but not exactly alike.

scarlet tanager   oriole   cardinal   goldfinch

Steve tried to think of details that would make a reader know which bird he was writing about. First, he thought of these details.

small, bright

These details are too general. They describe all four birds. Steve needed more precise details. This is what he added:

small, bright, mostly red

This still describes two of the birds. Steve added this.

small, bright, mostly red, feather "crown" on head

Now it is clear that Steve is describing a cardinal. The precise details show that this bird is different from the other three.

Steve added the precise details to his cluster map.

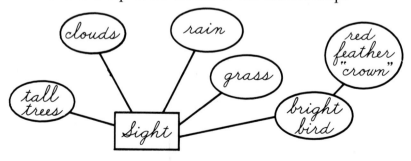

Practice

A. Write the descriptions below. Complete each one with the name of the cat that it describes.

Persian cat   Siamese cat   Himalayan cat   Burmese cat

1. The _____ has short, dark–brown hair and yellow eyes.
2. The _____ has long, white hair and orange eyes.
3. The _____ has short hair and blue eyes.
4. The _____ has long hair and blue eyes.

B. Write a description for each picture, using precise details. Each description should refer to only one picture.

5.   6.   7.   8.

Banana   Apple   Cherry   Lemon

9.   10.   11.   12.

Violin   Guitar   Clarinet   Flute

Add Precise Details

Look at your cluster map. Add details to make it more precise. Save your work to use in both your story and your poem.

Using Figurative Language

Writers often use figurative language to make descriptions more interesting. In figurative language, the usual meaning of a word or phrase is changed to create a special effect. Here are some kinds of figurative language that Steve found.

Comparisons

Several kinds of figurative language deal with comparisons. A **simile** is a statement that compares two things using the words *like* or *as*.

Read these examples of simile:

The sand was as soft as velvet.
The cactus was like a huge green pincushion.

Another kind of comparison is a **metaphor**. A metaphor is a statement that compares two things without using the words *like* or *as*. Here are some examples of metaphor:

The grass is a carpet of shining green silk.
The thunder was an angry lion's roar.

Sound Words

Sound words are words that imitate or suggest sounds. Words such as *squeak, screech, crash, ding-dong,* and *moo* are sound words.

The quiet tick-tock of the clock was the only sound in the room.
I heard the zoom of a car's engine down the road.

In his descriptive paragraph, Steve wanted to include some figurative language. He decided to compare the rain clouds to a curtain. Here is the figure of speech he wrote.

The clouds are a heavy, gray curtain over the sun.

His comparison is a metaphor because it does not use the words *like* or *as*.

Practice

A. Read each sentence. Write whether each sentence contains a simile, a metaphor, or a sound word.

1. The crow was a lonely messenger of spring.
2. The horse neighed in the field.
3. The dry leaves shook like rattles.
4. Like a herd of buffalo, the children raced through the field.
5. The trees were distant shadows hiding in the mist.
6. When the twig cracked, the dog yipped in surprise.
7. The wind was a cool breath on my skin.
8. The children's bright yellow raincoats made them look like giant flowers.
9. My rocking chair creaked when I rocked in it.
10. Each puddle was a hazy silver mirror.

B. Write each sentence. Add words to make each sentence into the type of figurative language in parentheses.

11. The lake _____. (simile)
12. The old oak tree _____. (metaphor)
13. Distant lightning _____. (simile)
14. The duck _____. (sound word)
15. My bicycle _____. (metaphor)

Use Figurative Language

Look at the details in your cluster map. Develop some of them using similes, metaphors, and sound words. Write the figurative language on a separate piece of paper. Keep the paper to help you later.

Writing a First Draft

Read the first draft of Steve's descriptive paragraph. Notice that there are some mistakes.

> It is raining when I first see the field. The clouds are a heavy gray curtain over the sun. Raindrops blow against my cheeks and drip on my hands as I stand on the edge of the feild. The grass touches my ankles. The smell of damp erth comes from the ground. Fog makes the grass look as faded as an old photograph. The only bright color is a red-crowned bird who sits by me. Wind hisses through the wet leaves of a nearby oak tree. Wet puddles are everywhere. I cant wait for the rain to stopp, to explore some more.

Steve didn't use every idea from his cluster map. That's all right. You can choose the ones you want to use.

Write Your First Draft

Use your cluster map to find ideas. You may want to discuss your ideas with your teacher or classmates. Then begin writing. Include the precise details and figurative language you wrote. Write on every other line of your paper. Save your draft to work on later.

Discussing a First Draft

After Steve finished his first draft, he wanted to improve it. He talked about it with his classmate Rosita.

Discussion Strategy

Stick to the topic. If you're talking about a paragraph describing a beach, talk about the paragraph. Don't start talking about what was on TV last night.

Content Checklist

✔ Does the paragraph tell about one particular place?
✔ Does it tell how the place looks, smells, sounds, feels, or tastes?
✔ Does it paint a clear picture with colorful words?

Revise Your First Draft for Content

To the Reader: Exchange papers with a classmate. Read your partner's paragraph. Try to imagine the place that is described. If you can't picture it in your mind, discuss details that might help give a clearer picture. Use the Content Checklist and the Discussion Strategy to discuss your partner's work.

To the Writer: After you have discussed your first draft with your partner, make content changes on your paper. Don't lose your corrected work.

Using a Thesaurus

Rosita said she had trouble picturing some of the things Steve described. Steve decided to use a thesaurus to find words that would create a clearer picture. A **thesaurus** is a book of synonyms, words with the same or similar meanings. In a thesaurus, words are listed alphabetically. For each word, there is a list of synonyms.

Here is what Steve's thesaurus lists for the word *touch*.

> **touch:** brush, handle, hit, pet, stroke, tag, tap, tickle

Here is how a sentence with the word *touch* can be improved using a thesaurus.

> Jim <u>touches</u> his dog, Ruff.
> Jim <u>pets</u> his dog, Ruff.

Here is a list of synonyms for *strong*.

> **strong:** firm, muscled, powerful, sturdy, tough,

Here is how a sentence with the word *strong* can be changed.

> Maggie spoke in a <u>strong</u> voice.
> Maggie spoke in a <u>firm</u> voice.

Here are some changes Steve made using the thesaurus.

Proofreading Marks
add
take away

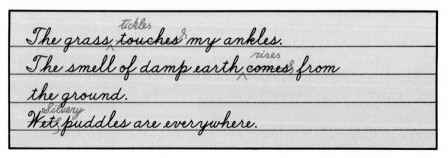

The grass ~~touches~~ *tickles* my ankles.
The smell of damp earth ~~comes~~ *rises* from the ground.
Wet *Silvery* puddles are everywhere.

198

Practice

A. One thesaurus lists these synonyms for the verb *to walk*. Use a different synonym to complete each sentence. Choose the word that best fits the meaning of the sentence.

 walk: hike, march, pad, plod, skip, stroll, tiptoe, waddle, wade

1. Let's walk through the woods and up Blue Mountain.
2. Walk out of the room or you'll wake the baby.
3. We watched the band walk proudly down the parade route.
4. Take off your shoes and walk in the water.
5. The cats walk silently on their soft paws.
6. Grandma and I walk through the park in the evening.
7. The ground shakes as the big workhorses walk by.
8. The fat geese walk down to the pond each morning.

B. Read this thesaurus entry for *noise*. Write a sentence for each synonym. Your sentence should give clues to the exact meaning of each synonym.

 **noise:** click, crash, creak, beep, racket, sound

Revising Checklist
- ✔ Have I included all the features of descriptive writing? (p. 185)
- ✔ Can I combine sentences with related ideas? (p. 32)
- ✔ Have I varied sentence beginnings? (p. 152)
- ✔ Where can I use a thesaurus to add descriptive language? (pp. 118, 198)

 ## Revise Your First Draft for Style
Check your first draft for everything on the Revising Checklist. You can use the thesaurus on page 429 for help. Mark your changes with the Proofreading Marks. Save your corrected draft.

Using Apostrophes

Steve often forgot to use apostrophes. So he looked up the rules about them. They are used in possessives and contractions. A **possessive** is a word that tells who or what has something. A **contraction** is a shortened form of two words. Here are the rules Steve found.

Rule	Example
To form the possessive of a singular noun, add an apostrophe and *s* ('s).	boy—boy's duck—duck's bush—bush's
To form the possessive of a plural noun that ends in *s,* add only an apostrophe (').	girls—girls' trees—trees' cats—cats'
To form the possessive of plural nouns that do not end in s, add an apostrophe and *s* ('s).	children—children's men—men's people—people's
Use an apostrophe in a contraction to show where a letter or letters have been left out. Many contractions contain a shortened form of *not*.	do not—don't is not—isn't would not—wouldn't cannot—can't will not—won't
Other contractions contain a shortened form of *to be, to have* or *will*.	I am—I'm she is—she's he had—he'd you will—you'll

Practice

A. Write each sentence. Write the possessive form of the underlined word.

    1. It is fun to read about other <u>people</u> travels.

    2. Helen Keller could not see or hear, but this <u>woman</u> words described scenes in unusual detail.

    3. She used her fingers to explore <u>nature</u> beauty.

    4. Her <u>friends</u> descriptions helped her learn how things looked and sounded.

B. Write each sentence. Write the correct contraction for the underlined words.

    5. <u>She is</u> famous for the descriptions that she wrote about her travels.

    6. <u>They have</u> amazed readers with their precise details for many years.

    7. Read her description of Niagara Falls, and you <u>can not</u> forget it.

    8. <u>It is</u> detailed and full of the excited feelings she felt visiting Niagara falls.

    9. She <u>did not</u> see or hear the waterfall, but she felt the vibrations of the thundering water.

Proofreading Checklist

✔ Have I capitalized the first word of each sentence? (p. 34)
✔ Have I indented the first word of my paragraph? (p. 34)
✔ Have I used apostrophes in possessive nouns and contractions correctly?
✔ Have I used the correct past tense of irregular verbs?

Proofreading Marks	
∧	add
⌇	take away
¶	indent
≡	capitalize
/	small letter
◯	check spelling
∼	transpose

Proofread Your Description

    Check your descriptive paragraph for correct use of apostrophes. Use the Proofreading Checklist. Make corrections on your draft. Save your work for the next lesson.

Checking Spelling/Writing a Final Copy

Spelling Strategy

You may have trouble remembering whether a word ends in *able* or *ible*. If so, say the word while stressing the syllable that gives you difficulty.

flexible (say "flex IH ble")
adorable (say "ador AY ble")

Here is Steve's revised and proofread paragraph.

> It is raining when I first see the field.
> The clouds are a heavy gray curtain over the
> sun. Raindrops blow against my cheeks and
> drip on my hands as I stand on the edge of
> the *field* feild. The grass *tickles* touches my ankles. The
> smell of damp *earth* erth *rises* comes from the ground.
> Fog makes the grass look as faded as an old
> photograph. The only bright color is a red,
> crowned bird who sits by me. Wind hisses
> through the wet leaves of a nearby oak tree.
> *Silvery* Wet puddles are everywhere. I can't wait for
> the rain to *stop* stopp, to explore some more.

Check Your Spelling

Use the Proofreading Marks to correct any spelling errors. Apply the Spelling Strategy. Add the words you changed to your Spelling Log. Then, write, proofread, and save your final copy.

Studying Poetry

Read this descriptive paragraph. Then read the poem.

We were at the beach at last! It was so wonderful to stand up after being hot and crowded in the car for an hour. The sun glittered on the waves. The scent of road fumes and hot highway tar was still in my mind. Now they were replaced with the ocean's salty smell. I opened the bottle of suntan lotion and began to rub the smooth, cool liquid on my arms and shoulders.

Driving to the Beach
by
Joanna Cole

On the road
smell fumes and tar
through the windows
of the car.

But at the beach
smell suntan lotion
and wind
   and sun
      and ocean!

Both the poem and the paragraph use some of the same sense images. The paragraph, however, gives many more details. The poem concentrates on just a few. In this way, each word in the poem is loaded with meaning. The way words are placed in a poem is also important. For example, the author wants you to be able to almost smell the wind, sun, and ocean. By placing each item on a separate line, she calls attention to each.

Poems can also use word sounds differently than paragraphs do. The words *car, tar, ocean,* and *lotion* are in both the poem and the paragraph. In the poem, they are used at the ends of lines. This makes you notice that they rhyme. It also gives the poem a sound pattern.

203

Read the following poems.

Bulgy Bunne	**bell**
by	**by**
Jack Prelutsky	**Valerie Worth**

Bulgy Bunne (the wonder builder)
built a boat of brass and wood,
Bulgy chose the finest lumber,
and the brass was just as good.

Every plank he picked was perfect,
there was not a knot in one,
for the best was barely suited
to the boat of Bulgy Bunne.

By flat tink
Of tin, or thin
Copper tong,
Brass clang,
Bronze bong,

The bell gives
Metal a tongue—
To sing
In one sound
Its whole song.

Rhyme and Rhythm

There are many ways to use sound in poems. **Rhyme** is one. Rhyming poems have words with the same final sound at the end of certain lines. The second and fourth lines of "Bulgy Bunne" rhyme. So do the sixth and eighth lines.

Rhythm, a pattern of strong beats, is another way to use sound in poetry. Every line in "Bulgy Bunne" has four strong beats. Read these two lines. Notice that each strong beat is shown with a ′ over it.

Búlgy Búnne (the wónder búilder)

búilt a bóat of bŕass and wóod,

Not all poems use rhyme and rhythm. The poem "bell" has only a few rhymes and no regular rhythm.

Alliteration

Alliteration is another way to give poems a catchy sound. Words with alliteration have the same beginning sound. "Bulgy Bunne" uses many words that start with b—*builder, built, boat, brass, best, barely,* and Bulgy's name. The poem's fifth line has many words starting with *p.*

204

You have already learned about **sound words** such as *hiss* and *pop*. Sound words can be used in poems, too. Some poets even make up sound words to get just the right effect. The poem "bell" uses words such as *tong, clang,* and *bang* to describe the sounds a bell makes.

Practice

A. Write whether each short poem contains an example of rhyme and rhythm, alliteration, or sound words.

  1. The moon sails softly across the night.
     The dark sea becomes silver
     Sliding over silver sand.

  2. Use red and green,
     and pink and blue.
     A rainbow shines
     When you are through.

  3. Three animals crossed a wooden floor.
     Frog plipped by in long, damp hops.
     Raccoon's feet clicked as he sped past.
     But huge, heavy-pawed Lion made no sound at all.

B. Write the short poems. Complete each one with the line that has the right rhyme and rhythm.

  4. Skáting óver shíning íce
     a. Ísn't óften dóne by míce.
     b. Tákes a lót of práctice.

  5. A stórm has cóme, and wínd has blówn,
     a. The léaves have fállen dówn.
     b. And whó knows whére the bírds have flówn?

  6. In schóol I léarned
     The sún's a stár.
     Are áll stars súns?
     a. Of cóurse they áre.
     b. They áre.

Using Simile and Metaphor in Poems
◆

When you wrote your descriptive paragraph, you learned how to use simile and metaphor. Remember that a **simile** is a comparison that uses *like* or *as*. A **metaphor** is a comparison that does not use *like* or *as* (page 194). These kinds of figurative language can also be used in poems.

Simile
The Fisherman's Wife
by
Amy Lowell
When I am alone,
The wind in the pine-trees
Is like the shuffling of waves
Upon the wooden sides of a boat.

Metaphor
Long Trip
by
Langston Hughes
The sea is a wilderness of waves,
A desert of water.
We dip and dive,
Rise and roll,
Hide and are hidden
On the sea.
    Day, night,
    Night, day,
The sea is a desert of waves,
A wilderness of water.

"The Fisherman's Wife" uses a simile to compare the wind in the trees to the sea's waves. "Long Trip" uses a metaphor to compare the sea to a desert. Both poems compare things on land to things in the water. Yet they create very different effects.

Notice that neither poem uses rhyme or rhythm. You may use rhyme and rhythm in your poem, but you don't have to.

Practice

A. Tell whether each short poem uses simile or metaphor.

   1. Leaves falling in a storm
      are green snowflakes
      that don't melt, even
      when they touch the ground.

   2. Snow, quiet and white
      Is a blanket for gardens
      To keep sleeping plants warm.

   3. This empty room
      Is as quiet
      As a dream
      That hasn't begun.

   4. Fireflies glowed
      like tiny flashlights
      in the deep darkness.

B. Write each comparison described below.

   5. Compare a whale to a ship, an elephant, or an island using
      a metaphor.

   6. Compare a butterfly to a jewel, a leaf, or a thought using a
      simile.

   7. Compare a rainbow to a bridge, a trail, or a dream using a
      simile.

Which detail will be best for a poem?

APPLY STEP BY STEP

Choose a Topic

Reread your descriptive paragraph and the cluster map you made for it. Choose one detail to use as the subject of your poem. If you prefer, pick a different subject. Think of some things to compare to your subject. Write your ideas and save them for later.

Writing and Discussing a Poem

Read this first draft of Steve's poem.

> *The wind blowing through the leaves*
> *Has a hissing sound.*
> *It sounds like voices whispering.*
> *Telling secrets.*

Use the Content Checklist to discuss Steve's poem with your class.

Content Checklist

✔ Does it have all the characteristics of descriptive writing? (p. 185)

✔ Does the poem rhyme? If so, which lines rhyme? (p. 204)

✔ Does the poem have a regular rhythm? (p. 204)

✔ Does it use alliteration? If so, which words start with the same sound? (p. 204)

✔ Does it make a comparison using a simile or a metaphor? (p. 206)

✔ Does the poem use any sound words? (p. 194)

Write and Revise Your Poem

Look at the notes you took in the last lesson. Write a poem comparing your subject to something in your notes. Your poem should contain a simile or a metaphor. You may use rhyme, rhythm, alliteration, and sound words, but you don't have to.

When you are finished, exchange poems with a classmate. Use the Content Checklist to discuss your partner's poem. Apply the Discussion Strategy on page 197. Then, revise your poem. Save your revised poem to share with your class.

Sharing Your Descriptive Writing

Speaking/Listening Strategy

Before reading aloud, read your work to yourself several times. That way, when you speak, you can look at your audience, not at your paper. If you're in the audience, look directly at the speaker. This shows you are interested and helps you understand what the speaker says.

Choosing a Way to Share

Here are some ways to share your descriptive writing.

Read Aloud   Read your poem or paragraph aloud as a riddle. Leave out words that directly name what you have described. Then, have your audience guess the topic from the details.

Give a Chalk Talk   Read your descriptive writing to the class. As you do, have a partner draw details from your description on the board. The drawings can be serious or funny.

Make a Travel Magazine   Put everyone's poems and paragraphs together to make a travel magazine. Use drawings, or cut-out pictures to illustrate it. Design a cover for the magazine. Display it in your school library.

Share Your Descriptive Writing
Choose the way you prefer to share your descriptive writing. Present it to your class.

Add to Your Learning Log
- Am I proud of my poem and my paragraph?
- Which did I enjoy writing more, the paragraph or the poem?
- What will I do differently in my next descriptive writing?

The Literature Connection: Pronouns

Have you ever taken a shortcut to get somewhere faster? In writing, **pronouns** are shortcut words that replace nouns. They save writers the trouble of repeating a name over and over again. They make sentences clear and easy to read. For example, read these sentences:

Jim saved Jim some time by calling Jim's friend. Jim saved *himself* some time by calling *his* friend. The second sentence is clearer and easier to read than the first. The writer avoided using Jim's name so many times by replacing it with the pronouns *himself* and *his*.

Read the poem below to see how pronouns let you use your imagination. The characters in this poem are named with pronouns, so you have more freedom to imagine who they are. You can picture them in any way you like. You can even pretend that you are one of them.

Anchored
by
Shel Silverstein

Our anchor's too big for our ship,
So we're sittin' here tryin' to think.
If we leave it behind we'll be lost.
If we haul it on board, we will sink.
If we sit and keep talkin' about it,
It will soon be too late for our trip.
It sure can be rough on a sailor
When the anchor's too big for the ship.

Discussion

1. Who is named by the word *we* in the poem?
2. What is named by the word *it* in the third line of the poem?
3. Replace the words *we* and *our* in the poem with other pronouns. Read the poem again using the pronouns you chose.

The Writing Connection:
Pronouns

◆

You can use a pronoun in your writing to replace any noun that is repeated too often. The examples below show how you might use pronouns to make your writing clear and easy to read.

Pete and Cindy looked at the anchor.
They looked at the anchor.

Cindy said, "Other people can help the sailors."
She said, "They can help us."

Activity

The sailors you read about on the facing page are shown in the picture above. Imagine that you are about to rescue them. Can you see why they are stuck? Write five sentences that tell what is happening. Don't use any of these pronouns: *I, he, she, it, they, him, her, them*. Then read your story to yourself. You probably repeated a lot of words. Now rewrite your story using the pronouns. Did your story improve?

Subject Pronouns

A **pronoun** is a word that replaces a noun or nouns.

A. One kind of pronoun is a subject pronoun.

A **subject pronoun** is used in place of a noun in the subject part of a sentence. *I, you, he, she, it, we,* and *they* are subject pronouns.

Henson traveled with Peary.   He traveled with Peary.

B. A pronoun should tell about the same kind and the same number of noun or nouns it replaces.

Subject Pronouns	Whom or What It Tells About
I	myself (the person speaking)
you	person or people I am talking to
he	one boy or man
she	one girl or woman
it	one thing
we	myself and one or more other persons
they	more than one person or thing

The men were brave.   They were brave.
Peary hiked through snow.   He hiked through snow.

Strategy

Don't use pronouns too often when you write. Use a subject pronoun as the subject of a sentence only if the reader knows what noun the pronoun replaces.

Check Your Understanding

A. Write the letter of the subject pronoun in each sentence.
    1. We read about the first journey to the North Pole.
        a. We   **b.** read   **c.** first   **d.** North Pole
    2. It was an important discovery.
        a. It   **b.** was   **c.** an   **d.** discovery

B. Write the letter of the subject pronoun that replaces the underlined word or words.

   3. Henson was the first person at the North Pole.
      a. It   **b.** They   **c.** He   **d.** You
   4. The men put an American flag in the ground.
      a. We   **b.** He   **c.** She   **d.** They

Practice

A. Write each sentence. Underline the subject pronoun.

   5. He worked with Peary on the voyage.
   6. They sailed to Greenland.
   7. It was very cold and windy.
   8. You must see the icebergs.

B. Write each sentence. Write the correct subject pronoun for the underlined word or words.

   9. Henson and Peary traveled by dogsled. (They, He)
   10. Peary wrote a book about the trip. (He, You)
   11. Sara and I read about the Arctic Ocean. (I, We)
   12. Sara gave a report about Peary's trip. (She, You)

C. Mixed Practice Write each sentence. Write a subject pronoun for the underlined word or words.

   13. The explorers sailed on a ship called the *Roosevelt*.
   14. Maggie found a picture of the *Roosevelt*.
   15. The camp was 450 miles from the North Pole.
   16. Peary sent many of the men back to camp.
   17. The people traveled in the harsh weather.
   18. Maggie and I learned a lot about the North Pole.
   19. Years later, Richard E. Byrd flew to the North Pole.
   20. Peary, Henson, and four Eskimos reached the Pole.

Apply: Work with a Partner

Write five newspaper headlines telling what has happened at your school or in your neighborhood. Then rewrite the headlines replacing the noun in the subject part with a subject pronoun.

Object Pronouns

A. Another kind of pronoun is an object pronoun.

An **object pronoun** is used in place of a noun that follows an action verb. It is found in the predicate part of the sentence. *Me, you, him, her, it, us,* and *them* are object pronouns.

People admired Lindbergh.   People admired him.
Lindbergh received a medal.   Lindbergh received it.

B. The chart below shows what each object pronoun stands for.

Object Pronoun	Whom or What It Tells About
me	myself (the person speaking)
you	person or people I am talking to
him	one boy or man
her	one girl or woman
it	one thing
us	myself and one or more other persons
them	more than one person or thing

Lindbergh flew the plane.   Lindbergh flew it.
Planes interested the men.   Planes interested them.

Strategy

When you are asked to replace a noun with a pronoun, be sure you do not use another noun.

Sentence: The pilot landed the plane.
Sentence with a pronoun: The pilot landed it.
Sentence with another noun: The pilot landed the jet.

Check Your Understanding

A. Write the letter of the object pronoun.
1. People told him about a special airplane.
    a. people   **b.** told   **c.** him   **d.** airplane
2. Lindbergh and other men designed it.
    a. Lindbergh   **b.** other   **c.** men   **d.** it

B. Write the letter of the object pronoun that replaces the underlined words.

    3. He named the plane the *Spirit of St. Louis*.
        a. it   **b.** him   **c.** them   **d.** us

    4. The teacher told Greg and me about the flight.
        a. me   **b.** him   **c.** us   **d.** them

Practice

A. Write each sentence. Underline the object pronoun.

    5. Charles Lindbergh took it to New York.

    6. Reporters met him on the field.

    7. Charles told them about the route.

    8. The librarian helped me with the report.

B. Write each sentence. Write the correct object pronoun for the underlined word or words.

    9. Raymond Orteig offered a prize. (them, it)

    10. Joy asked Juanita and me about Lindbergh. (me, us)

    11. The plane carried Lindbergh into the sky. (him, her)

    12. Lindbergh saw people on the ground. (them, him)

C. Mixed Practice Write each sentence. Write an object pronoun for the underlined word or words.

    13. Lindbergh flew the plane over the Atlantic Ocean.

    14. Friends called the pilot the Lone Eagle.

    15. Lindbergh wrote a book about the flight.

    16. People in France saw Lindbergh in the sky.

    17. Charles Lindbergh won the prize.

    18. Charles married Anne Morrow two years later.

    19. Ms. Torres gave Juan, Sara, and me Lindbergh's book.

    20. Charles Lindbergh received a prize and a medal.

Apply: Test a Partner

Make a list of object pronouns. Then make another list of words that can be replaced by the object pronouns. Write the words in a different order from that of the pronouns. Trade papers with a partner. Match each object pronoun with the word or words it can replace.

I and Me; We and Us

A. *I* is a subject pronoun. Use *I* in the subject part of a sentence.

> I went to Dinosaur National Monument.

Me is an object pronoun. Use *me* in the predicate part of a sentence.

> Dinosaur skeletons interest me.

Sometimes *I* or *me* is used with the name of a person. When you speak or write, always use *I* or *me* last to be polite.

> Lola and I looked at the fossils.
> The size of the dinosaurs surprised Lola and me.

B. *We* is a subject pronoun. Use *we* in the subject part of a sentence.

> We listened to the tour guide.

Us is an object pronoun. Use *us* in the predicate part of a sentence.

> The guide told us about the Indians.

Strategy

Sometimes it's hard to know whether to use *I* or *me* with the name of a person. To decide, say the sentence aloud with the pronoun only. Which pronoun sounds right? That is the word to use.

Check Your Understanding

A. Write the letter of the correct word or words.
    1. _____ found the fossils in the rocks.
      a. I   **b.** Me
    2. The guide told _____ about the early tools.
      a. Dad and I   **b.** Dad and me   **c.** Me and dad

B. Write the letter that names the underlined word.

    3. The museum guide expected <u>us</u>.

        a. subject pronoun   **b.** object pronoun

    4. <u>We</u> saw the large canyons.

        a. subject pronoun   **b.** object pronoun

Practice

A. Write each sentence. Write the correct pronoun.

    5. _____ saw sketches of the dinosaurs. (I, me)

    6. The guide took _____ to the Yampa River. (I, me)

    7. Jan and _____ watched a movie about dinosaurs. (I, me)

    8. The dinosaurs interested Jan and _____. (I, me)

B. Write each sentence. Write the correct pronoun.

    9. _____ also learned about the plant life. (We, Us)

    10. The pilot flew _____ to Utah. (we, us)

    11. _____ saw a model of an Indian's tepee. (We, Us)

    12. Ming followed _____ to the Green River. (we, us)

C. Mixed Practice Write each sentence. Write the correct pronoun.

    13. _____ stayed for one week. (We, Us)

    14. The dinosaurs amazed _____. (I, me)

    15. Dad took _____ to the visitor center. (we, us)

    16. _____ studied the dinosaur's skeleton. (I, Me)

    17. Mom and _____ walked down the trails. (I, me)

    18. Dad asked Junko and _____ about the fossils. (I, me)

    19. Sandy, Junko, and _____ brought knapsacks. (I, me)

    20. _____ gave _____ a tour of the canyons. (She, Her) (we, us)

Apply: Learning Log

   What part of this lesson did you find most difficult? Think of a way to help yourself remember when to use *I* or *me* and *we* or *us*. Write your idea in your learning log.

Possessive Forms of Pronouns

◆

Possessive forms of pronouns tell who or what owns or has something. They take the place of possessives.

A. The possessive forms of pronouns are *my, your, her, his, its, our,* and *their*.

> My book is about Annie Smith Peck.
> The picture shows her mountain-climbing equipment.

B. Use the possessive form of the pronoun that tells about the same kind and number as the possessive it replaces.

Possessive Pronoun	Whom or What It Tells About
my	belonging to myself
your	belonging to you
his	belonging to one boy or man
her	belonging to one girl or woman
its	belonging to one thing
our	belonging to myself and one or more other persons
their	belonging to more than one person or thing

Strategy

Study the chart carefully so that you will use the possessive forms of pronouns correctly. Remember that possessive forms of pronouns usually come before nouns.

Check Your Understanding

A. Write the letter of the possessive form of the pronoun.
  1. Our book shows pictures of Annie Smith Peck.
     a. Our   **b.** of   **c.** Annie Smith Peck
  2. His father saw Mount Huascaran.
     a. His   **b.** father   **c.** Mount Huascaran

B. Write the letter of the possessive form of the pronoun that replaces the underlined word.
  3. Annie's first trip was in Switzerland.
     a. She   **b.** Her   **c.** Her's
  4. They climbed the mountain's steep side.
     a. their   **b.** his   **c.** its

Practice

A. Write each sentence. Underline the possessive form of the pronoun.

    5. Her age surprised many people.

    6. Our book tells about Mount Huascaran.

    7. Your map shows Mount Huascaran in Peru.

    8. Snow covers its peaks.

B. Write the second sentence. Replace the underlined word or words with a possessive form of the pronoun.

    9. Annie's journeys amazed other people.

          _____ journeys amazed other people.

   10. Annie climbed Mount Matterhorn's peak first.

          Annie climbed _____ peak first.

   11. An ice pick was one of the guides' tools.

          An ice pick was one of _____ tools.

   12. The climbers' path went through a lot of ice.

          _____ path went through a lot of ice.

C. Mixed Practice Write each sentence. Replace the possessive with the correct possessive form of the pronoun.

   13. The mountain climbers' trip took four days.

   14. The mountain's peak was 6,768 meters high.

   15. The cold weather froze Annie's food.

   16. The men's ice picks cut steps in the ice.

   17. Annie's guides hiked tall mountains in Europe.

   18. Annie also climbed New Hampshire's Mount Madison.

   19. The state's peaks are popular with climbers.

   20. This was the woman's last climb.

   21. Annie's age at the time was 82.

   22. Huascaran's north peak was named in Annie's honor.

   23. Jason's book tells about the climbers' journey.

Apply: Work with a Group

   Write ten sentences about an imaginary place where your group would like to travel. Describe your group's special place. Use possessive forms of pronouns.

Contractions

A **contraction** is a shortened form of two words that are joined together. An apostrophe (') takes the place of the missing letters.

A. Pronouns can be combined with the verbs *am*, *is*, and *are* to form contractions. Look at the chart below.

Contraction	Meaning
I'm	I am
you're	you are
we're	we are
they're	they are
she's	she is
he's	he is
it's	it is

B. Pronouns can also be combined with the verbs *will* and *have* to form contractions. Look at the charts below.

Contraction	Meaning
I'll	I will
you'll	you will
she'll	she will
he'll	he will
we'll	we will
they'll	they will

Contraction	Meaning
I've	I have
you've	you have
we've	we have
they've	they have

An apostrophe stands for a missing letter in a contraction. So, *it's* must be the contraction for *it is*.

Strategy

Is it hard to decide whether to use *it's* or *its*? Remember:

it's = it is   its = belonging to it

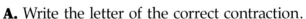

Check Your Understanding

A. Write the letter of the correct contraction.

1. I am writing a report about Sally Ride.
   a. Im   **b.** I's   **c.** I'm
2. She is the first American woman astronaut.
   a. Sheis   **b.** She's   **c.** She're

B. Write the letter of the correct contraction.

   3. She will go into space again.
      a. She'll   **b.** Shew'll   **c.** Shel'l
   4. We have read about Ms. Ride.
      a. We'eve   **b.** We've   **c.** Weh've

Practice

A. Write each sentence. Use the correct contraction for the underlined words.

   5. It is a long journey into space.
   6. They are preparing the spaceship for another flight.
   7. We are learning about Ride and the other astronauts.
   8. She is a scientist also.

B. Follow the instructions for Practice A.

   9. They will prepare for the next flight.
   10. We will learn more about space.
   11. They have studied the moon.
   12. She will fly with other astronauts.

C. Mixed Practice Write each sentence. Use the correct contraction for the underlined words.

   13. He is the captain of the crew.
   14. You will remember her.
   15. They have trained for many years.
   16. It is hard work.
   17. They will wear special suits.
   18. She will do experiments in space.
   19. We will find out if they are ready to fly again.
   20. You have read where she will go on the next trip.

Apply: Journal

In your journal, write five sentences about traveling to an imaginary planet. Use contractions when you can. Underline each contraction that you write.

Context Clues

A. You can often figure out the meaning of a word from its **context**, the words around it. Context clues may be synonyms or antonyms that appear in the same sentence as the unfamiliar word.

> When Dad mentioned a trip to the Grand Canyon, I answered with an eager, enthusiastic yes. I had felt drowsy before, but now I felt alert.

Which word in the first sentence is a synonym for *enthusiastic*? What does *enthusiastic* mean? Which word is an antonym for *drowsy*? What does *drowsy* mean?

B. Context clues may also appear in another sentence.

> We walked down a crowded corridor at the airport. The hallway was filled with people.

What do you think *corridor* means? What context clues tell you the meaning?

Strategy

If you cannot find a clue to an unfamiliar word in the same sentence, look at nearby sentences.

Check Your Understanding

A. Circle the letter of the meaning of the underlined word.
  1. We heard a myth, not a true story, about the canyon.
     a. true story   **b.** newspaper story   **c.** made-up story
  2. The flight to Arizona was pleasant and delightful.
     a. bumpy   **b.** boring   **c.** enjoyable

B. Follow the directions for Check Your Understanding A.
  3. The canyon is immense. I never saw anything so big.
     a. large   **b.** small   **c.** far away
  4. We stood on a plateau. It is cool on this high plain.
     a. mountain   **b.** valley   **c.** high plain

Practice

A. Write the meaning of the underlined words. Use context clues to help you.

5. Cougars, or mountain lions, live in the Grand Canyon.

6. The Colorado River eroded, or wore away, layers of rock.

7. The sight is memorable, not forgettable.

8. The canyon broadens, not narrows, at the top.

B. Follow the directions for Practice A.

9. The canyon walls contain the hardened remains of animals and plants. Scientists study these fossils.

10. Spaniards made an expedition to the canyon 400 years ago. This special journey was the first by Europeans.

11. The canyon's elevation is more than 9,000 feet. At that height, the air is cool.

12. The canyon attracts millions of visitors each year. Its natural beauty draws them.

C. Mixed Practice Write the meaning of each underlined word.

13. The Grand Canyon's colors are varied, not all the same.

14. Many species, or kinds, of birds live around the canyon.

15. Burros eat much of the plant life. Other animals also eat the vegetation.

16. Certain animals are unique to the canyon. They are not found anywhere else.

17. The boundaries of four states meet in Arizona. The edges join at a place called Four Corners.

18. The Colorado River is swift, not sluggish.

19. Park rangers conserve rather than use up the plants here.

20. They prohibit hunters in the canyon. They make a rule against hunters.

Apply: Work with a Partner

Write three sentences. Leave out the main noun in the subject part of each sentence. Include clues so that your partner can figure out the missing words. Trade papers and see if you can fill in the missing words from the clues.

A Group Discussion

Your class wants to take a trip. Where should you go? You have a group discussion to pick a place. What do you do?

People have group discussions to share ideas and solve problems. Here are some tips about group discussions.

- Be prepared to participate. Think about what you want to say before the discussion begins.
- Listen to what other people say. Consider their opinions.
- Don't talk on and on. Say what you want to say, but say it simply and quickly.
- Don't interrupt. Wait your turn to speak. If you want to be sure to remember what you want to say, write it down.
- Stick to the topic. You may want to say something that has nothing to do with the subject. It may be funny or interesting. Save it for after the discussion.
- You may disagree with someone. Say so politely and pleasantly. Never raise your voice.

Practice

On a separate piece of paper, answer the following questions.

1. You want to say something, but someone is speaking. You are afraid that you'll forget what you want to say. What should you do?
2. You disagree with someone. How should you say so?
3. You want to say something, but it's off the subject. What should you do?
4. What should you do before the discussion begins?

Apply

Have a group discussion in your class. Ask your teacher to suggest a topic and to pick a discussion leader.

HISTORY OF LANGUAGE

American and British English

Monica was visiting her cousin Colin in England. Colin suggested going to the *cinema*. Unfortunately, his *motor* was out of *petrol*. They had to take a *coach*. On the way, he bought a bag of *crisps*. For dinner that night, they ate stuffed *marrow*. Colin's father bought the marrow from a *lorry* parked near the *carriageway* exit. By the time dinner was over, Monica was completely confused. Was this English they were speaking?

The British and the American people speak the same language. However, many words are not the same in British and American English.

This chart gives the American word for the British words used in the story above.

British	American	British	American
cinema	movie theater	crisps	potato chips
motor	car	marrow	zucchini
petrol	gasoline	lorry	truck
coach	bus	carriageway	highway

Activity

Write the American words. Next to them, write the British words that mean the same thing.

1. elevator
2. garbage can
3. mailbox
4. to call on the phone
5. to mail

a. dustbin
b. to ring up
c. lift
d. to post
e. letter box

225

UNIT REVIEW

Descriptive Writing (*pages 185-189*)
 1. Write three features of descriptive writing.

Using Figurative Language (*pages 194-195*)
Write what kind of figurative language each sentence contains.
 2. Whoosh, the wind blew my hat away.
 3. The flowers were as colorful as an Indian blanket.
 4. The snow was a soft blanket covering the mountaintop.

Using a Thesaurus and Using Apostrophes (*pages 198-201*)

> talk: shout, speak, whisper

Use a synonym from the box to replace each underlined word.
 5. Mr. Jones will talk about his hiking trips to our class.
 6. Don't talk on the mountain; you could scare the deer.
 7. You should talk if you don't want them to hear.

Combine the underlined words. Write each new word.
 8. We are glad we went hiking.   9. I hope we will go again.

Write each sentence making the underlined words possessive.
 10. The flowers smell was sweet.   11. My sister hat was lost.

Studying Poetry (*pages 203-205*)
Write the line that has the right rhyme and rhythm for each poem.
 12. The sky is dark, the wind is blowing
     a. I feel like crowing.   **b.** I like mountains when it's snowing.
 13. Oh, deer, do come here
     a. I said, but he fled.   **b.** I said, but he ran away.

Subject and Object Pronouns (*pages 212-215*)
Write each sentence. Replace the underlined words with a pronoun. Write
whether it is a *subject pronoun* or an *object pronoun*.
 14. Jesse Owens was one of the century's greatest athletes.
 15. Owens won gold medals in the 1936 Olympics.
 16. The gym coach told Carlos and me about Owens.
 17. Young people admired Jesse Owens.
 18. Sylvia once heard Jesse Owens give a speech.

I and Me; We and Us (pages 216-217)

Write each sentence. Write the correct pronoun.

19. My parents and _____ flew to Australia. (I, me)

20. The farmer gave _____ a tour of the sheep farm. (we, us)

21. _____ visited the city of Sydney. (I, Me)

22. Some friends took Aretha and _____ to Port Jackson. (I, me)

23. The woman showed _____ the sheep ranch. (we, us)

24. Mom drove Sabrina and _____ to the boat races. (I, me)

25. _____ also watched a camel race. (We, Us)

Possessive Forms of Pronouns (pages 218-219)

Write each sentence. Replace the underlined possessive with the possessive form of the correct pronoun.

26. Mary Akeley's explorations began in 1909.

27. Mary studied the Indians' customs in Canada.

28. Mary's home was in Mystic, Connecticut.

29. Mary taught young girls about explorers' adventures.

30. Carl Akeley's trip to Africa was very important.

31. In Mount Mikeno, Mary observed the gorillas' habits.

32. Mary protected the animals' homes.

33. Mary climbed a mountain's steep side.

Contractions (pages 220-221)

Write a contraction for each pair of words.

34. I am

35. we have

36. she is

37. they are

38. it is

39. you will

40. they will

41. I have

Context Clues (pages 222-223)

Use the context clues to write the meaning of each underlined word.

42. Pablo Picasso began to sketch, or draw, even before he had learned how to write.

43. Picasso's father often painted placid, or calm, bird scenes.

44. Pablo's paintings were usually not dark. He used luminous colors.

45. He was the creator, or maker, of many famous works of art.

46. Picasso did a lot of hard work on his art. A great deal of labor was needed to complete each piece.

47. People all over the world adore Picasso's art. They love and admire his work.

Book Report

◆

Adjectives

What Do You Know?

"What a great book! I felt like I was there."

Has anybody ever said something like that to you? A good book can make you feel like you have traveled to a distant land. The trick is finding books that interest you, about topics you like. One way to choose is to get another person's opinion. Perhaps a friend or relative has read it already and can tell you what she or he thinks of it. Many newspapers have a book review section. In school, students often write book reports. These are all good places to find someone else's opinion before selecting a book to read.

Thinking About Book Reports

What is a Book Report

A **book report** has these features:

- It gives the title and author of the book.
- It tells where and when the story takes place.
- It describes the main characters.
- The first part tells about events in the book without giving away the ending.
- The second part explains why the book is or is not interesting or worth reading.

On TV and in newspapers, book reviews are presented regularly. In school, book reports are done regularly. One reason for writing a book report is to share your knowledge and opinion of a book with your classmates. This information will be helpful to them when they choose a book. Their book reports can also help you choose a book.

Another good reason for writing a book report is that it makes your ideas about a book sharper. If you just read a book and put it away, you might forget it pretty quickly. Writing a book report makes you think about the book and how you felt about it. This will help you remember the book much better.

Discussion

1. What are the last three books you read?
2. How did you decide to read each of them?
3. What would you tell a friend who asked what you thought of each of them?

229

Reading a Book Report

You have learned how book reports help readers. Read the book report below. Use the information in the report to decide if you might like to read this book.

The title and the author are given here.

This tells who the main character is, and when and where the story takes place.

Another main character is introduced.

This tells about a main event without giving away the ending.

This part tells why the book is interesting and why you might want to read it.

The Long Winter by Laura Ingalls Wilder is a story based on real life. Young Laura Ingalls lived with her pioneer family on the prairies of the Dakota Territory in the late 1800s. One October, Pa Ingalls thinks a bad winter is on the way. Pa is right. Big snowstorms start that month, and they don't stop until April. In a sudden storm, Laura, her teacher, and her classmates are trapped at school. They can't stay in school because there isn't enough coal to last until the storm ends. They try to get to a house in town. The snowstorm makes it impossible to see. It would be easy to wander into the prairie. At one point, Laura loses sight of everyone but her little sister Carrie. Then she makes a discovery that helps her find the path again. Laura and her family have many other adventures before the terrible winter ends.

If you like exciting stories set in pioneer days, you'll love *The Long Winter*. It tells about many thrilling events as well as describing everyday pioneer life. The characters are interesting, too. You will feel like you know the people you meet in these pages.

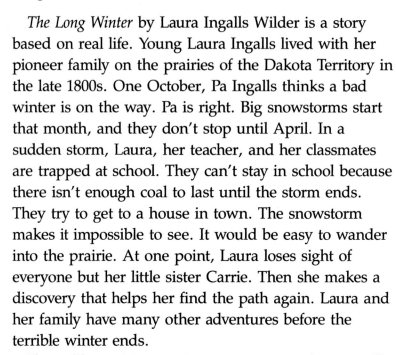

Understanding What You've Read

Answer the questions about the book report.

1. What are the book's title and author?
2. Where and when does the story take place?
3. Why doesn't the writer of the book report tell how Laura finds the path again in the storm?
4. Based on this book report, would you like to read the book? Explain why or why not.

Writing Assignment

Imagine that one of your classmates is taking a trip. She asks you to suggest a book to read on the plane. You agree to give her a two-paragraph report about a book you've read recently. Your book report will give her a short summary of the book in the first paragraph and your opinion of it in the second paragraph.

The **audience** for your report will be one of your classmates. Your **purpose** will be to share what you know about the book. You will also see how Bill, another student, writes his book report.

Make a List of Books

Make a list of three or four books you have read recently. Include the author's name if you remember it. The books may be ones you liked a lot or ones you didn't like. You may also make a short list of books you want to read. It's your choice!

231

Using a Library

Bill just read and enjoyed a book called *Pippi in the South Seas*. He decided to write his book report about it. To be sure of the details of the story, Bill decided to take it out of the library again.

Inside the library, Bill found this floor plan. It shows where different types of books are found.

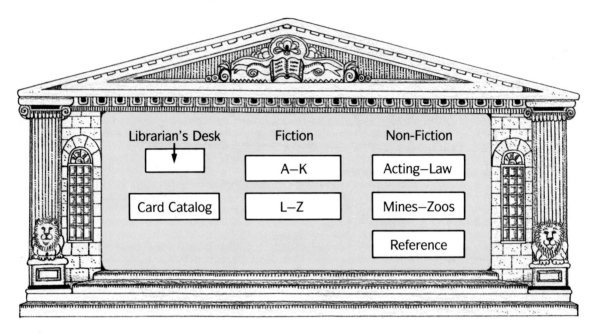

Library books are divided into two main categories: fiction and nonfiction. Nonfiction books give facts and information. They are about real people and events. Nonfiction books are grouped by subject. All the history books are together. All the science books are together, and so on.

Reference books are special nonfiction books. Encyclopedias and dictionaries are reference books; so are atlases, which are books of maps. Reference books usually have their own special section and can only be used in the library.

Fiction books are made-up stories. They come from an author's imagination. In the library, fiction books are put on the shelf in alphabetical order by the author's last name. For example, Laura Ingalls Wilder's book about prairie life would be on the *W* shelf in the fiction section.

Practice

A. Tell which letter you would look under to find each of these fiction books on a library shelf.

    1. *When the Rattlesnake Sounds* by Alice Childress

    2. *The One and Only Mr. Mahoney* by Dennis Baselice

    3. *The House at Three Rivers* by Louisa Wong

    4. *Get That Dog Out of Here!* by Danny Allocco

    5. *Dragons: A Punch-Out Book* by David Kawami

B. Tell in which section of the library—fiction, nonfiction, or reference—you would find each book.

    6. *The Only One for Me* by Sharon Hull is a fun story about a boy and his great-great-aunt.

    7. *Rosa Parks* is the true story of a woman's fight for equality.

    8. *Fairy Tales of Puerto Rico* by David Garcia is a collection of stories from the island of Puerto Rico.

    9. *The Encyclopaedia Britannica* is a set of 20 books filled with facts on many subjects.

    10. *Blue Whale* by Lila Young provides information about the life and habits of the largest animal of all.

    11. *Where's Johnny?* by Kaye Cupo is a mystery about a young boy who finds his missing brother.

    12. *The American School Dictionary* has definitions for more than 20,000 English words.

What book should I write about?

Choose Your Book

Look at the list of books you made. Choose one to write about in your book report, or choose one of these books:

Pippi Longstocking by Astrid Lindgren
Mary Poppins by P.L. Travers

Circle the name of the book you choose. Write in which part of the library you will find it.

Using a Card Catalog

Bill knew that fiction books were listed by the author's last name, but he didn't know who wrote *Pippi in the South Seas*. The librarian showed Bill the card catalog. The **card catalog** is a set of drawers containing cards filed in alphabetical order. They give information about every book in the library. There are three kinds of cards in the catalog.

Author cards list books by the author's last name. **Title cards** list books by the first important word in the title. Bill found the title card under *P*, for Pippi. It had the author's name.

Nonfiction books have a third kind of card, a **subject card**. On subject cards, books are listed by topic. Bill wanted to learn more about the South Seas, where Pippi went. He looked up a subject card for South Seas. Here are the cards Bill found.

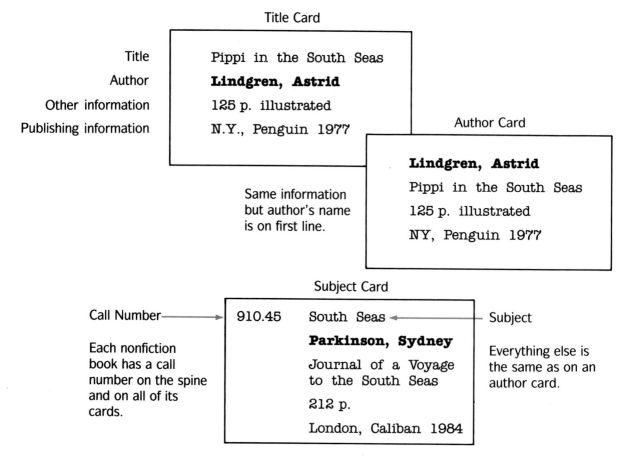

Title Card

Title	Pippi in the South Seas
Author	**Lindgren, Astrid**
Other information	125 p. illustrated
Publishing information	N.Y., Penguin 1977

Same information but author's name is on first line.

Author Card

Lindgren, Astrid
Pippi in the South Seas
125 p. illustrated
NY, Penguin 1977

Subject Card

Call Number ⟶ 910.45   South Seas ⟵ Subject

Each nonfiction book has a call number on the spine and on all of its cards.

Parkinson, Sydney
Journal of a Voyage to the South Seas
212 p.
London, Caliban 1984

Everything else is the same as on an author card.

In some libraries this information is on a computer, too.

Practice

A. Write which kind of card—author, title, or subject—you would use to find each book described below.

1. a biography of Frederick Douglass
2. a story by Sonia Sanchez
3. a book called *The Jungle Book*
4. a story by Langston Hughes
5. a book about trains in India
6. a story called *Stone Soup*

B. Study these cards from the card catalog. Use them to answer the questions.

Card A

D	**Dalgleish, Alice**
	The Courage of Sarah Noble
	Charles Scribner's Sons, 1954
	54 pp.
	In 1707, Sarah Noble goes into the Connecticut wilderness to help her father build a cabin.

Card B

J 629.45 O	Space Travel
	Sally Ride and the New Astronauts
	O'Connor, Karen
	Watts, 1983
	This book describes the experiences of the first American woman astronaut.

7. Is Card A an author card or a title card?
8. Is Card B an author card or a subject card?
9. Which card is for a fiction book?
10. What is the call number on Card B?
11. Who wrote the book on Card A?
12. What is the title of the book on Card B?

Find Your Book

If you don't know the author of your book, look it up in the title catalog. Then, find your book and check it out of the library.

Making a Story Map

Bill reread his book very carefully. The first paragraph of his book report was going to be a summary of the story. So Bill decided to do a story map to help him summarize the story.

Bill put the following information in his story map:

Setting: where and when the story takes place
Characters: the people and animals in the story
Plot: the important events that make up the story

Bill divided the plot into three parts:

Problem: something that prevents the characters from doing or getting what they want
Solution attempts: ways the characters try to solve the problem; solution attempts add humor, mystery or excitement to the story
Outcome: the result, how the story ends

Here is Bill's story map for *Pippi in the South Seas.*

Setting: a town in Sweden and Kurrekurredutt Island		
Characters: Pippi and her father, Tommy, Anika, and a shark		
Plot: Problem	Solution Attempts	Outcome
Pippi's friends Tommy and Anika have the measles. Pippi is bored.	Pippi's father invites them to an island in the South Pacific. The warm weather will be good for Tommy and Anika. Pippi will have many adventures, from talking to sharks to fighting bandits.	After the adventure, they are happy to go home.

Bill knew that a book report never gives away the ending of a story. When he writes his report later, he will leave out the information in the *Outcome* part of his story map.

Practice

A. Read this story. Correct the map that follows so that it matches the events from the story.

On his first plane trip, José was scared. Seeing Boston below him cheered him up. The main part of the flight was only an hour, but the plane circled for an hour before landing. José talked to the flight attendants until he wasn't scared anymore. When the plane finally landed, José knew that he would never be scared to fly again.

SETTING:		
CHARACTERS:		
PLOT: Problem	**Solution Attempts**	**Outcome**
José is scared.	José looks out the window.	The plane was late.

B. Make a story map for this story.

The wagon carrying Anna's family west forded the river on the third day of the trip. The horses had to swim across, pulling the wagon. Anna was afraid the wagon would tip over, but they made it across. By October, the wagon train reached the desert. The hot sun beat down on everything. The grass was all dried up, and the horses didn't have enough to eat. Her grandmother dumped books and tools to lighten the horses' load. Anna thought the traveling would never end. At last they reached Oregon. Everyone cheered. Anna could see that the new land was a good one. The journey was worth it!

Make a Story Map

Make a story map for the book you read. Save the map. You will use the information in it to write the first paragraph of your book report.

Distinguishing Fact and Opinion

What exactly is a fact? Bill found this definition.

A **fact** is a piece of information that can be checked and proved to be true. You can check facts in books, or you can observe something yourself to see if it is true.

Bill wrote these facts.

Astrid Lindgren wrote Pippi in the South Seas in 1958. In it, Pippi sails to Kurrekurredutt Island.

Checking these facts is easy. By reading the book, you could check whether Pippi sailed to Kurrekurredutt Island. The book would also list the author's name and when it was published.

In the second paragraph of his book report, Bill planned to give his opinions of the book. An **opinion** is what a person thinks or feels about something. Opinions can not be proved true or false. They may be true for one person but not for another. Opinions can be supported with facts.

Read Bill's opinions, which are supported with facts.

Opinion: *Pippi is a very unusual child.*
Fact: *She talks to sharks.*

Opinion: *Pippi in the South Seas is an exciting book.*
Fact: *Pippi fights off bandits all by herself.*

Practice

A. Read these statements from a book report. Tell whether each statement is a fact or an opinion.

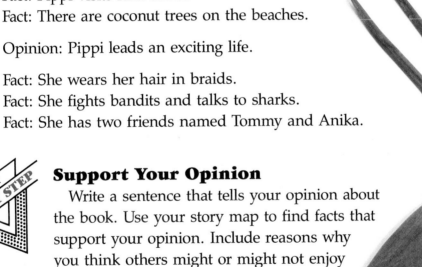

What facts will support my opinion?

  1. The best book you can read is *The 21 Balloons*.
  2. William Pene DuBois wrote and illustrated the book.
  3. *The 21 Balloons* is full of amazing people and events.
  4. The main character in the story, William Sherman, flies over the Pacific Ocean in a hot air balloon.
  5. Part of the story takes place on an island just before an earthquake begins.

B. Underline the fact that supports each opinion below.

  6. Opinion: Kurrekurredutt Island is very beautiful.

   Fact: Pippi's father lives on Kurrekurredutt Island.
   Fact: Pippi visits him there.
   Fact: There are coconut trees on the beaches.

  7. Opinion: Pippi leads an exciting life.

   Fact: She wears her hair in braids.
   Fact: She fights bandits and talks to sharks.
   Fact: She has two friends named Tommy and Anika.

APPLY STEP BY STEP

Support Your Opinion

Write a sentence that tells your opinion about the book. Use your story map to find facts that support your opinion. Include reasons why you think others might or might not enjoy it. Save your notes for later.

COMPOSING

Writing a First Draft

Before you write your first draft, read Bill's. It's a first draft, so watch out for mistakes.

> Pippi in the South Seas is about an amazing girl named Pippi Longstocking. Pippi lives in a small town in Sweden. where she does silly things. Every day for two weeks she does acrobatic tricks to cheer up her friends when they have the measles. One day. Pippi's father sends her a letter. It says to come visit him on Kurrekurredutt Island. It is a warm. sunny island. It is a colorful island. Pippi has many adventures there. She convinces a shark not to bite children any more. She fights off bandits bravely. She fights them off courageously.
>
> Allmost every page in this book has another advenchur. If you like exciting stories. you'll love Pippi in the South Seas. I liked it because it had lots of surprizes. from the tricks Pippi did in Sweden to talking to sharks in the South Seas.

Write Your First Draft

You may want to discuss your ideas with your teacher or a classmate before writing. If you prefer, you may just start writing. It's your choice. Start with the title and author of the book. Use the map you made to write the summary for the first paragraph. Put the opinions you wrote in the second paragraph. Save your work for later.

Discussing a First Draft

Discussion Strategy

Your comments about your partner's draft should be specific. Point out sentences in the draft that show what you mean. Bill's partner, Brooke, said, "This is a pretty good book report but you left out some stuff." That wasn't specific enough. It would help Bill more if Brooke said something specific, such as, "You didn't say who wrote the book."

Use the Content Checklist to discuss Bill's first draft with your class.

Content Checklist
- ✔ Are the title and author of the book given?
- ✔ Is the first paragraph a summary of the story?
- ✔ Does the second paragraph give an opinion of the book?

APPLY STEP BY STEP

Revise Your First Draft for Content

To the Reader: Use the Content Checklist to discuss your partner's first draft. When you comment on your partner's work, use the Discussion Strategy. Avoid comments such as, "I love it!" or "It's too hard." or "Nice."

To the Writer: Take notes on all of your partner's comments. Keep them to refer to later when you revise your first draft.

Combining Sentences

Many short sentences that describe the same thing can make a paragraph choppy and hard to read. You can often combine short sentences that describe the same person, place, or thing. Use commas to separate describing words in a series.

Read these sentences.

We saw tall mountains.	>	We saw tall, snowy mountains.
We saw snowy mountains.		

At sunset, the sky was pink.	>	At sunset, the sky was pink, orange, and purple.
At sunset the sky was orange.		
At sunset, the sky was purple.		

You may also combine short sentences that describe the same action. Two describing words connected with *and* don't need a comma. When there are three or more describing words, separate them with commas.

Look at these examples.

The deer ran swiftly.	>	The deer ran swiftly and silently.
The deer ran silently.		

The plane flew high.	>	The plane flew high, quickly, and noiselessly.
The plane flew quickly.		
The plane flew noiselessly.		

Now read Bill's revised first draft. See where he combined describing words in a series.

One day, Pippis father sends her a letter. It says to come visit him on Kurrekurredutt Island. It is a warm, _{and} sunny, island. It is a colorful island. Pippi has many adventures there. She convinces a shark not to bite children any more. She fights off bandits bravely. _{and} She fights them off courageously.

Practice

Combine each group of sentences by linking words that describe nouns or action. Write your new sentence.

1. The fluffy clouds floated over the mountain.
   The white clouds floated over the mountain.
2. The tall trees swayed in the wind.
   The thin, young trees swayed in the wind.
3. We walked quickly. We walked quietly.
4. We swam in the clear lake. We swam in the clean lake. We swam in the cool lake.
5. Our short vacation was fun. Our summer vacation was interesting.

Revising Checklist

✔ Have I included all the characteristics of a book report?
✔ Can I combine sentences with like subjects or predicates? (p. 32)
✔ Can I use a thesaurus to add descriptive language? (pp. 118, 198)
✔ Can I vary my sentence beginnings? (p. 152)
✔ Can I combine short sentences into one sentence with describing words in a series?

Revise Your Book Report for Style

Using the checklist above, revise your book report. If you can, combine some sentences by linking describing words. Use the proofreading marks to make your changes. Save your work for the next lesson.

Proofreading Marks	
∧	add
ᶳ	take away

243

Writing Titles

A book report includes the complete title of the book. Bill looked up the rules for writing titles.

Rule	Example
Capitalize all important words in a title. Always capitalize the first and last words, too.	<u>Pippi</u> in the <u>South</u> <u>Seas</u> <u>Make</u> <u>Way</u> for <u>Ducklings</u>
Do not capitalize unimportant words such as *a, an, and, in, of, the,* and *on* unless they begin or end the title.	<u>On</u> the <u>Banks</u> of <u>Plum</u> <u>Creek</u> <u>And</u> to <u>Think</u> <u>That</u> <u>I</u> <u>Saw</u> <u>It</u> on <u>Mulberry</u> <u>Street</u>
Underline all book titles. That helps a reader distinguish between the title and other words in a sentence or paragraph.	<u>The</u> <u>Phantom</u> <u>Tollbooth</u>
The titles of short stories, poems, and songs are capitalized in the same way as book titles. However, the titles of these short works are not underlined. Instead, quotation marks are placed around them.	Short Story: "Stone Soup" Poem: "Alligator on the Escalator" Song: "Row, Row, Row Your Boat"
When the title of a short work is at the end of a statement, the period goes inside the quotation mark.	We love to sing "Home on the Range."

Practice

Write each sentence. Add correct capitalization and punctuation for the titles.

1. Another book by Astrid Lindgren is pippi goes aboard.
2. Kenji read from the earth to the moon for his book report.
3. Another excellent book is a wrinkle in time.
4. My favorite short story is the ransom of red chief.
5. This book, america's best-loved songs, has the words of my favorite song, the yellow rose of texas.
6. One well-known poem in the book is swift things are beautiful.
7. Yesterday, Mr. Vasquez read us a story called the wish at the top.
8. Let's sing america the beautiful or my country 'tis of thee.

Proofreading Checklist
- ✔ Did I capitalize the first word of each sentence? (p. 34)
- ✔ Did I use apostrophes in contractions and possessives? (p. 200)
- ✔ Did I capitalize the book title correctly and underline it?
- ✔ Do my pronouns refer to the correct nouns?

Proofreading Marks	
∧	add
ϟ	take away
¶	indent
≡	capitalize
/	small letter
◯	check spelling
∼	transpose

Proofreading Your Book Report

Use the Proofreading Checklist to improve your book report. Be sure to follow the rules for capitalizing and underlining titles. Don't worry if your page looks messy. You will have a chance to recopy it later.

Checking Spelling/Writing a Final Copy

Spelling Strategy

Sometimes a memory hint can help you spell a word.
Example: Which spelling is correct, *friend* or *freind*?
Use this memory hint: I'll be your fri*end* to the *end*.

Choose a word you misspelled lately. Make your own memory hint to help you spell it correctly.

Here is Bill's revised and proofread book report.

---

a book by Astrid Lindgren

~~Pippi in the South Seas~~ is about an amazing girl named Pippi Longstocking. Pippi lives in a small town in Sweden. where she does silly things. Every day for two weeks she does acrobatic tricks to cheer up her friends when they have the measles. One day. Pippi's father sends her a letter. It says to come visit him on Kurrekurredutt Island. It is a warm. *and* sunny, island. It is a ~~colorful island.~~ Pippi has many adventures there. She convinces a shark not to bite children any more. She fights off bandits bravely. *and* ~~She fights them off courageously.~~

Almost
~~Allmost~~ every page in this book has another *adventure* ~~advenchur~~. If you like exciting stories. you'll love Pippi in the South Seas. I liked it because it had lots of *surprises* ~~surprizes.~~ from the tricks Pippi did in Sweden to talking to sharks in the South Seas.

Check Your Spelling

Correct your spelling errors. Use the Spelling Strategy and put any misspelled words in your spelling log. Then, write a clean, final copy of your book report.

Sharing Your Book Report

Speaking/Listening Strategy

Make sure you know your material well before you read it aloud. This will help you avoid long pauses. If you are listening, at the end you may ask questions about things you didn't understand.

Choosing a Way To Share

Here are some ideas for sharing your book report.

Reading Aloud   Read your book report to the class. As you read, pretend you are a bookseller. Your job is to persuade others to buy and read the book. After you finish, answer any questions your "customers" may have. Then ask how many want to "buy" the book.

Presenting a Puppet Show   Perform your book report as a puppet show. Make a puppet for each character you talk about in the report. Your puppets can be simple paper cutouts taped to sticks or pencils. Use the puppets to act out the story events.

Make a Book Cover   Make a book cover to share your book report. On the front of the cover, draw a picture that shows an important event in the book. On the flaps of the cover, write your summary of the story. Your opinions can go on the back of the cover.

Share Your Book Report

Choose one of the ideas above to present your book report to your class.

Add to Your Learning Log

Answer these questions in your learning log.

- Am I proud of my book report? Explain.
- Which part of my book report was the most fun to do?
- What will I do differently in my next book report?

The Literature Connection:
Adjectives

Reading is a way of traveling. When you read about a faraway place, it is almost like going there.

In some stories, writers take you to imaginary places. To tell about these imaginary places, writers use adjectives. **Adjectives** are words that tell how things look, sound, smell, feel, and taste.

In the selection below, the author tells about a hobbit's home. A hobbit is an imaginary creature that lives underground. Notice how the adjectives in the selection make the hobbit's home seem real.

A Hobbit's Home
by
J. R. R. Tolkien

In a hole in the ground there lived a hobbit. Not a nasty, dirty, wet hole, filled with the ends of worms and an oozy smell, nor yet a dry, bare, sandy hole with nothing in it to sit down on or to eat: it was a hobbit-hole, and that means comfort.

It had a perfectly round door like a porthole, painted green, with a shiny yellow brass knob in the exact middle. The door opened on to a tube-shaped hall like a tunnel: a very comfortable tunnel without smoke, with panelled walls, and floors tiled and carpeted, provided with polished chairs, and lots and lots of pegs for hats and coats—the hobbit was fond of visitors.

Discussion

1. What adjectives in the selection tell how the door of the hobbit's hole looks?
2. Which adjectives in the selection describe how things feel or smell?
3. After reading about the hobbit's home, can you guess what a hobbit itself would look like? Think of adjectives that describe your idea of a hobbit.

The Writing Connection: Adjectives

You can use adjectives to make your writing seem more real. Each adjective tells how something feels, looks, sounds, smells, or tastes. Here are some ways you could use adjectives to tell about a hobbit.

> The hobbit has furry feet.
> The hobbit has a pleasant smile.

Activity

Imagine that you were a hobbit like one of those in the picture. Describe *how* you would look. Write five sentences about your size, your eyes, your fur, your fingers and toes, and your clothes. Use adjectives in each sentence. Then exchange papers with a friend to see if the friend can decide which hobbit you are most like. A sample sentence is completed for you.

> I would wear a green vest.
> I would have curly hair.

Adjectives

An **adjective** is a word that tells about a noun.

A. Many adjectives give a clearer picture of a noun by telling *what kind*. They do this by telling how the noun looks, sounds, smells, tastes, or feels.

> Yellowstone is a large park.
> (*Large* tells how the park looks.)
> The loud waterfall crashes over the rocks.
> (*Loud* tells how the waterfall sounds.)

B. Other adjectives tell *how many* there are.

> Four rangers lead the hike.
> (*Four* tells how many rangers.)

Some adjectives, such as *many*, *some*, and *several*, tell how many but do not give an exact number.

> They visited some campsites.
> (*Some* gives an idea of how many campsites.)

Strategy

To look for an adjective, first find a noun. If the word before the noun tells *what kind* or *how many*, the word is an adjective.

Check Your Understanding

A. Look at the underlined noun. Write the letter of the adjective that tells about the noun.

1. The campers see tall trees.
   a. campers   **b.** see   **c.** tall   **d.** trees
2. The rangers protect wild animals.
   a. rangers   **b.** protect   **c.** wild   **d.** animals

250

B. Follow the directions for Check Your Understanding A.

    3. Tourists visit two <u>parks</u> in Wyoming.

        a. tourists **b.** visit **c.** two **d.** parks

    4. Many <u>people</u> sleep in tents.

        a. many **b.** people **c.** sleep **d.** tents

Practice

A. Look at the underlined noun. Write each sentence.
Underline the adjective that tells about the noun twice.

    5. White <u>snow</u> covers the mountains.

    6. Travelers see ancient <u>volcanoes</u>.

    7. Helpful <u>rangers</u> direct the campers.

    8. Campers take pictures of young <u>deer</u>.

B. Follow the directions for Practice A.

    9. Many <u>Indians</u> lived in the area long ago.

  10. The park has several <u>lakes</u>.

  11. Six canoes sail on the <u>river</u>.

  12. One <u>park</u> in Minnesota is near Canada.

C. Mixed Practice   Write each sentence. Underline each adjective twice. Underline the noun it tells about once.

  13. Yellowstone Lake is twenty miles long.

  14. White pelicans swim on the river.

  15. The park has five entrances.

  16. Hot springs amaze the tourists.

  17. Eager campers drive through the campgrounds.

  18. People ride snowmobiles up beautiful mountains.

  19. One park has fifty glaciers.

  20. Many bears roam the large forest.

Apply: Work with a Group

Work with a group to describe a person, place, or thing that everyone in the class knows. Write five sentences using an adjective in each sentence. Trade papers with another group. Try to guess who or what the other group described.

Articles

The words *a*, *an*, and *the* are special adjectives. They are called **articles**.

A. An article is used before a noun to point to the noun.

A and *an* are used before singular nouns only.

> A traveler enjoys Africa.
> Two children ride an elephant.

The is used before singular or plural nouns.

> Africa lies on the equator.
> The travelers see unusual animals.

B. *A* and *an* are used differently.

Use *a* before a noun that begins with a consonant sound.

> a lion   a woman   a house

Use *an* before a noun that begins with a vowel sound.

> an antelope   an airplane   an honor

Strategy

If you have trouble deciding whether you should use *a* or *an*, say the noun with the article aloud. Usually only the correct article sounds right. This is especially helpful with words that begin with *h*.

Check Your Understanding

A. Write the letter of the article in each sentence.
   1. A desert covers northern Africa.
      a. A   **b.** desert   **c.** northern   **d.** Africa
   2. Winds blow the sand into mountains.
      a. Winds   **b.** blow   **c.** the   **d.** sand

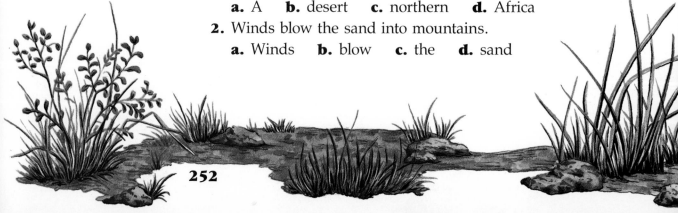

B. Write the letter of the correct article.

    3. _____ mountain rises from the desert.

      a. A   **b.** An

    4. Some people see _____ elk in the forest.

      a. a   **b.** an

Practice

A. Write each sentence. Underline each article.

    5. Few rivers flow through the desert.

    6. Large boulders surround a volcano.

    7. The country has many jungles.

    8. An antelope eats grass.

B. Write each sentence using the correct article.

    9. _____ swamp covers much of West Africa. (A, An)

   10. Tourists walk along the path for _____ hour. (a, an)

   11. _____ hippopotamus lives near water. (A, An)

   12. Explorers find _____ entrance to small caves. (a, an)

C. Mixed Practice Write each sentence using the correct article.

   13. Rocks protect _____ harbor. (a, the)

   14. Few people see _____ buffalo in the forest. (a, an)

   15. Many animals make _____ home in forests. (a, an)

   16. It is very hot near _____ equator. (a, the)

   17. Women look for _____ herb near the river. (a, an)

   18. Madagascar is _____ island near Africa. (a, an)

   19. _____ monsoon damages many of _____ homes.
      (A, An) (a, the)

   20. _____ rivers run into _____ ocean. (A, The) (a, an)

Apply: Exploring Language

Think of a place you would like to visit. Write five sentences that tell why you would like to travel to that place. Do not use any articles. What does this show you about articles?

Comparing with *er* and *est*

Adjectives can be used to compare two or more nouns.

A. Add *er* to an adjective to compare two nouns. Add *est* to an adjective to compare three or more nouns.

> The rowboat is long.
> The sailboat is longer than the rowboat.
> The houseboat is the longest boat of the three boats.
> The houseboat is the longest boat of all.

B. Some adjectives change when you add *er* or *est*.

Type of Adjective	Spelling	Example	er Form	est Form
word ending with e	drop the final e; then add er or est	nice	nicer	nicest
word ending with consonant + y	change y to i; then add er or est	dry	drier	driest
one-syllable word ending with vowel + consonant	double the final consonant; then add er or est	hot	hotter	hottest

Strategy

To compare *two* nouns, use the *two*-letter ending, *er*. To compare *three* or more nouns, use the *three*-letter ending, *est*.

Check Your Understanding

A. Write the letter of the correct adjective.
  1. The Nina was the _____ of the three ships of Columbus.
    a. small   **b.** smaller   **c.** smallest
  2. Magellan's trip was _____ than Columbus's trip.
    a. long   **b.** longer   **c.** longest

B. Write the letter of the correct adjective.

    3. His trip was the _____ trip of all.

        a. early   **b.** earlier   **c.** earliest

    4. A steamboat is _____ than a rowboat.

        a. large   **b.** larger   **c.** largest

Practice

A. Write each sentence using the correct form of the adjective in parentheses.

    5. The voyage of Cook was the (hard) of all.

    6. The Mediterranean is (warm) than the Baltic.

    7. The mainmast is the (high) of four masts.

    8. The Indian Ocean is (small) than the Atlantic.

B. Follow the directions for Practice A.

    9. Great Salt Lake is (salty) than the ocean.

  10. The blue whale is the (big) animal of all.

  11. The Indian Ocean is (large) than the Arctic Ocean.

  12. The Pacific Ocean is the (wide) of the five oceans.

C. Mixed Practice   Write each sentence using the correct form of the adjective in parentheses.

  13. The Caribbean Sea is (hot) than the Laptev Sea.

  14. Giant kelp is the (large) seaweed of all.

  15. A wave in a storm is (foam) than a wave in calm weather.

  16. The Antarctic is the (cold) ocean of the five oceans.

  17. The bottom of the Kara Sea is (flat) than the bottom of the North Atlantic.

  18. The Pacific Ocean is the (deep) ocean of all.

  19. The Atlantic is the second (large) of all the oceans.

  20. You get (wet) on a small boat than on a large ship.

Apply: Learning Log

What part of this lesson was the hardest? Think of a way to help you remember how to write adjectives when comparing two or more nouns. Write your method in your learning log.

Comparing with *More* and *Most*

Remember that *er* or *est* is added to adjectives when comparing nouns. However, for many adjectives with two or more syllables, use *more* or *most* before the adjective instead of adding an ending.

A. Study the chart to learn the correct form of an adjective when comparing two nouns.

Type of Adjective	Rule	Example	
most adjectives with one syllable	add <u>er</u>	small	small<u>er</u>
most adjectives with two or more syllables	use <u>more</u>	beautiful	<u>more</u> beautiful

Margaret Mead traveled to a <u>beautiful</u> island in Samoa. An island is <u>more beautiful</u> than a desert.

B. Study the chart to learn the correct form of a adjective when comparing three or more nouns.

Type of Adjective	Rule	Example	
most adjectives with one syllable	add <u>est</u>	small	small<u>est</u>
most adjectives with two or more syllables	use <u>most</u>	beautiful	<u>most</u> beautiful

Upolu Island is the <u>most beautiful</u> island of all.

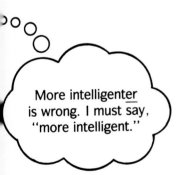

More intelligent<u>er</u> is wrong. I must say, "more intelligent."

Strategy

Never use *more* or *most* with an adjective that already ends with *er* or *est*.

Check Your Understanding

A. Write the letter of the correct form of the adjective.
   1. The trip to Samoa was _____ than the trip to Russia.
      a. more dangerous   **b.** dangerouser   **c.** dangerous
   2. Her first book is _____ than her second book.
      a. popularer   **b.** popular   **c.** more popular

256

B. Write the letter of the correct form of the adjective.

    3. The language was the ____ language of all.

        a. difficultest   **b.** difficult   **c.** most difficult

    4. The fruit was the ____ fruit of all.

        a. deliciousest   **b.** most delicious   **c.** delicious

Practice

A. Write each sentence using the correct form of the adjective in parentheses.

    5. Samoan culture is (unusual) than American culture.

    6. A hut is (comfortable) than a tent.

    7. The night was (peaceful) than a night in a big city.

    8. The society was (ancient) than American society.

B. Follow the directions for Practice A.

    9. The book about Samoa was her (famous) book of all.

    10. The land of Samoa was the (magnificent) land of all.

    11. Upolu is the (beautiful) island of the three islands.

    12. The report on Samoa was the (important) report of all.

C. Mixed Practice   Write each sentence using the correct form of the adjective in parentheses.

    13. The Samoan forest is (wonderful) than the village.

    14. The winter in Russia was the (terrible) winter of all.

    15. Russia was (modern) than Samoa.

    16. America was the (modern) country of all.

    17. The coral was the (beautiful) coral of all.

    18. The book about Samoa was (helpful) than the movie.

    19. The people Mead studied were the (unusual) in all the world.

    20. Upolu is the second (big) island of the three islands.

Apply: Test a Partner

Make a list of five adjectives. Trade papers with a partner. In a column, write the form of each adjective for comparing two nouns. Then, in another column, write the form of each adjective for comparing three or more nouns. Check your partner's paper.

Comparing with *Good* and *Bad* ◆

The adjectives *good* and *bad* have special forms for comparing two or more nouns.

A. *Good* has special forms for comparing more than one noun.

> Mexico has good soil.
> The soil in Cocula is better than the soil in Gallego.
> The soil in southern Mexico is the best soil of all.

Use *better* when you compare two nouns.
Use *best* to compare three or more nouns.

Adjective	To Compare Two Nouns	To Compare Three or More Nouns
good	better	best

B. *Bad* has special forms for comparing more than one noun.

> He sailed through a bad storm.
> A hurricane is worse than a thunder storm.
> A hurricane is the worst storm of all.

Use *worse* to compare two people, places, or things.
Use *worst* to compare three or more people, places, or things.

Adjective	To Compare Two Nouns	To Compare Three or More Nouns
bad	worse	worst

Strategy

Never add *er* or *est* to the words *good* or *bad*.

Incorrect: gooder   badder

Correct: better   worse

Check Your Understanding

A. Write the letter of the correct form of *good*.

  1. A modern ship is ____ than an old ship.

    a. good   **b.** better   **c.** best   **d.** gooder

  2. The vacation in Mexico was the ____ vacation of all.

    a. good   **b.** better   **c.** best   **d.** goodest

B. Write the letter of the correct form of *bad*.

  3. The afternoon flight was the ____ flight of all.

    a. bad   **b.** worse   **c.** worst   **d.** baddest

  4. Gina's trip was ____ than Leslie's trip.

    a. bad   **b.** worse   **c.** worst   **d.** badder

Practice

A. Write each sentence using the correct form of *good*.

  5. The Aztec empire was the ____ empire of all.

  6. Tourism in Acapulco is ____ than tourism in Juarez.

  7. The farmlands in the south are the ____ of all.

  8. Round houses are ____ than rectangular houses.

B. Write each sentence using the correct form of *bad*.

  9. Hot weather is ____ than rain for an avocado plant.

  10. The weather in the desert is the ____ weather of all.

  11. A Russian winter is ____ than a Mexican winter.

  12. Storms in the south are the ____ storms of all.

C. Mixed Practice   Write each sentence using the correct form of the adjective in parentheses.

  13. The summer rainfall is (bad) than the winter rainfall.

  14. The rainfall in Veracruz is the (bad) rainfall of all.

  15. The northwest area is the (good) of all areas for minerals.

  16. The mountain is (good) than the desert for crops.

  17. Roads in Mexico were (bad) than roads in Iowa.

  18. Corn is the (good) and (important) crop of all.

  19. Mexico City is (big) and (famous) than Ocampo.

Apply: Journal

  Write five sentences in your journal using the adjectives *good* and *bad* to compare two places you would like to visit.

Prefixes

A **base word** is a word to which other word parts can be added. A **prefix** is a word part that is added to the beginning of a base word.

A. Study the prefixes in the chart below.

Prefix	Meaning	Example
dis	the opposite of, not	disappear
im	not	impatient
in	not	incorrect
mis	badly, wrong	misspell
pre	before	preview
re	again	rewrite
un	the opposite of, not	unclear

B. Adding a prefix to a base word changes the meaning of the base word. The new word has the meaning of its two parts. You can often make new words by adding a prefix to words you already know.

Prefix + Base Word		New Word	Meaning
un +	clear	unclear	not clear
mis +	behave	misbehave	behave badly
pre +	pay	prepay	pay before

Strategy

Sometimes you can figure out the meaning of a word you don't know. If the word has a prefix, add the meaning of the prefix to the meaning of the base word.

Check Your Understanding

A. Write the letter of the prefix of the underlined word.

1. We reread all the books about Hawaii.

    a. ad   **b.** re   **c.** er   **d.** read

2. They were uncertain about the trip.

    a. certain   **b.** cer   **c.** un   **d.** tain

B. Write the letter of the word or words that tell the meaning of the underlined word.

    3. Many people dislike airplane flights.

        a. like before   **b.** like again   **c.** opposite of like

    4. They were unaware of the length of the trip.

        a. aware again   **b.** not aware   **c.** very aware

Practice

A. Write each sentence. Underline the word with a prefix. Underline the prefix twice.

    5. The children repack their suitcases.

    6. A rocky flight is unpleasant.

    7. Many passengers misunderstand the schedules.

    8. The workers unload the luggage.

B. Write a new word by adding the prefix to the base word. Write the meaning of the new word.

    9. in + expensive   **13.** pre + heat

  10. un + kind   **14.** re + check

  11. dis + agree   **15.** mis + judge

  12. im + possible   **16.** un + known

C. Mixed Practice Write each sentence. Underline the word that has a prefix. Then, write the meaning of the word.

  17. Some people feel uncomfortable on an airplane.

  18. The tourists rejoin their group each evening.

  19. Travelers reset their watches to the correct time.

  20. The plans for the trip were impractical.

  21. Many tourists preplan summer vacations.

  22. The islands have many inactive volcanoes.

  23. We must rewrite the report on Hawaii without any misspellings.

  24. The unpleasant waiter dissatisfied us.

Apply: Work with a Partner

Work with your partner to make as many new words as you can by adding different prefixes to the base words in the box. Check your words in the dictionary.

appear	read
fold	cost

LANGUAGE IN ACTION

Using the Phone Book

Imagine you want to call your friend Jenni. You know her last name. You know where she lives, but you don't know her phone number. What do you do? You use the phone book.

The phone book lists people's names, addresses, and phone numbers. It is a very helpful book. Here are some tips for using the phone book.

- ◆ People are listed alphabetically by last name. After the name, the address and phone number are given.
- ◆ Two key names are at the top of each page. These are the first and last names on the page. A page with *Edburg-Evans* at the top would have all the names that come between Edburg and Evans alphabetically. *Ekblad*, for example, would be on that page because *Ek* falls between *Ed* and *Ev*.
- ◆ Usually, there is only one person listed for each family. Your friends' phone numbers are probably listed under one of their parents' names.

Practice

Look at this page from a phone book. Then, on a separate sheet of paper, answer the following questions.

Scully, B.	Smith J.
31 Westgate Ct. 723-3372	12 Orange St. 836-0224
Segal, E.	Stannard, B.
744 Vandelinda Ave. . . . 493-7623	674 E. Main St. 493-7362

1. What is Eli Segal's phone number?
2. Where does Barbara Stannard live?
3. Your friend Otis Scully lives on Westgate Court. What is his phone number?

Apply

When you go home today, get out the phone book. Look up the phone numbers of three of your classmates. Bring them in tomorrow and see if you were right.

TEST TAKING

Using Time Well

When you take a test, use your time well. In this way you will have a chance to answer every question you know and get the best score possible.

Here are some steps to follow to help you use your time better when you take a test:

- Read through the whole test once. As you read, answer the questions whose answers you know. If there is a question you don't know, skip it and go on.
- After going through the test the first time, go back to the beginning. This time through, work on the questions you didn't know the first time. If you find a problem that is still too difficult, skip it.
- After the second time, go back and work on any questions you still haven't finished.
- If you have finished the test and there is still some time left, go back and check your answers.

Practice

Answer each question below.
1. What should you do if you get stuck on a problem the first time you go through the test?
2. Why should you go through the test a second time?
3. What should you do if you've gone through the test twice and there are still a few problems you haven't answered?
4. What should you do if you've answered every question on the test and there is still some time left?

Apply

Learning Log Decide what things from this lesson you found helpful. Write them in your learning log.

UNIT REVIEW

Book Reports   *(pages 229-231)*
   1. Write three features of a book report.

Using a Library and a Card Catalog   *(pages 232-233)*
Tell in which section of the library you would find these books.
   2. *Moishe's Invention* by Sam Bernstein is a book about a real boy who won the Young Inventor's Award. (100 pages, Chicago, Brown Books 1980   718.2)
   3. *The Short Giraffe* by Charlie Wynn is a funny story about a giraffe. (50 pages, New York, Orange Press 1982)
   4. *Webster's Dictionary* contains the definitions of many words.
   5. *How to Do Origami* by Jane Wong explains how to make fun shapes out of colored paper. (75 pages, illus. New York, Marks & Co., 1976   501.3)
   6. Now, make an author card for *Moishe's Invention*.
   7. Make a title card for *The Short Giraffe*.
   8. Make a subject card for *How to Do Origami*.

Combining Sentences and Writing Titles *(pages 242-245)*
Combine each pair of sentences into one sentence.
   9. a. The passengers were noisy.   **b.** The passengers were friendly.
   10. a. My train trip was exciting.   **b.** My train trip was new.
Add the correct capitalization and punctuation. Write each sentence.
   11. Ira wrote his book report on the boy who never said yes.
   12. My favorite song is on a clear day.
   13. I read the short story how the zebra got his stripes.

Adjectives   *(pages 250-251)*
Write each sentence. Underline each adjective twice. Underline the noun it tells about once. Do not underline articles.
   14. An orangutan is a hairy ape.
   15. The ape has long arms.
   16. They are peaceful animals.
   17. Two orangutans are in the tree.
   18. They eat wild fruits.
   19. Some orangutans travel alone.
   20. Orangutans are large apes.
   21. Many scientists study them.

Articles   *(pages 252-253)*

Write each sentence, using the correct article.

22. _____ eagle looks fierce. (A, An)

23. It builds _____ nest on high cliffs. (a, an)

24. You see golden eagles in _____ (a, the) mountains.

25. The scientist observed the eagle for _____ hour. (a, an)

Comparing with *er* and *est*   *(pages 254-255)*

Write each sentence, using the correct form of the adjective in parentheses.

26. Mount Whitney is the (high) mountain in California.

27. The Matterhorn is (small) than Mount McKinley.

28. Mount Everest is the (big) mountain of all.

29. Land in a desert is (dry) than land near a river.

Comparing with *More* and *Most*   *(pages 256-257)*

Write each sentence, using the correct form of the adjective in parentheses.

30. Italy is the (popular) country of all in Europe for tourists.

31. Rome is (famous) than Milan.

32. Tourism is the (important) business of all there.

33. Northern Italy is (modern) than southern Italy.

Comparing with *Good* and *Bad*   *(pages 258-259)*

Write each sentence, using the correct form of the adjective in parentheses.

34. The land near the Nile River is the (good) farmland of all.

35. Cotton is a (good) crop than wheat in Egypt.

36. The desert is the (bad) area of all for crops.

37. Weather in Aswan is (bad) than weather in Cairo in summer.

Prefixes   *(pages 260-261)*

Write a new word by adding the prefix to the base word. Write the meaning of the new word.

38. un + healthy

39. in + active

40. re + built

41. re + schedule

42. pre + heat

43. dis + approve

44. un + popular

45. in + dependent

MAKING ALL THE
CONNECTIONS

You and several classmates will now write a character description as a group. What you have learned about descriptive writing will help you.

You will do the following in your character description:

- Tell about a character from a book, movie, TV show, or other fiction story
- Describe the character's looks.
- Tell how the character acts, speaks, or feels.
- Tell what the character likes or does not like.
- Tell what other people think of the character.

Reading a Character Description

Read the following character description. It tells about Wilbur, the piglet who discovers the world outside his barn, in the story "Escape" by E. B. White. Notice the side notes that point out the features of a character description. Discuss the paragraph with a group of classmates. Then, your group will write a character description together.

The writer tells:
- where the character comes from
- how the character looks
- what the character likes
- how the character feels
- what other people think of the character
- how the character acts

Wilbur, a pig, is a character from the story "Escape" by E. B. White. Born a runt, Wilbur quickly grows big and healthy. He loves buckets of slops and soft mud. Wilbur sometimes feels lonesome and afraid, but his good friend Charlotte the spider helps to cheer him up. She convinces Wilbur he is "terrific" and "radiant." The judges at the County Fair agree with this opinion. Although Wilbur is not very smart, he is a lovable pig and a loyal friend.

Speaking and Listening

Your teacher will assign you to a group. Choose a group leader. Talk about these questions.

1. In the character description you read on page 266, what did you learn about the way Wilbur looks?
2. What did you learn about the way Wilbur acts and feels?
3. How did other people in the story feel about Wilbur?
4. What can you learn about Wilbur from the picture above?

Thinking

Brainstorming

Choose one person from your group to be a note taker. Have the person take notes as you discuss these questions. Save your notes.

1. Which characters from books, movies, or TV shows do you think are most interesting?
2. What do the characters look like?
3. How do the characters act, speak, or feel? Tell about the things they like or do not like.
4. What do other people in the story think of the characters?
5. If you could draw a picture of each character, what details would the picture include?

MAKING ALL THE CONNECTIONS

Organizing

When you prepare a character description, it helps to put your details in a chart. Study the chart below about Wilbur the pig.

Looks	Acts/Speaks/Feels
runt, then big, healthy	sometimes afraid, lonesome; not smart but loyal, lovable

Likes/Dislikes	Others' Opinions
likes slops, soft mud	Charlotte the spider and judges think he is terrific, radiant.

With your group, choose the most interesting person you know from a fiction story. Tell what each of you knows about the character. Have one group member take notes and write them in a chart like the one above.

Writing a Character Description

Imagine that your school were organizing a Character Hall of Fame. Your group was asked to choose an interesting character to describe. Your description will hang in the Hall of Fame under a picture of the character that your group will make. You will use the chart of details you made to help write the paragraph.

Planning

- Review the chart you made as a group. Add any new details you may think of now.
- Decide which details from the chart you will include in your paragraph.
- Organize your information in an outline. First write the character's name and the fiction story from which the character comes. Underneath, write your details in the order you wish to present them. For example, you might begin with what the character looks like.

Composing

- Work with your group to write the character description. Choose one member to write the first draft as everyone suggests ideas.
- Decide exactly how to word the first sentence. It will name the character and the story he or she is from.
- Next, decide exactly how to word the other sentences, which tell important details about the character.

Revising

- As a group, read over your character description sentence by sentence. Think of ways to improve the content.
- Check that your first sentence names the character and the story he or she is from.
- Check that all other details in the paragraph are clear and in order.

Proofreading

As a group, proofread your character description. Choose one group member to make the changes on your draft. Answer these questions:

- Does each sentence have the correct end punctuation?
- Are all pronouns used correctly?
- Is the character described with clear, precise adjectives?
- Are all words spelled correctly?

Presenting

- Choose one group member to write a neat, final copy of your character description.
- Find a magazine or newspaper picture of your character, or draw your own. Hang your picture on the classroom wall and attach the character description beneath it.

Cumulative Review

A. Write the letter of the group of words that is a sentence. (*pages 40-41*)

1. **a.** Mary visited Norway.
   b. Saw many farms.
   c. One farmer

2. **a.** The capital city.
   b. Mary reached Oslo.
   c. Rode on a bus.

B. Write the letter of the word that names each kind of sentence. (*pages 42-43*)

3. George Gershwin wrote exciting music.
   a. exclamation   **b.** statement   **c.** command   **d.** question

4. Listen to this song by Gershwin.
   a. exclamation   **b.** statement   **c.** command   **d.** question

C. Write the letter of the sentence with one line under the complete subject and two lines under the complete predicate. (*pages 44-47*)

5. **a.** Elsa knits a hat.
   b. Grace weaves fast.
   c. The boys make quilts.

6. **a.** Juan dyes the cloth.
   b. Eva makes clay pots.
   c. Rita paints a dish.

D. Write the letter of the word that is a noun. (*pages 78-79*)

7. The red bird flew.
   a. red   **b.** bird

8. The eagle flew very high.
   a. eagle   **b.** very

E. Write the letter of the correct plural noun. (*pages 80-81*)

9. fox   **a.** foxies   **b.** foxs   **c.** foxes
10. dress   **a.** dresses   **b.** dresse   **c.** dress
11. story   **a.** storys   **b.** stories   **c.** storyes
12. way   **a.** ways   **b.** waies   **c.** wayes

F. Write the letter of the correct possessive of each noun. (*pages 84-87*)

13. birds   **a.** bird's   **b.** birds'   **c.** birds's
14. women   **a.** women's   **b.** womens'   **c.** womens's
15. flag   **a.** flags'   **b.** flags's   **c.** flag's

G. Write the letter of the correctly written proper noun. (*pages 82-83, 88-89*)

16. **a.** Mond., April 14   **b.** tues., feb. 8   **c.** Wed., Oct. 1
17. **a.** mrs. Jane Won   **b.** Mr. Goro Sato   **c.** Miss. Ana Diaz

H. Write the letter of the word that names each verb. (*pages 126-129*)

   18. A deer <u>forms</u> new antlers each year.

      a. action verb   **b.** linking verb

   19. A moose <u>is</u> really a kind of large deer.

      a. action verb   **b.** linking verb

I. Write the letter of the correct tense of the verb. (*pages 130-131*)

   20. Anthony <u>baked</u> three loaves of bread.

      a. present tense   **b.** past tense   **c.** future tense

   21. The two boys <u>will make</u> sandwiches for the family.

      a. present tense   **b.** past tense   **c.** future tense

J. Write the letter of the correct spelling for each underlined verb, using the tense in parentheses. (*pages 132-135*)

   22. Mark <u>clip</u> an article from the newspaper. (past)

      a. clipped   **b.** cliped   **c.** clippd

   23. Aunt Lena <u>study</u> the newspaper article. (past)

      a. studied   **b.** studyed   **c.** studdied

   24. Aunt Lena <u>pass</u> the article back to Mark. (present)

      a. pass   **b.** passes   **c.** passs

K. Write the letter of the correct helping verb. (*pages 160-161*)

   25. The Sterling Seed Company ____ mailed Sandy a catalog.

      a. has   **b.** was   **c.** is

   26. Sandy ____ reading the catalog.

      a. has   **b.** had   **c.** is

L. Write the letter of the correct past-tense verb. (*pages 162-165*)

   27. Jesse Owens ____ many races.

      a. run   **b.** ran   **c.** runned

   28. Al Oerter ____ the discus in four Olympic Games.

      a. thrown   **b.** throwed   **c.** threw

   29. Richard Meade ____ a horse to victory many times.

      a. has rided   **b.** has rode   **c.** has ridden

M. Write the letter of the correct contraction. (*pages 166-167*)

   30. do not   **a.** do'nt   **b.** don't   **c.** do n't

   31. should not   **a.** shon't   **b.** should'nt   **c.** shouldn't

N. Write the letter of the correct subject pronoun to replace the underlined word or words. (*pages 212-213*)

32. Dad and I climbed Mount Washington.
   a. He   **b.** They   **c.** We

33. The mountain is in New Hampshire.
   a. It   **b.** He   **c.** They

34. Aunt Wanda also climbed to the top.
   a. We   **b.** She   **c.** I

O. Write the letter of the correct object pronoun to replace the underlined word or words. (*pages 214-215*)

35. Bees built a hive near Uncle Doug's farm.
   a. them   **b.** it   **c.** her

36. The hive protected the bees from bad weather.
   a. them   **b.** us   **c.** it

37. Uncle Doug told Harry and me about the hive.
   a. me   **b.** us   **c.** them

P. Write the letter of the correct pronoun. (*pages 216-217*)

38. ____ run outside.
   a. We   **b.** Us

39. ____ play tag.
   a. We   **b.** Us

40. Jim chases ____.
   a. I   **b.** me

41. ____ will hide in here.
   a. I   **b.** Me

42. Nicky finds ____.
   a. I   **b.** me

43. Mom calls ____ inside.
   a. we   **b.** us

Q. Write the letter of the possessive form of the pronoun that replaces each possessive. (*pages 218-219*)

44. The building's walls are very thick.
   a. His   **b.** Their   **c.** Its

45. Jane's room is on the third floor.
   a. My   **b.** Her   **c.** Their

46. You can see the Baxters' home from here.
   a. their   **b.** our   **c.** his

R. Write the letter of the correct contraction for each group of words. (*pages 220-221*)

47. I am   **a.** I'me   **b.** I'm   **c.** I'am
48. you have   **a.** you've   **b.** you'ave   **c.** you'hve

S. Write the letter that tells whether the title is written correctly. (*pages 244-245*)

49. I read the story "Rags The Dog."   **a.** correct   **b.** incorrect
50. The book Be a Star Now is good.   **a.** correct   **b.** incorrect
51. Here is the song Night and Day.   **a.** correct   **b.** incorrect

T. Write the letter of the word that is an adjective. (*pages 250-251*)

52. The deep snow covers a field.
    a. deep   **b.** snow   **c.** covers
53. A man walks three dogs through the snow.
    a. man   **b.** three   **c.** dogs
54. The happy dogs leap into the snowdrifts.
    a. happy   **b.** dogs   **c.** snowdrifts

U. Write the letter of the correct article. (*pages 252-253*)

55. We put on ____ play.
    a. a   **b.** an
56. ____ curtain rises.
    a. An   **b.** The
57. ____ actor speaks.
    a. A   **b.** An

58. The play lasts ____ hour.
    a. a   **b.** an
59. The end is ____ surprise.
    a. a   **b.** an
60. ____ audience claps.
    a. A   **b.** The

V. Write the letter of the correct adjective. (*pages 254-259*)

61. Death Valley is the ____ place of all.
    a. hotter   **b.** hottest
62. Reno, Nevada, is ____ than Portland, Oregon.
    a. drier   **b.** driest
63. Mount Rushmore is ____ than Granite Peak.
    a. more famous   **b.** most famous
64. Mount McKinley is the ____ mountain of all.
    a. more magnificent   **b.** most magnificent
65. Gordon is the ____ dancer of all in our family.
    a. better   **b.** best
66. I dance ____ than Mom does.
    a. worse   **b.** worst
67. Greg is the ____ dancer of all.
    a. worse   **b.** worst

PART FOUR

Curiosities

"Curiouser and curiouser!" cried Alice (she was so much surprised, that for the moment she quite forgot how to speak good English).

from *Alice's Adventures in Wonderland* by Lewis Carroll

◆

Curiosities are things that will surprise you. Some strange curiosities really do exist. Other curiosities may exist only in your imagination. In these units, think about the surprises you may find when you search for curiosities.

Story

◆

Adverbs

What Do You Know?

"Tell me another story, please."

When you were younger, you probably had a story that you loved to hear over and over. A good story creates a special, imaginary world to visit. There you meet interesting characters and learn about odd curiosities.

What about writing stories? Perhaps that's the best way to reach that special world. As a writer, you can create your own characters and curiosities. What's more, you're in charge of everything that happens. Each story you write is an invitation to the reader to visit your special world.

Thinking About Stories

What is a Story?

A story has these features:

- It has **characters,** people or animals who do things.
- It has a **setting,** the time and place of the events.
- It has a **plot,** the series of events that happen.
- The plot starts with the **introduction,** which describes the characters and the setting.
- The **problem** tells what difficulty a character faces.
- The **solution attempts** tell how the character tries to solve the problem.
- The **outcome** tells the result of the problem and the solution attempts.

Storytelling has always been a way for people to share feelings and experiences. Early people made up stories to explain the world around them. Telling stories was a good way to describe and remember important events, too. Later, storytellers wandered from castle to castle and from country to country entertaining people. Today, we find stories in books and magazines.

Discussion

1. When you were younger, what stories did you most like to hear?
2. What good stories have you read recently?
3. Who are your favorite story characters?

277

Reading a Story

Read this story about a family who found something curious in its barn.

The Enormous Egg
by
Oliver Butterworth

MAMMOTH EGG LAID IN FREEDOM

FREEDOM, N.H., June 24 Freedom, New Hampshire, may be a small town, but it sure can produce a big egg. A hen belonging to the Walter Twitchell family of this town recently laid an egg which may turn out to be the largest hen's egg in history.

Their hen laid this astonishing egg on June 16, Mr. Twitchell declared. She had shown some signs of uneasiness before laying the remarkable egg, which measures almost a foot and a half around, and weighs nearly three and a half pounds.

Mr. and Mrs. Twitchell have two children, a girl, Cynthia, 10, and a boy, Nathan, aged 12. Mr. Twitchell is the owner and editor of the *Freedom Sentinel*, a country newspaper with a circulation of about 800. The family has decided to let the hen sit on the egg, in hopes that it will hatch out. Mr. Twitchell admits that he doesn't know what will come out of the egg. "Something surprising," Mr. Twitchell guesses.

Well, the three weeks were finally up. That's the time it takes for a hen's egg to hatch out, in case you didn't know. But nothing happened. I kept going out to the nest every little while all day long, but nothing doing. Pop went out three times after supper. No luck. I must have looked pretty glum, and Mom said not to worry, maybe an egg this size needed more time than a regular one.

A whole week went by this way, and even Mom didn't seem to have much hope for it any more. Pop looked really discouraged. I think he'd kind of set his heart on that egg hatching out, almost as much as I had. One evening, after a whole month had gone by, he looked at me for a while with his face sort of screwed up.

"Nate," he said, "you counted on that egg hatching out, didn't you?"

I said yes I had.

"And you've worked hard all this time taking care of the egg, and feeding the hen specially, and now it almost looks as if you wouldn't have anything to show for your pains, doesn't it?"

I nodded, but I didn't say anything.

He walked over to me and put his hand on my shoulder. "Well, Nate, I guess we have to expect a certain amount of hard luck every now and then, and we just have to take it. After all, it was pretty amazing just to find an egg like that, even if it doesn't hatch out."

"What are you going to do with it?" Mom wanted to know.

"Well, it isn't strictly fresh anymore," Pop said. "I suppose we might give it to some museum. They could preserve it somehow, and put a card on it saying it was the gift of Nathan Twitchell, of Freedom, New—"

"I don't want to give it to a museum yet," I said. "I want to be sure about it first. It might be a five-week egg. You never can tell about something like this. It's not like an ordinary egg."

Pop sat down on the sofa and stretched out his legs. "Now, Nate," he said, "you deserve a lot of credit for keeping at this thing the way you have. Just don't try to follow a lost cause farther than it's worth, will you?"

"Oh no," I said. But I guess I was more disappointed than I let on. Just to myself I decided that I would give that egg one more week, and if nothing happened then—well, that would be the end of it.

Here are some of Nate's solution attempts.

That next week went by awfully slowly. I went out to look at the egg about every half hour, I guess. After what Dr. Ziemer had said about the egg maybe hatching, I was getting pretty anxious to see what was going to happen. But every time I looked in the nest, the egg was just lying there, just as it had for a month and a half. The hen was beginning to look kind of bored too, as if she didn't really care any more whether the old thing hatched or not. That was a bad sign, because this was no time to quit, just when the end was in sight. If the hen had walked off the job now, I think I would have sat on the egg myself.

Well, Saturday came around at last, but no news from the egg. I'd been out to see it so many times that morning that Mom had said, "A watched pot never boils, Nate." I never could figure out how grownups could be so patient about things all the time. We were having dinner, and I could hardly sit still.

Pop had been looking at me for a while. "You know, Nate," he said, "you don't want to get your heart set on this thing too much. If you get too eager about it, you're going to be awfully hard hit if that old thing doesn't hatch. I kind of suspect we're running on borrowed time anyway. I never heard of an egg that took more than five weeks."

"But Dr. Ziemer said it might hatch within a week."

"And who is Dr. Ziemer?" Mom wanted to know. "Just because he's a doctor, that doesn't mean he knows everything. Why, a city doctor like him probably doesn't know the first thing about poultry."

"But Dr. Ziemer talked as if he knew a lot about it," I said. "He said he collected eggs, or something like that."

"So do we," Pop said. "We collect them twice a day."

"Besides," Mom said, "this one is something new. I don't imagine he's seen anything like this before. How could he know what it's likely to do?"

Pop grinned. "Don't know that you could call a six-week egg exactly *new*. Except compared with a dinosaur egg, perhaps. Maybe Dr. Ziemer collects dinosaur eggs."

"Dinosaur eggs, indeed!" Mom said.

We didn't say much until after the pie was all gone. After dinner I went out to look at the egg again, but nothing doing.

Nothing doing at suppertime either, or at bedtime.

In the morning I crawled out of bed feeling pretty gloomy about things. I went down to the cellar and got old Ezekiel the rooster out of his box. As usual, he flapped his wings and clawed around a lot, and I stumbled up the cellar stairs with his wing feathers in my face. By the time I got him out to the chicken yard I was about ready to give up everything that had anything to do with chickens or eggs or anything like that.

That was probably why I didn't notice anything different at first. I just went over to the nest and put a little grain down for the poor old hen, and started to turn away, when I realized all at once that something had changed. The hen wasn't sitting on the nest any more. She was walking back and forth with a kind of wild look in her eye and every time she came near the nest she gave a little hop and fluttered away again. I bent down to look in the nest, and —*wow*! There was something in there, and it was alive! It was moving around.

I thought at first that it was a rat or something that had busted the egg and eaten it. But after I got a good look I could see that it wasn't any rat. It was about the size of a squirrel, but it didn't have any hair, and its head—well, I couldn't believe my eyes when I saw it. It didn't look like anything I'd ever seen before. It had three little knobs sticking out of its head and a sort of collar up over its neck. It was a lizardy-looking critter and it kept moving its thin tail slowly back and forth in the nest. The poor hen was looking pretty upset. I guess she hadn't expected anything like this, and neither had I.

I just stood there for a minute. I was so surprised all I could do was look. Then I started yelling, and lit out across the yard as fast as I could go. When I busted into the kitchen Mom was so startled that she dropped a saucepan in the sink. Pop came running down the stairs with the lather over one side of his face and a razor in his hand, and Cynthia was right behind.

"For goodness' sakes!" Mom said. "What's the matter with you?"

"It's alive!" I shouted. "It's alive! And it moves around, and it wiggles its tail and has horns and it looks like a lizard, and it doesn't have any fur, and the hen's running round and round and doesn't know what to do about it, and—"

"Hold on there, Nate," Pop said. "You look as if you'd seen a ghost. What's all the excitement about?"

I was so out of breath that I couldn't talk for a while. "It's the egg," I said. "It's hatched!"

"*What!*" Pop shouted. "It did? Why didn't you say so?" And he ran out the door and down the steps, still holding on to his razor. I grabbed Mom's hand and pulled her along, and Cynthia was just ahead of us. She'd forgotten to put on her shoes, and Mom was saying, "All this excitement over an egg. My goodness!"

When we all got out to the nest, Pop was leaning over, looking hard at it. Mom was still saying, "Why we should all come running out here only half dressed, just to see an egg that hatched out—I can't see anything in there, it's too dark."

Pop was still leaning over staring at that thing in the nest. All he said was, "By jing!" under his breath, sort of. By that time Cynthia had squeezed in beside Pop. She took one good look and then let out a screech you could have heard way down to the post office. That started the hen off, and she began squawking and flapping around in circles, and Ezekiel started crowing, and the goat started bleating. There was an awful lot of commotion, and everybody was talking at the same time and nobody could hear anything.

When it quieted down a little, Pop said, "Nate, you better run into the house and call Dr. Ziemer. He wanted to be told first thing. Remember, he's at the MacPhersons' place."

Dr. Ziemer arrived while we were still staring at the thing in the nest. He jumped out of his car and came running to us in the backyard. He was wearing a red bathrobe over his pajamas, and he looked pretty excited.

He ran up to the nest and looked in. His eyes opened up wide and he knelt down on the ground and stared and stared and stared. After a long while he said softly, "That's it. By George, that's just what it is." Then he stared for another long time and finally he shook his head and said, "It can't be true, but there it is."

"An amazing thing's happened," he said, in a kind of whisper. "I don't know how to account for it. It must be some sort of freak biological mixup that might happen once in a thousand years."

"But what is it?" I asked.

Dr. Ziemer turned and pointed a trembling finger at the nest. "Believe it or not, you people have hatched out a *dinosaur*."

We just looked at him.

"Sounds incredible, I know," he said, "and I can't explain it, but there it is. I've seen too many Triceratops skulls to be mistaken about this one."

"But—but how could it be a dinosaur?" Pop asked.

"Goodness gracious!" Mom spluttered. "And right here in our backyard. It doesn't seem hardly right."

Cynthia was pretty interested by now, and kept peeking into the nest and making faces, the way she did when Pop brought a bowl of frogs' legs into the kitchen one time. I guess girls just naturally don't like crawly things too much. To tell the truth, I don't either sometimes, but this thing that had just hatched out looked kind of cute to me. Maybe that was because I had taken care of the egg so long. I felt as if the little dinosaur was almost one of the family.

The outcome of the story is told here.

Understanding What You've Read

Write the answers to these questions.

1. How many children are there in the Twitchell family?
2. What is special about the egg in the story?
3. What problems does the egg pose for Nate's family?
4. What is the outcome of the story?
5. What problems might Nate have owning a baby dinosaur?

Writing Assignment

Imagine that each desk in your classroom is a castle. You are a storyteller who will go from castle to castle to entertain the people who live there. You will also see how a student named Tracy writes a story.

Your classmates are your **audience.** Your **purpose** is to entertain them.

Choose an Event

Professional storytellers keep a list of story ideas. In it, they write strange or amusing events they have seen or imagined. Each event is a good starting point when it's time to write a story. You, too, can keep an idea list. Has anyone played a joke on you lately? Has your pet done something unusual? Perhaps you heard a strange item on the news. List a few ideas. Then choose the one you want to use for your story. Write some notes about the characters and the plot. Save your details for later.

Making a Character Sketch

"What a character!" You've probably heard people say that. The word *character*, in that sentence, means a person who is funny or hard to forget.

Character can also mean a person or animal in a story. Story characters should be hard to forget, too. They should make an impression on readers by being unusual or special in some way.

To plan a character, you can make a character sketch. Artists use lines and colors to sketch people. Writers use lists of information to make a character sketch. A character sketch answers certain questions:

What is the character's name?
How old is the character?
Is the character male or female?
What does the character do?

The sketch can also tell what a character is like. Is the character calm or nervous, helpful or mean, funny or serious? It can tell what the character likes or dislikes. It can also tell about the character's interests. It should say what is special about the character. Knowing these things about the characters can be a big help when writing a story.

Here is a character sketch that Tracy prepared for the main character in her story.

—girl named Karen Wong
—twelve years old
—sixth-grade student at a school for the deaf
—interested in collecting rocks and fossils
—shy, but learning to speak out about important things

Practice

A. Answer these questions about the character described in the sketch on the last page.

   1. What is the character's name?

   2. How old is she?

   3. What might she enjoy doing on holidays and vacations?

   4. What is unusual about her school?

   5. What other details could you add to the sketch?

B. Write this incomplete character sketch on your paper. Then fill in the blanks with your own ideas about what the character is like. Make the character interesting.

> **6.** —_____-year-old boy called _____
> **7.** —goes to a school _____
> **8.** —collects _____
> **9.** —is very _____ and a little _____

Make a Character Sketch

   Look at the notes you wrote about your characters. To help you decide more about them, make sketches for at least two characters. Hold on to your sketches for later.

Planning the Parts of a Story

Tracy knows that the characters, setting, and plot are the three main parts of a story. She already worked on her main characters. Now, she will plan a setting and plot. She decides to make a story chart (page 236) to help plan her story. Her story chart will have the characters and setting. It will also have the introduction, problem, solution attempts, and outcome of her story.

A story's **setting** is where and when the events take place. It can be a forest at dawn, the cafeteria at noon, or a park at night. It may be the same for the entire story. Different events may happen in different settings.

The events that occur in a story make up the **plot**. The first events, or **introduction**, present the setting and characters. Later, there is a **problem** that one or more characters face. How the characters work to solve the problem are the **solution attempts**. The **outcome** tells the result of the problem and the solution attempts. It is usually the end of the story.

Look at the story chart Tracy made.

Characters: Karen Gray, road workers, a TV news reporter

Setting: a roadwork site during the day, in town

Plot: Introduction	Problem	Solution Attempts	Outcome
Karen is looking for rocks at a road construction site. She finds a dinosaur bone.	Workers plan to blast the site.	Karen can't convince them to change their plans. She decides to picket.	A TV news team sees Karen. Her story gets on TV, and the bones are saved.

Practice

A. Answer these questions about the chart on the last page.
1. What is the setting of the story?
2. Besides Karen, what other characters will be in the story?
3. What problem does Karen face in the story?
4. Which attempt of Karen's to solve the problem doesn't work?
5. Why was Karen's next attempt successful?
6. What other ideas can you think of that could have solved the problem?

B. The chart below is for an imaginary story. Copy the chart on your paper. Think of interesting details to fill in the story.

Characters: Captain Aguilar and _____			
Setting: the planet Mars in the year 2072			
Plot:			
Introduction	**Problem**	**Solution Attempts**	**Outcome**
In her small spaceship, Captain Aguilar leaves Mars for _____ in order to _____	Near Mars, a large starship seizes Aguilar's craft. Aguilar is forced to _____ _____.	Friendly _____ try to help Aguilar by _____ _____. When that fails, they _____ _____.	At last, Captain Aguilar _____. and in the end is able to _____.

Make a Story Chart

Make a chart that shows the characters, setting, and plot of your story. The plot should include these story parts:

- an introduction
- a problem
- solution attempts
- and an outcome

Keep your chart to help you write your story.

COMPOSING
Writing a First Draft

Read the first few paragraphs of Tracy's first draft. Notice that she has made some mistakes.

> Karen biked to the construction site early. She hoped there would be some good rocks to collect. Then, she spotted something much better. A dinosaur bone was sticking out of a large rock. It was in perfect shape.
>
> Suddenly, Karen felt a hand on her shoulder. "You have to leave now," a worker said. "We've got to blast the rest of this rock." Karen was deaf, but she could read lips.
>
> Karen didn't like to talk to strangers much. She hesitated. "Sir, you can't dynamite an allosaurus," she finally said.
>
> "Yes, I can. It's my job. We've got work to do, kid. You have to leave." Karen pedaled away furiously. She had to find a way to save that fossil.

Write Your First Draft

APPLY STEP BY STEP

If you are ready to write the first draft of your story, start writing now. If you prefer, discuss your ideas with your teacher or a classmate first. Use your character sketches and story chart to help you. Put the introduction in the first paragraph. In the next paragraphs, describe the problem and the solution attempts. The last paragraph will tell the outcome. Save your first draft to work on later.

290

Discussing a First Draft

Discuss your first draft with a partner. Your partner may have some good ideas for improving it.

Discussion Strategy

Listen carefully and quietly to your partner's comments. Put yourself in his or her place. Give your partner's suggestions the respect you would like your partner to give your suggestions. Use the Content Checklist as you discuss Tracy's first draft with your class.

Content Checklist
✔ Are the characters described well?
✔ Is the setting stated in the story?
✔ Does the plot have an introduction, a problem, solution attempts, and an outcome?

Revise Your First Draft for Content

To the Reader: While reading your partner's story, try to identify the characters and setting. Try to identify the different parts of the plot, too. Use the Content Checklist to discuss ways to make the plot clearer.

To the Writer: Use the Discussion Strategy when you listen to the suggestions your partner makes. After you revise your work, be sure not to lose it.

291

Varying Sentences

Tracy's partner, Paul, noticed that all her sentences were statements. They are all the same length, too.

Here are some ways to change a statement into another type of sentence. The idea of the sentence stays the same.

Statements	Other Sentence Types	
I am very hungry.	Wow, how hungry I am!	(exclamation)
I wonder what time it is.	What time is it?	(question)
You should open your present.	Open your present.	(command)

Here are some ways to change sentence length. When many sentences are the same length, you can make some shorter. You can also combine two or three sentences into one longer one. Here are some sentences that have been made longer or shorter. Again, the idea of each sentence stays the same.

Proofreading Marks	
∧	add
⅄	take away
≡	capitalize
/	small letter
∿	transpose

Then, the sun started to shine.	The sun shone.
He got his notebook. He got his pencil. He got his eraser.	He got his notebook, pencil, and eraser.
He got his things together. He started to write.	He got his things together, and he started to write.

Read this part of Tracy's revised story.

Boom, how
The ground shook from the blast! What a hurry Karen was in!
Karen had to hurry. She
What should she do?
didn't know what to do. Suddenly, she had a good idea. She
decided to buy cardboard, tape, and markers. She wrote her
and
message in large letters. She paraded through town with her
sign. She had to hurry up, hurry, hurry.

Practice

A. Rewrite each statement to make the type of sentence in parentheses. You will have to add some words and take away others, but keep the same idea.

1. That is a huge animal. (exclamation)
2. I wonder if it is a dinosaur. (question)
3. It's strange to see a dinosaur here. (exclamation)
4. I think it might be heading toward us. (question)
5. You should turn the car around quickly. (command)
6. Let's watch out for dinosaur footprints. (command)

B. Rewrite this paragraph. Vary the length of the sentences to make some short and others long.

> Having a pet dinosaur is not very easy. Mine has already eaten all the trees in town. The neighbors get mad when it crushes their cars. Huge crowds stand outside and ruin our lawn. I charge for rides, but that barely pays for food. My dinosaur gets lonely sometimes and looks for other dinosaurs.

Revising Checklist
✔ Have I included all the characteristics of a short story? (p. 277)
✔ Can I combine sentences with related ideas? (p. 32)
✔ Is my information complete? (p. 70)
✔ Where can I use a thesaurus to add descriptive language? (pp. 118, 198)
✔ Can I combine adjectives and adverbs in a series? (p. 242)
✔ Are my sentences varied in length and type?

Revise Your First Draft for Style

Check for the items on the Revising Checklist. Revise your short story to make sure you have sentences of different types and lengths. Save your work.

Using Commas

When speaking, you pause at certain times. When writing, you use commas to tell a reader when to pause. Commas help to make the meanings of your sentences clear. Here are some rules for using commas in sentences.

Rule	Example
Use a comma to set off the name or title of a person spoken to directly. Use commas before and after the name when it is in the middle of the sentence.	Sir, you can't dynamite an alosaurus. We've got work to do, kid. You know, Karen, you're a bright kid.
Use a comma after *yes*, *no*, and *well* when they begin a sentence.	Yes, I can.
Use commas to separate the items in a series of three or more words listed together.	She decided to buy cardboard, tape, and markers.
When you join two complete thoughts as one sentence, use a comma before the word *and*.	She wrote her message, and she paraded through town.

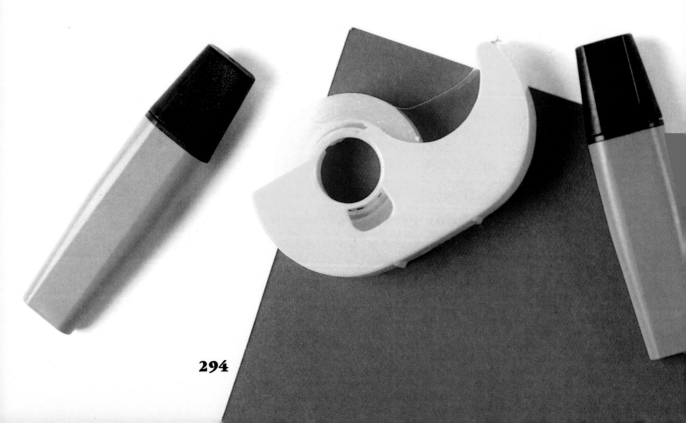

Practice

A. Rewrite each sentence. Add commas where necessary.

   1. Why is it John that you sleep on top of that lamp?
   2. Well I'm a light sleeper Mr. Fernandez.
   3. Lupe do you think heat travels faster than cold?
   4. Yes I do Aretha because it's easy to catch cold.
   5. Lin do you know what's worth more upside down?
   6. Yes Dee I do. It's the number six.

B. Rewrite the paragraph. Add commas where necessary.

(7)Wind rain and machines uncover fossils. (8)People see them and they tell scientists where they are. (9)Then, they are coated with plaster and the fossils are sent to a museum university or laboratory. (10)Lab workers clean study and repair the bones and then they start to rebuild the skeleton. (11)If some bones are missing, wood plaster or plastic copies are used to replace them.

◆━━━━━━━━━━━━━━━━━━━━━━━━━━━━━━◆

Proofreading Checklist

✔ Did I indent the first word of each paragraph? (p. 34)
✔ Did I punctuate conversation correctly? (p. 120)
✔ Did I use apostrophes properly? (p. 200)
✔ Did I write my title correctly? (p. 244)
✔ Did I use commas correctly?
✔ Have I used the correct form of an adjective to compare two or more nouns?

◆━━━━━━━━━━━━━━━━━━━━━━━━━━━━━━◆

APPLY STEP BY STEP

Proofread Your Story

Use the Proofreading Checklist as you reread your story. Make sure you have used commas correctly where they are needed. Save the draft on which you have made your corrections.

Proofreading Marks
∧ add
⌇ take away
¶ indent
≡ capitalize
/ small letter
◯ check spelling
∿ transpose

Checking Spelling/Writing a Final Copy

Spelling Strategy

If a long word is hard to spell, break it into syllables. The spelling may be easier for you that way.

Example: *composition* com po si tion

Here is the outcome of Tracy's story. She has proofread it for punctuation and spelling mistakes.

DON'T DYNAMITE THE DINOSAUR *Karen's sign said.*
People in cars, trucks, and buses saw the sign.
    Then, the TV News Center truck drove down the road. "Look at that girl with the sign," the reporter said. "I'm stopping. It might be a good story."
    She pulled to the curb next to Karen. The twelve-year-old girl told her about the fossil, the ~~construktion~~ *construction site, and the workers.*
    Then, things started to happen fast. ~~Sientists~~ *Scientists came from a museum. Karen met with the mayor. They held up the sign for the* ~~photgriphers~~ *photographers. Best of all, the workers agreed to stop blasting.*
    "Who says rock collecting is dull?" Karen thought.

Make a Final Check for Spelling

Look for spelling errors to correct. Add any words you spelled wrong to your spelling log.

Write a Final Copy

Write a neat, final copy of your story. Proofread your final copy, too. Save it to share with your class.

Sharing Your Story

Speaking/Listening Strategy

Say each word clearly when reading aloud. Use your voice to show feelings such as fear or excitement. This will make your reading come alive for your audience.

Choosing a Way to Share

Here are some ways to share your story with your class.

Reading Aloud Go from "castle" to "castle" (from desk to desk) practicing your story until you can read it without mistakes. Then, record it on tape. Change your voice slightly for each character in the story. You can even add some sound effects. Play your tape for your class. Then, send it to a friend or relative.

Presenting a Play Perform your story as a play. Ask classmates to play the different characters. You can narrate the parts of the story that are not dialogue. Use a few simple props, such as a hat or a sign. Let the audience use its imagination.

Making a Book Make an illustrated cover for your story. Write the title on it, and staple it to your story. Put it in a special story corner of the classroom. You can add a few sheets of blank paper at the end of the story for readers to write their comments.

Share Your Story

Choose one of these ways to share your story. Present it, and see how your audience likes it.

Add to Your Learning Log

Answer these questions in your learning log.

- ◆ What pleases me most in my story?
- ◆ What part of the story was easiest to write?
- ◆ How would I change the plot if I could write my story over?

The Literature Connection: Adverbs

Imagine a world where everyone acted the same. What a dull place it would be! Fortunately, people are not like that. We all do things differently. Some of us eat quickly. Others eat slowly. Some days we play outdoors. Other days we stay inside.

Words that tell how we do things are called **adverbs**. Adverbs can help us describe our actions to others.

Using adverbs in writing can tell readers exactly how an action is done. For example, a singer might sing *beautifully*, *rapidly*, or *softly*. Each adverb gives us a different picture of the action. A runner in a race may run *awkwardly*, *swiftly*, or *determinedly*. Are these actions the same? Certainly not! Each adverb creates a completely new image in our minds.

This poem tells about things that a crocodile does. Look for the words that tell how it does them.

The Crocodile
by
Lewis Carroll
How doth the little crocodile
   Improve his shining tail,
And pour the waters of the Nile
   On every golden scale!

How cheerfully he seems to grin,
   How neatly spreads his claws,
And welcomes little fishes in
   With gently smiling jaws!

Discussion

1. How does the crocodile seem to grin? Name the word in the fifth line that tells you.
2. How does he spread his claws? Name the word in the sixth line that tells you.
3. What are some other things a crocodile might do? Use adverbs to tell how it would do them.

The Writing Connection: Adverbs

In your own writing, adverbs can help give a clearer picture of the actions you describe. Read the following sentence.

The lion leaps.

The sentence tells you only a little about what the lion does. An adverb can tell *how* the lion does it. Read these sentences.

The lion leaps quickly.   The lion leaps fiercely.
The lion leaps suddenly.   The lion leaps bravely.

Do you see how adverbs help? Use adverbs to make your writing more interesting.

Activity

Have you ever been to a children's zoo? Look at the picture above and describe what is happening. Write each sentence. Use an adverb ending in *-ly* to tell more about what you see. The suggested topics below may help you.

• how the parents stand by the fence
• how Jimmy pets the pony
• how Melba rides the pony
• how the boys watch the lamb
• how the sheep cares for the lamb

Adverbs That Tell *How*

An **adverb** is a word that tells more about an action.

A. Some adverbs tell *how* an action is done.

> The wind blows hard. (*Hard* tells how the wind blows.)

To find the adverb in a sentence, first find the verb. Then, ask a question about the verb starting with *how*.

> The wind blows hard. (How does the wind blow? hard)
> The land warms quickly. (How does the land warm? quickly)

B. Many verbs that tell how an action is done end in *ly*.

dimly	gently	selfishly	safely
brightly	sharply	sadly	wisely

When you look for an adverb in a sentence, find the word right after the verb. Adverbs that tell *how* often follow the verb.

Strategy

Remember that many words that end in *ly* are adverbs. Ask a *how* question about the verb in a sentence to be sure that the word is an adverb.

Check Your Understanding

A. Write the letter of the question that shows you the adverb.
   1. Air moves quickly in a storm.
      a. How does air move?   **b.** What moves quickly?
   2. The wind blew harshly against the rocks.
      a. What did the wind blow?
      b. How did the wind blow?

B. Write the letter of the adverb.

    3. We listened carefully to the scientist.

        a. We   **b.** carefully   **c.** scientist

    4. The branches of the tree snap loudly.

        a. The   **b.** snap   **c.** loudly

Practice

A. Write the answer to the question in parentheses.

    5. Winds blow gently. (How do winds blow?)

    6. Oceans warm slowly. (How do oceans warm?)

    7. The flag waves lazily. (How does the flag wave?)

    8. The wind changes fast. (How does the wind change?)

B. Write each sentence. Look at the underlined verb. Underline the adverb twice.

    9. A beach heats quickly.

    10. Hot air rises gradually in some areas.

    11. Hurricane winds blow strongly.

    12. A sea breeze drifts smoothly from water to land.

C. Mixed Practice   Write each sentence. Look at the underlined verb. Underline the adverb twice.

    13. Dark clouds drift steadily.

    14. Waves move roughly in a hurricane.

    15. Air pressure drops rapidly in a storm.

    16. It rains fiercely near the center of a hurricane.

    17. The wind of a storm pushes hard against buildings.

    18. The temperature changes slowly from hour to hour.

    19. The weather has changed suddenly.

    20. Scientists report the weather accurately.

Apply: Work with a Group

Write five sentences about today's weather. Use an adverb in each sentence. Discuss your sentences with the other groups.

Adverbs That Tell *Where* or *When*

You learned that some adverbs tell *how* an action is done. Other adverbs tell *where* or *when* an action is done.

A. Some adverbs tell *where* an action takes place.

> We walked there. (*Where* did we walk? there)
> The tide went out. (*Where* did the tide go? out)

Here is a chart of some adverbs that tell *where*.

here	in	inside	down	everywhere
there	out	outside	up	nearby

B. Some adverbs tell *when* an action is done.

> Now the tide rises. (*When* does the tide rise? now)
> It changes daily. (*When* does it change? daily)

Here is a chart of some adverbs that tell *when*.

today	yesterday	always	once	later	soon
tomorrow	now	then	early	daily	again

An adverb that tells when an action happens often comes at the beginning or the end of a sentence.

> Today I went to the beach. I went to the beach today.

Strategy

To find an adverb in a sentence, first find the verb. Then ask a *when, how,* or *where* question about the verb. The word that answers one of the questions is an adverb.

Check Your Understanding

A. Write the letter of the question that shows you the adverb.
   1. The tide went out.
      a. Where did the tide go?
      b. How did the tide go?
   2. An ocean flows nearby.
      a. How does an ocean flow?
      b. Where does an ocean flow?

B. Follow the directions for Check Your Understanding A.

    3. Later we saw low tide.   **a.** When did we see low tide?

                                        b. How did we see low tide?

    4. The tide rose early.   **a.** Where did the tide rise?

                                        b. When did the tide rise?

Practice

A. Write the answer to the questions in parentheses.

    5. Water flows there. (Where does water flow?)

    6. The waves crash here. (Where do the waves crash?)

    7. Water levels go down. (Where do water levels go?)

    8. The water rushes up. (Where does the water rush?)

B. Write the answer to the questions in parentheses.

    9. Soon the earth turns. (When does the earth turn?)

    10. High tide comes again. (When does high tide come?)

    11. Now we know about tides. (When do we know about tides?)

    12. The moon pulls the ocean then. (When does the moon pull the ocean?)

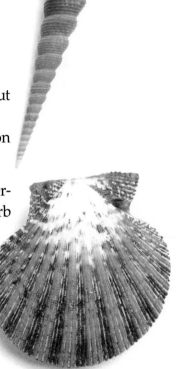

C. Mixed Practice   Write each sentence. Look at the underlined verb. Underline the adverb twice. Write what the adverb tells about the verb.

    13. The water goes out at low tide.

    14. People dig for clams then.

    15. Some scientists study the tides hourly.

    16. The moon changes the tides daily.

    17. Snails in the sand rise up in low tide.

    18. Large ships travel nearby in high tide.

    19. The tides change slowly.

    20. Once, people did not know what caused tides.

Apply: Journal

Write five sentences in your journal about a place you like to visit, such as a beach, a park, or a playground. Use adverbs that tell *how*, *when*, and *where* to help you describe what people and things do there.

Adverbs That Compare

An adverb can be used to compare two or more actions.

A. Add *er* or *est* to adverbs of one syllable.

Adverb	Compares Two Actions	Compares Three or More Actions
fast hard	faster harder	fastest hardest

Earth turns faster than Mars.
Jupiter turns fastest of all the planets.

B. Use *more* or *most* before most adverbs ending with *ly*.

Adverb	Compares Two Actions	Compares Three or More Actions
softly quickly	more softly more quickly	most softly most quickly

Earth goes around the sun more quickly than Mars.
Mercury goes most quickly of all the nine planets.

Strategy

The adverb *early* shows comparison in an unusual way. Although it ends in *ly*, you don't use *more* or *most* before the adverb. You must add *er* or *est*: earlier, earliest.

Check Your Understanding

A. Write the letter of the correct form of the adverb.
  1. Jan studied _____ of all for the test on planets.
     a. hard   **b.** harder   **c.** hardest
  2. Mercury moves _____ than Earth through space.
     a. fast   **b.** faster   **c.** fastest

B. Write the letter of the correct form of the adverb.
  3. We see Jupiter _____ than Uranus.
     a. clearly   **b.** more clearly   **c.** most clearly
  4. We have mapped our moon _____ of all the moons.
     a. fully   **b.** more fully   **c.** most fully

Practice

A. Write each sentence using the correct form of the adverb.

5. Earth is (larger, largest) than Mercury.

6. Russia sent a spaceship to Venus (later, latest) than the United States.

7. Mercury orbits the sun (faster, fastest) of all planets.

8. A spacecraft observed Venus (sooner, soonest) than the moon.

B. Write each sentence using the correct form of the adverb.

9. Venus turns (more slowly, most slowly) of all.

10. Venus shines (more brightly, most brightly) than Mars.

11. Scientists learned about Mars (more easily, most easily) than Venus.

12. The moon shines (more brightly, most brightly) of all the objects in the sky.

C. Mixed Practice   Write each sentence using the correct form of the adverb.

13. Mars is (more rugged, most rugged) of all the planets.

14. Scientists look (harder, hardest) for Mars than Venus.

15. Venus rotates (more slowly, most slowly) than Jupiter.

16. Uranus tilts (more sharply, most sharply) of all the planets.

17. Neptune was found (later, latest) than Uranus.

18. Pluto was found (later, latest) of all the planets.

19. Scientists knew about Mars (earlier, more early) than Uranus.

20. The sun heats the earth (quickly, more quickly).

Apply: Test a Partner

Make a list of five adverbs. Include adverbs with more than one syllable. Trade papers with a partner. Then, write the form of each adverb for comparing two actions and for three or more actions.

Adverb or Adjective?

An adverb can tell *how, where,* or *when* about a verb. An adjective can tell *what kind* or *how many* about a noun.

A. Remember that an adjective tells about a noun and an adverb tells about a verb. Many adverbs end with *ly.*

> The bright star shines.
> (The adjective *bright* tells about the noun *star.*)
>
> The star shines brightly.
> (The adverb *brightly* tells about the verb *shines.*)

B. It is sometimes hard to know when to use the words *good* and *well. Good* is an adjective. Use it to tell about a noun. *Well* is an adverb. Use it to tell about a verb.

> The good student studies.
> (The adjective *good* tells about the noun *student.*)
>
> The student studies science well.
> (The adverb *well* tells about the verb *studies.*)

Sometimes *well* is used to mean *not sick.* When it is used this way, *well* is an adjective. Any other time it is an adverb.

Strategy

Good is an adjective. *Well* is an adverb. Remember this sentence to help you to use the words correctly.

A good student studies well.

Check Your Understanding

A. Write the letter of the correct word for the sentence.
  1. A _____ star appears.
     a. new   **b.** newly
  2. Many stars fade _____.
     a. slow   **b.** slowly

B. Write the letter of the correct word for the sentence.

    3. The _____ scientist studies many stars.

      a. good   **b.** well

    4. This book describes stars _____.

      a. good   **b.** well

Practice

A. Write each sentence. Write if the underlined word is an *adjective* or an *adverb*.

    5. Some stars are <u>bigger</u> than the sun.

    6. Vega is a <u>blue</u> star.

    7. The star glows <u>strongly</u>.

    8. A star cools <u>slowly</u>.

B. Write each sentence, using the correct word.

    9. A (good/well) teacher explains the stars with pictures.

   10. We see (good/well) with a telescope.

   11. The book shows many (good/well) pictures of stars.

   12. Henrietta Leavitt studied (good/well) for many years.

C. Mixed Practice   Write each sentence, using the correct word. Then, write if the word is an *adjective* or *adverb*.

   13. Some dim stars burst (sudden/suddenly).

   14. The star changes (gradual/gradually) to yellow.

   15. The (bright/brightly) sun shines light on the earth.

   16. She wrote a (good/well) report about the stars.

   17. A scientist works (good/well) in a laboratory.

   18. Some old stars shrink (quick/quickly).

   19. The sun is the (closest/closely) star to the earth.

   20. She felt (good/well) after the science trip.

Apply: Work with a Partner

Imagine that you and your partner have discovered two new planets. Write five sentences that compare the two planets. Use adjectives and adverbs in your sentences. Share your sentences with the class.

Using Words That Mean No

A. *Not* is an adverb that makes a sentence mean *no*. A contraction formed by combining a verb with *not* ends with *n't*. A contraction ending with *n't* also makes a sentence mean *no*.

> We do <u>not</u> know all the answers.
> We <u>can't</u> explain many things about dinosaurs.

The chart shows some other words that make a sentence mean *no*.

no	nowhere	nothing
never	nobody	nowhere

<u>Nothing</u> was known about dinosaurs before 1800.

B. Use only *one* word to mean *no* in a sentence. It is incorrect to have two *no* words in one sentence when one is enough.

> Incorrect: <u>No</u> dinosaurs <u>don't</u> roam the earth today.
> Correct: Dinosaurs <u>don't</u> roam the earth today.

You can correct a sentence with two *no* words by taking out one of the words that mean *no*.

I can also write:
<u>No</u> dinosaurs roam the earth today.

Strategy

Remember to check that each sentence you write has only one word meaning *no*.

Check Your Understanding

A. Write the letter of the word that means *no* in each sentence.
  1. Nobody is sure about the last years of the dinosaur.
    a. Nobody   **b.** sure   **c.** last   **d.** dinosaur
  2. Dinosaurs weren't the same size.
    a. Dinosaurs   **b.** weren't   **c.** same   **d.** size

B. Write the letter of the word that should be removed to correct the sentence.

    3. Some dinosaurs didn't never eat meat.

        a. some   **b.** never   **c.** eat   **d.** meat

    4. Not all dinosaurs weren't that large.

        a. Not   **b.** all   **c.** that   **d.** large

Practice

A. Write each sentence. Underline the word that means *no*.

    5. We don't know much about that time.

    6. Dinosaurs were not the only animals then.

    7. None of the dinosaurs had fur.

    8. Nobody thought dinosaurs moved quickly.

B. Write each sentence. Underline the word or words that mean *no*. Write correct or incorrect after each sentence.

    9. No dinosaurs do not look like modern reptiles.

    10. Many of the plants from that time do not grow now.

    11. Much of the land wasn't separated by the sea.

    12. The climate wasn't never very cold.

C. Mixed Practice   Write each sentence. Choose the word that will form a sentence with one *no* word.

    13. We (do, don't) know many things about long ago.

    14. Dinosaurs (did, didn't) have fur.

    15. Some dinosaurs never (could, couldn't) live in a cold climate.

    16. No fossils (were, weren't) studied before 1800.

    17. Usually scientists (do, don't) find all the bones.

    18. Certain dinosaurs (did, didn't) live with a herd.

    19. People didn't know (anything, nothing) about them.

    20. No one (can, can't) explain (everything, nothing).

Apply: Learning Log

What part of this lesson was the most difficult? Think of a way to help you remember what you learned about words that mean *no*. Write your method in your learning log.

Suffixes

A **base word** is a word to which other word parts can be added. A **suffix** is a word part that is added to the end of a base word.

A. Study the suffixes in the chart below.

Suffix	Meaning	Example
er	a person or thing that	wor<u>ker</u>
or	a person or thing that	inspect<u>or</u>
able	able to be	read<u>able</u>
less	without	hope<u>less</u>
ful	full of	care<u>ful</u>
y	having	dirt<u>y</u>
ly	in a _____ way	sad<u>ly</u>

B. Adding a suffix to a base word changes the meaning of the base word. The meaning of the new word is based on its two parts. Compare these examples:

Base Word + Suffix		New Word	Meaning
hope	+ ful	hopeful	<u>full of</u> hope
direct	+ ly	directly	<u>in a</u> direct <u>way</u>

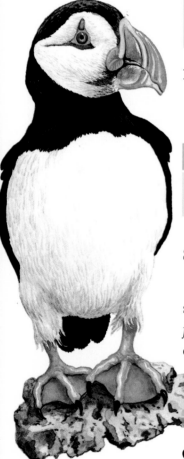

Strategy

Some words are made up of a base word and more than one suffix. The word *wonderfully*, for example, is made from *wonder + ful + ly*. When you try to figure out the meaning of a word you don't know, look at each suffix.

Check Your Understanding

A. Write the letter of the suffix of the underlined word.
1. The <u>friendly</u> puffin lives in Norway.
   a. ly   **b.** y   **c.** less   **d.** friend
2. Puffins are very <u>playful</u> birds.
   a. ly   **b.** play   **c.** ful   **d.** ul

B. Write the letter of the words that tell what the underlined word means.

    3. Each puffin is a good <u>fisher</u>.
        a. without fish   **b.** person or thing that fishes
        c. having fish
    4. Puffins take a <u>lengthy</u> trip south every winter.
        a. having length   **b.** in a lengthy way
        c. without length

Practice

A. Write each sentence. Underline the word with a suffix. Underline the suffix twice.

    5. Flamingos have colorful pink feathers.
    6. Its neck is long and shapely.
    7. The flamingo's legs are unusually thin.
    8. Flamingos live in swampy areas.

B. Write a new word by adding the suffix to the base word. Write the meaning of the new word.

    9. build + er   **12.** harm + ful
   10. break + able   **13.** act + or
   11. fear + less   **14.** itch + y

C. **Mixed Practice** Write each sentence. Underline the word that has a suffix. Then write the meaning of the word.

   15. A robin sings a cheery song.
   16. Fearless falcons command the sky.
   17. The nightingale is a fine singer.
   18. Pelicans put on an enjoyable show.
   19. Little egrets hunt for fish cautiously.
   20. Sea gulls travel in noisy groups.
   21. Most ducks are excellent swimmers.
   22. Muddy waters provide food for the beautiful flamingos.

Apply: Work with a Partner

Work with your partner to make as many new words as you can by adding different suffixes to the base words in the box. Check your words in a dictionary.

taste	care
read	work

LANGUAGE IN ACTION

Filling Out Forms

Let's say that you want a library card. You go to the public library and ask the librarian how to get one. The librarian hands you a piece of paper covered with lines, spaces, words, and boxes. What are you supposed to do with it?

You may have already filled out some forms for your school. You will fill out many more as you get older. Forms are a part of modern life. Here are some tips on filling out forms.

- ◆ Remember that neatness counts. Always print. If you make a mistake, cross it out neatly. If you make too many mistakes, ask for a new form.
- ◆ Answer each question. Some questions might not apply to you. If one doesn't, draw a line through the answer space.
- ◆ When you finish, read everything over. Make sure you filled everything in. Check that all your answers are correct and in the right place.

Practice

On a separate piece of paper, answer the following questions.
1. How should you write when you fill out a form?
2. What should you do with a question if it doesn't apply to you?
3. When should you ask for a new form?
4. What should you do if you make a mistake?
5. What is the last thing you do when filling out a form?

Apply

Work with a partner. Each of you will make up a form. It may be an application for a library card, a pet license, or anything else you choose. Exchange papers and fill out the form your partner made.

HISTORY OF LANGUAGE

Planet Names

Thousands of years ago, the people of Rome studied the sun, the moon, the planets, and the stars carefully. They discovered the planets Mercury, Venus, Mars, Jupiter, and Saturn. These are the planets that are closest to the earth. They are the easiest ones to see using only your eyes or a simple telescope. Without powerful telescopes, they couldn't see Uranus, Neptune, or Pluto.

Astronomy, the study of stars and planets, was very important to the Romans. They named the planets they knew after their gods. They tried to name each planet for a god who was like the planet in some way. For example, the god Mars was associated with the color red. The planet Mars got its name because it is red.

Modern astronomers gave the planets they discovered Roman gods' names, too. They wanted to continue that tradition started long ago in Rome.

Activity

Read the descriptions of the Roman gods. Then write each sentence. Fill in the blank with a god's name. Choose the god whose description best matches the planet's description.

Roman Gods and Goddesses

Mercury was the messenger of the gods. He ran very fast.
Jupiter was the king or leader of the gods.
Venus was the goddess of love and beauty.
Saturn was the god of agriculture. He was almost as important as Jupiter.

1. _____ is the biggest planet.
2. _____ is the planet that shines the most brightly. It is very beautiful to see.
3. _____ goes around the earth the fastest.
4. _____ is the second largest planet.

UNIT REVIEW

Stories   *(pages 277-285)*

1. Write three features that make this paragraph a story.

   Once upon a time, a little boy lived in a gigantic shoe. The shoe was very big because it used to be a shoe store. The problem was that rain got in through the holes for the laces. Then the boy had an idea. He searched all over his house. He found a jar of waterproof shoe wax that was left in his house from when it was a shoe store. He polished his house and never got wet again.

Planning the Parts of a Story   *(pages 288-289)*

2. List and describe the three parts of a story. Then, list and describe the four parts of a plot.

Varying Sentences and Using Commas   *(pages 292-295)*

Rewrite each sentence to make it the type of sentence in parentheses. You may add or take away words, but keep the same idea.

3. That is a big shoe. (exclamation)
4. I wonder why it's so big. (question)
5. I want you to ask why it's so big. (command)

Rewrite each sentence. Add commas where necessary.

6. Rayvonne please show me that.
7. Do you want to see the nautilus shell the seahorse or the sand dollar?
8. I want to see the shell and may I see the starfish, too?
9. Yes of course you may. Here it is.

Adverbs That Tell *How, Where,* or *When*   *(pages 300-303)*

Write each sentence. Look at the underlined verb. Underline the adverb twice. Write whether the adverb tells *how, where,* or *when.*

10. Marianne waters the garden daily.
11. The sun shines down on the cool earth.
12. Then tiny green leaves sprout.
13. Marianne watches eagerly for the first flowers.
14. Beautiful flowers grow everywhere.

314

Adverbs That Compare *(pages 304-305)*

Write each sentence, using the correct form of the adverb.

15. A goldfish moves (more quickly, most quickly) than a turtle.

16. A sailfish swims (faster, fastest) than a goldfish.

17. An ostrich runs (more quickly, most quickly) than an elephant.

18. The cheetah runs (faster, fastest) of all land animals.

19. Many birds fly (more rapidly, most rapidly) than a cheetah runs.

20. A duck hawk flies (more quickly, most quickly) than any other bird.

Adverb or Adjective? *(pages 306-307)*

Write each sentence, using the correct word. Then write whether the word is an adjective or an adverb.

21. The carpenter measures the wood (careful, carefully).

22. She takes a (good, well) look at the plans.

23. The window box will fit (perfect, perfectly).

24. The carpenter sands the wood (good, well).

25. She cuts the (smooth, smoothly) wood into pieces.

26. She (quick, quickly) hammers nails into the wood.

27. The window box is painted a (light, lightly) color.

Using Words That Mean *No* *(pages 308-309)*

Write each sentence. Choose the word that will form a sentence with one *no* word.

28. Auks (are, aren't) like most birds.

29. They (do, don't) fly well.

30. Auks (can, can't) walk well either.

31. They (are, aren't) good at nothing but swimming and diving.

32. They don't eat (anything, nothing) except fish.

33. Today there (are, aren't) not many auks in the world.

Suffixes *(pages 310-311)*

Write a new word by adding the suffix to the base word. Write the meaning of the new word.

34. inspect + or

35. sand + y

36. hope + ful

37. reach + able

38. thought + less

39. joy + ful

40. fix + able

41. teach + er

42. glad + ly

43. govern + or

Research Report

◆

Sentences II

What Do You Know?

"I wonder . . ."

What things do *you* wonder about? The world is full of curiosities to explore. What makes it rain? Why do leaves change color? How does a telephone work? You may wonder about these things and more. One way to answer your questions is to do research and then to write a report on your findings.

Writing a research report is helpful in two ways. First, it shows you exactly what you learned about your topic. Second, by sharing your report with friends, they can learn about your topic, too.

Thinking About Research Reports

What Is a Research Report?

A **research report** has these features:

♦ It gives information on a topic.
♦ It requires research because it must include information you found out for the report.
♦ The topic may be divided into two or more main ideas.
♦ Each main idea is supported with facts.
♦ All information in the report is true. It does not contain opinions.

Teachers often ask you to write research reports in school. They may be on topics in science, social studies, or literature. You might explain how the Grand Canyon was formed, what caused the Revolutionary War, or how books are printed. Nearly anything you are curious about can be discussed in a report.

Research reports are fun to read and write, but they take some work to do well. In this unit, you will learn how to find, organize, and present information on a topic that interests *you*.

Discussion

1. What things in nature, such as rainbows or snowflakes do you wonder about the most?
2. What questions do you have about these wonders?
3. Where do you think you might find the information to answer your questions?

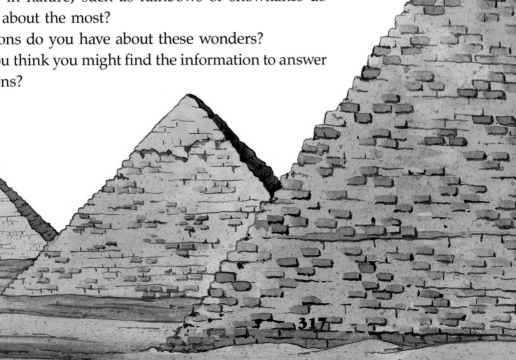

Reading a Model Research Report

Read this research report about archaeology. Notice how the main idea in each paragraph has facts to support it.

This is the first main idea.
These facts support the main idea.

Archaeologists study objects from long ago to learn how people lived in the past. There are two kinds of things archaeologists study. One kind is small objects such as tools, cooking pots, and jewelry. These things tell us how people worked, cooked, and dressed long ago. Archaeologists also study large objects that cannot be moved, such as houses and temples. They tell us where people lived and how they made their buildings. A place where these things are found is called an archaeological site.

This is the second main idea.
These facts support it.

Archaeological sites can be found above ground, underground, and underwater. For example, the great pyramids in Egypt are a very famous aboveground site. A famous underground site is the tomb of King Tutankhamen. Sunken ships in the Mediterranean Sea are underwater sites that tell us about ancient Greece and Rome. Sometimes, sites are found by accident. In 1940, some French children were looking for a lost dog. They found a cave. Its walls were covered with paintings done by people who had lived there thousands of years before. The cave is now called the Lascaux Cave. It has some of the best ancient art in the world.

Understanding What You've Read

Write the answer to each of these questions.

1. What do archaeologists do?
2. What are the two types of objects archaeologists study?
3. How was the Lascaux Cave found?
4. What is the main idea of the second paragraph?
5. What facts are given to support the main idea in the second paragraph?
6. What can an arrowhead tell you about the people who made it and how they used it?

Writing Assignment

Imagine that your class is planning a Fact Fair for June. Each student will share information on a subject he or she knows well. To prepare for the fair, you will write a research report on a topic of your choice.

Your **audience** for the report will be your teacher and classmates. Your **purpose** will be to study a subject you are curious about and to share your findings with others.

Choose a Topic

Make a list of five topics you are interested in, such as birds, rainbows, or Niagara Falls. Then, choose the topic that interests you the most, and circle it on your list.

"I wonder what I wonder about . . ."

Making a Topic Wheel

Tiffany decided to do a two-paragraph research report about the telephone. She knew this topic was too general for a brief report. She would have to narrow her topic to more specific ideas about the telephone.

Tiffany decided to make a topic wheel. A **topic wheel** lists many questions about a general topic. You write your topic in the center of a piece of paper and write your questions around the topic. Later you choose the specific questions you will discuss in your report.

Look at Tiffany's topic wheel below. First, she listed the questions that interested her most about the telephone. Then, under each question, Tiffany wrote down information she already knew. Finally, she planned to find more information in books and magazines to answer each question.

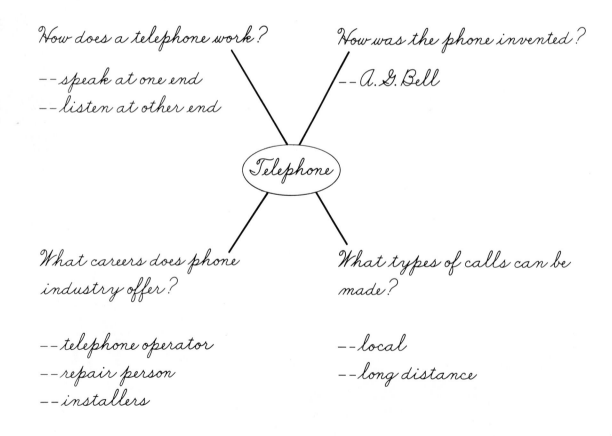

How does a telephone work?

--speak at one end
--listen at other end

How was the phone invented?

--A. G. Bell

Telephone

What careers does phone industry offer?

--telephone operator
--repair person
--installers

What types of calls can be made?

--local
--long distance

Practice

A. Make a topic wheel for each general topic below. Write at least four questions that interest you about each topic.

1. airplanes
2. calendars
3. hair
4. radio

5. popcorn
6. mirrors
7. Alaska
8. pencils

B. Choose two of the topic wheels you made in Practice A. Under each question, write down all the information you already know. Then write where you could look to find out more about the topic.

Make a Topic Wheel

Look at the topic you chose. Make a topic wheel that lists at least four questions you have about that topic. If you chose Niagara Falls, you could ask how they were formed. Where does the water go after the falls is another possible question. Under each question, write anything you already know. Then write where you might look to find more information about the topic. Save your topic wheel for the next lesson.

Using an Encyclopedia

Tiffany decided to do a research report about the telephone. She wanted to use the encyclopedia to find information on her topic. An encyclopedia has articles on different topics. Usually, it has many volumes, which are numbered and in alphabetical order. The topics within each volume are also arranged in alphabetical order.

To find a particular article in the encyclopedia, look in the volume with the same first letter as your topic. Tiffany found the article on the telephone in Volume 19, the *T* volume. An article on Niagara Falls would be in Volume 13, the *N* volume.

To find an article on a person, look in the volume with the same first letter as the person's *last* name. Tiffany used Volume 2, the *B* volume, to find the information on Alexander Graham *B*ell.

Sometimes, your topic may be a phrase with several words. In that case, choose the **key word**, the most important word, in the phrase. For example, suppose your topic were *the world's tallest mountains*. Since the key word is *mountains*, you would look in the *M* volume. If your topic were *generals in the Revolutionary War*, you would look in the *R* volume under *Revolutionary War*.

Practice

Use the encyclopedia shown on the previous page. Write the key word you would look up and the number of the volume in which you would find information on each topic below.

1. the invention of the refrigerator
2. George Washington Carver
3. snowflakes
4. the state of Alaska
5. the causes of rainbows
6. how pencils are made
7. Susan B. Anthony
8. how food is packaged and shipped
9. black-and-white televisions
10. different kinds of birds

APPLY
STEP BY STEP

Find Your Topic in the Encyclopedia

Use an encyclopedia to find more information on your topic. Look in each volume that might contain helpful articles. For example, Tiffany used two volumes for her report: the *T* volume for *telephone* and the *B* volume for *Bell*. Write down the page number in each volume you plan to use. Save your work for the next lesson.

Understanding the Parts of a Book

Tiffany wanted to answer these two questions in her research report:

How was the telephone invented?
How does a telephone work?

Tiffany found many books on the subject of telephones. Which books could help her most? Tiffany examined the main parts of each book to learn more about the content.

The Life of Alexander Graham Bell

by Clinton Maynard

Education Book Company
Boston, Massachusetts

The **title page** appears at the front of a book. It names the book title, the author, the publishing company, and the company's location. On the back of the title page, the copyright date tells when the book was first published.

Table of Contents

The **table of contents** follows the title page. It lists the chapter or unit titles in the order in which they appear. It shows the beginning page number for each chapter.

Index

The **index** appears at the back of the book. It lists, in alphabetical order, all the main topics discussed in the book. Some topics may have more specific subtopics listed under them. The index shows the page or pages on which each topic and subtopic can be found.

Practice

Use the title page, table of contents, and index on the previous page to answer these questions.

1. Who is the author of *The Life of Alexander Graham Bell*?

2. What company published the book?

3. What is the first chapter of the book about?

4. On what page does Chapter 3 begin?

5. Which chapter tells about Bell's career as a teacher of the deaf?

6. Bell also developed a method for making wax phonograph records. Which chapter would include information on that invention?

7. On what page in the book could you find mention of science awards that Bell won?

8. What page in the book tells who Thomas Watson was?

9. On which page could you discover where Bell first demonstrated the telephone?

10. Why would someone writing a research report be interested in the date that a book was published?

Find Books on Your Topic
♦ Find books on the topic you chose. Use your textbooks or library books. (pp. 232, 234)
♦ Check the title page, table of contents, and index of each book to learn more about the contents.
♦ List the titles of the books that can help you answer your questions about the topic.
♦ List the numbers of the pages that have information on your questions. Choose the two questions about which there is the most information.
♦ Save your work.

Taking Notes in Your Own Words

Tiffany found book and encyclopedia articles to use for her report. Next she took notes on the subjects.

Taking notes means writing down only the most important information you find. Your notes may be in phrases or complete sentences. Put the notes in your own words. Do not copy sentences directly from a book.

Here is one article Tiffany used for her report. Below it are notes she took on it.

Today's telephones are much more sophisticated than the one Alexander Graham Bell invented in 1876. Now when someone speaks into a telephone, the sound of the voice enters a transmitter. This device converts the sound into a pattern of electric waves that travel over wire. On the other end of the line, a receiver converts the waves into sound again. It reaches the ear of the listener, who hears the speaker's words.

A person can make three types of telephone calls — local, long distance, and overseas. Over 90 percent of all calls in the United States are local, which are limited to nearby areas. Long distance calls, generally more expensive, go to other city or state locations. A caller in the United States can reach about 220 overseas countries and territories.

How was the telephone invented?

-- *invented 1876*

How does a telephone work?

-- *person talks into transmitter*
-- *voice changes into electric waves*
-- *waves pass through wire to receiver*
-- *waves change back to sound*
-- *listener hears words*

Look at the notecards. At the top of each one, Tiffany wrote one of the questions she wanted to answer in her report. This helped her decide which information to include. Tiffany took no notes on the second part of the article, because it did not relate to her questions.

Tiffany's first card did not have much information. She still needed another source to help her answer the question of how the telephone was invented.

Practice

A. Read the following article Tiffany found. Take notes that Tiffany could use to answer the question of how the telephone was invented.

> The invention of the telephone, believe it or not, came about by accident. Alexander Graham Bell had been experimenting on a different type of instrument—the harmonic telegraph. He worked together with his assistant, Thomas A. Watson. One evening a reed on the telegraph became stuck, and Watson attempted to loosen the reed by snapping it. To Bell's amazement, the sound traveled to the receiver in the next room, where the inventor was sitting. Bell realized that electric waves had transmitted the sound to the receiver. After further experimentation, Bell managed to apply his new-found knowledge to the telephone. Soon his first telephone was completed, and he demonstrated it later at a fair in Philadelphia in June of 1876.

B. Imagine you were doing a research report on different types of telephone calls. Take notes on the second paragraph of the article on page 326. Put the notes in your own words. Above your notes, write the question that your notes answer.

Take Notes for Your Report

Write each question you chose at the top of a piece of paper or notecard. Then, take notes from the books and encyclopedia articles you chose. Put each note under the question that it helps answer. Write only the most important information. Put the notes in your own words. Save your notes for later.

Making an Outline

After taking enough notes, Tiffany was ready to organize them. She decided to make an outline.

An outline helps you put your information in the best order. Each question you asked about the topic becomes a main idea in the outline. Each main idea appears next to a Roman numeral. All details about that main idea are listed next to capital letters under the Roman numeral. Later, when you write your report, each main idea and its details will make up one entire paragraph.

Here is how Tiffany organized her notes in an outline.

How was the telephone invented?
-- A. G. Bell invented by accident
-- invented 1876
-- working on harmonic telegraph
-- Watson loosened stuck reed
-- Bell heard sound in receiver.
-- Applied knowledge to telephone
-- Displayed phone in Philadelphia

How does a telephone work?
-- person talks into transmitter
-- voice changes into electric waves
-- waves travel thru wire to receiver
-- waves change back to sound
-- listener hears words

I. Bell invented telephone by accident
  A. Created phone in 1876
  B. Worked on telegraph at time
  C. Assistant loosened stuck reed
  D. Bell heard sound in other room
  E. Figured out how to send words
  F. Displayed phone at Philadelphia fair
II. Telephone works on transmitter, receiver, wire
  A. Person talks into transmitter
  B. Changes voice into electric waves
  C. Waves travel over wire
  D. Receiver changes waves to sound
  E. Listener hears words

Practice

A. Answer these questions about Tiffany's outline.

    1. What are the two main ideas in the outline?

    2. How many details support the first main idea?

    3. What is the first detail that supports the second main idea?

    4. How many paragraphs will this report have, based on this outline?

B. Read the two main ideas below and the details that follow. Make an outline by listing each main idea and the details that belong under it.

      I. Niagara Falls was created in an interesting way.

      II. Many tourists enjoy Niagara Falls each year.

    A. About 10 million people visit the falls yearly.

    B. Long ago, melting ice caused Lake Erie to overflow.

    C. The overflow caused the Niagara River.

    D. Most visitors see the falls between April and October.

    E. The *Maid of the Mist* boat carries guests near the falls.

    F. Many people view the falls from Prospect Point.

    G. The Niagara River ran over a high cliff.

    H. Over the years, the river formed Niagara Falls.

Make an Outline

Look at the notes you took in the last lesson. Put your notes into an outline. Write your two main ideas next to Roman numerals I and II. List your details next to numbers under each main idea. Save your outline for the next lesson.

Writing a First Draft

Read the first draft of Tiffany's research report. Notice there are some mistakes in her work.

Alexander graham Bell ivented the telephone by acident. He made his discovery in 1876. Bell had been working on a new kind of telegraph. One night, a reed on the telgraph stuck. Bell's assistant. Thomas A watson. snapped the reed to loosen it. Bell was in another room. He managed to hear the sound in his receiver. The inventor realized that the reed had sent electric waves to the reciever. Bell needed a little more time. He soon figured out how to send words over the telephone. Bell displayed his new instrument at a fair in philadelphia in june. 1876.

A telephone has three main parts: a transmitter. a receiver. and a wire. A person talks into the transmitter. It changes the voice sound into electric waves. The waves then travel through the wire. which is connected to the receiver. The receiver changes the elctric waves back into sound. The listener hears the speaker's words.

Write Your First Draft

You may discuss your ideas with your teacher or a classmate, or start working by yourself. Follow your outline. Begin with your first main idea. Then, write the details that tell more about it. Do the same in the second paragraph. Keep your first draft to correct later.

Discussing a First Draft

Tiffany finished her first draft. Then she wanted to improve it. She discussed the report with Adam, a classmate.

Discussion Strategy

Sometimes, two people simply don't agree. In that case, make your opinion clear, and go on to the next subject. Don't waste time trying to change a person's mind. Adam didn't think Tiffany needed to mention when Bell first displayed the telephone. Tiffany, however, thought it was important. Adam told Tiffany he disagreed, and then went to his next comment.

Use this Content Checklist to discuss with your class the research report that Tiffany wrote.

Content Checklist
- ✔ Does the research report give information on one topic?
- ✔ Does each paragraph discuss a separate main idea?
- ✔ Do details in each paragraph help explain the main idea?
- ✔ Are all details in the report facts and not opinions?

APPLY STEP BY STEP

Revise Your First Draft for Content

To the Reader: Read your partner's report. Try to identify the main idea in each paragraph. If anything is unclear, discuss ways to improve the report. Use the Content Checklist and Discussion Strategy for help.

To the Writer: Listen to what your partner says. Then revise your draft for content. Save your work for later.

331

Combining Sentences

You may write two sentences that are related in their ideas. To improve your writing, you can combine the sentences with the word *and*, *but*, or *or*.

Use *and* to add one idea to another.

> Bell was in one room. His assistant stayed in another.
> Bell was in one room, **and** his assistant stayed in another.

Use *but* to show a contrast.

> The man worked hard. His discovery took awhile.
> The man worked hard, **but** his discovery took awhile.

Use *or* to show choice.

> Watson spoke loudly. Bell would not hear him.
> Watson spoke loudly, **or** Bell would not hear him.

Here is how Tiffany combined some of the sentences in her draft.

A comma always goes before *and*, *but*, and *or* in combined sentences.

Proofreading Marks	
∧	add
✗	take away
/	small letter

Alexander graham Bell ivented the telephone by acident. He made his discovery in 1876. Bell had been working on a new kind of telegraph. One night, a reed on the telgraph stuck. Bell's assistant. Thomas A watson. snapped the reed to loosen it. Bell was in another room. He managed to hear the sound in his receiver. The inventor realized that the reed had sent electric waves to the reciever. Bell needed a little more time. He soon figured out how to send words over the telephone. Bell displayed his new instrument at a fair in philadelphia in june. 1876.

Practice

Combine each pair of sentences into one sentence by using the word *and*, *but*, or *or*. Write your new sentence.

1. a. Frédéric Bartholdi designed the Statue of Liberty.
   b. It stands as a symbol of freedom.

2. a. One person designed the statue.
   b. It took a crew to put it together.

3. a. The statue was built in France.
   b. It was given to the United States as a gift.

4. a. The statue is made of metal.
   b. The base is made of stone.

5. a. The statue arrived in New York in 1885.
   b. It wasn't inaugurated until 1886.

6. a. Visitors may climb steps all the way up.
   b. They can remain at the base instead.

Revising Checklist
- ✔ Have I included all the features of a research report? (p. 317)
- ✔ Is my information complete? (p. 70)
- ✔ Are my sentence beginnings varied? (p. 152)
- ✔ Are my sentences varied in type and length? (p. 292)
- ✔ Where can I combine sentences with the word *and*, *but*, or *or*?

Revise Your First Draft for Style
Check for the items on the Revising Checklist. Where possible, combine sentences by using *and*, *but*, or *or*. Mark your changes on the draft. Hold on to your work.

Proper Nouns, Titles, and Initials

Tiffany used several proper nouns in her research report. She checked the following rules for writing proper nouns, titles, and initials.

Rule	Examples
Begin every important word in a proper noun with a capital letter.	Grand Canyon Statue of Liberty Alexander Graham Bell
Capitalize the initials in a person's name. Place a period after each initial.	Thomas A. Watson T. Adams Watson T. A. Watson
Begin the title of a person with a capital letter. If the title is an abbreviation, place a period after it.	Dr. Bell Mr. Watson Miss Valenzuela

Practice

Write each sentence correctly. Use capital letters and periods where necessary.

1. The eiffel tower is a huge tower in paris, france.
2. alexander g eiffel designed the 984-foot tower.
3. The tower was presented at the World's Fair Of 1889.
4. Soldiers in world war I watched planes from the tower.
5. It overlooks the seine river.
6. ms m falk has called the tower "the greatest ever built."
7. mr eiffel also worked on the statue of liberty.
8. In addition, a g eiffel designed the duoro River Bridge.

Proofreading Checklist

✔ Did I write sentences and paragraphs correctly? (p. 34)
✔ Did I use apostrophes properly? (p. 200)
✔ Did I use commas where necessary? (p. 294)
✔ Did I write proper nouns, titles, and initials correctly?
✔ Do the pronouns in my sentences refer to the right nouns?

APPLY STEP BY STEP

Proofread Your Research Report

Check for correct capitalization and punctuation. Use the Proofreading Checklist. Use the proofreading marks to make changes on your draft. Save your work for the next lesson.

Proofreading Marks	
∧	add
⅄	take away
¶	indent
≡	capitalize
/	small letter
◯	check spelling
∿	transpose

Checking Spelling/Writing a Final Copy

Spelling Strategy

Sometimes a memory hint can help you spell a word. *Example*: Which spelling is correct, *receiver* or *reciever*? Use this memory hint: *i* before *e*, except after *c* (re*ce*iver).

Now read Tiffany's revised and proofread report.

Alexander graham Bell *invented* ~~ivented~~ the telephone by *accident* ~~acident~~. He made his discovery in 1876. Bell had been working on a new kind of telegraph *and* One night, a reed on the ~~telgraph~~ *telegraph* stuck. Bell's assistant. Thomas A. watson. snapped the reed to loosen it. Bell was in another room *but* He managed to hear the sound in his receiver. The inventor realized that the reed had sent electric waves to the ~~reciever~~ *receiver*. Bell needed a little more time. *but* He soon figured out how to send words over the telephone. Bell displayed his new instrument at a fair in philadelphia in june. 1876.

A telephone has three main parts: a transmitter. a receiver. and a wire. A person talks into the transmitter *and* It changes the voice sound into electric waves. The waves then travel through the wire. which is connected to the receiver. The receiver changes the ~~elctric~~ *electric* waves back into sound. *and* The listener hears the speaker's words.

Check Your Spelling

Look for spelling mistakes to correct. Apply the Spelling Strategy. Add the words you needed to correct to your spelling log. Then, write a neat, final copy of your research report. Proofread your work. Keep your final copy.

Sharing Your Research Report

Speaking/Listening Strategy

When you are speaking, try to stand still. Talk with your voice, not your hands. While listening, you may want to take notes about an interesting or difficult idea.

Choosing a Way to Share

Here are some ways to share your research report.

Reading Aloud Imagine you are speaking at the class Fact Fair. Make a poster that shows your main ideas in pictures or drawings. Explain the information to your audience. Attach your report to the poster.

Presenting a Show Put on a show using costumes and props to explain your report. Tiffany dressed up as Alexander Graham Bell, and her classmate dressed up as Thomas Watson. Together they acted out a scene showing how Bell invented the telephone. Tiffany also brought a real phone to class to show the main parts and explain how they work.

Making a Book Put all the class reports into a *Class Book of Curiosities*. Make a title page, table of contents, and index for the book. Display it in your school or local library.

Share Your Research Report

Choose a way you prefer to share your report. After presenting it, ask your audience if they have any questions about the topic.

Add to Your Learning Log

Answer these questions in your learning log.

♦ What makes me happiest in my research report?

♦ What was the most interesting thing I learned?

♦ When I write another research report, what will I do differently?

The Literature Connection: Sentences

Have you ever read a story about something that could never happen in real life? Many of our favorite stories tell about impossible things. These tales are fun to read because they make strange things seem real. In reading them, we "see" the fantastic people or places in the story.

How do we "see" the imaginary events taking place in a story? We must concentrate on the details in the story, just as we do for a story about real people and places. We try to picture the action as clearly as possible as we read. Then we add one magical ingredient—*imagination*.

With imagination, our minds form a picture of something we have never seen. A story gives us ideas to help make this new picture. The ideas are written in **sentences**.

Read the poem below. Then see how well you can imagine what the poet describes.

Curious Something
by
Winifred Welles

If I could smell smells with my ears,
　If sounds came buzzing in my nose,
If in my lips were looks and tears,
　Tongues in my eyes, do you suppose

　That I should have this kind of face,
　Or something curious in its place?

Discussion

1. How do the images in the poem make you feel? Tell whether you find them funny or scary.
2. How well were you able to picture the things in the poem? Tell how the picture looked to you.
3. Imagine that you could develop a new way to use your senses. Would this change the way you look?

338

The Writing Connection: Sentences

In your own writing, you can express fantastic ideas such as those in the poem. You can record on paper things that you imagine. In fact, you can write about anything that your mind can picture!

How can you tell a reader about something only you have imagined? You can express your thoughts through sentences. Look at this sentence.

I see many thunderclouds.

It tells what one person sees. Now read this sentence.

I see an ocean of clouds rushing in waves across the sky.

Can you see the part imagination plays in this sentence?

Activity

Did you ever look at something and imagine that it was something else? Look at the picture above and think about each thing the boy is imagining. Write five sentences to tell what you might imagine. The first sentence is provided for you.

When I see the moon, I imagine a huge, silver mirror.

Simple Subjects

A. You have learned that a sentence has a complete subject.

The **complete subject** tells whom or what the sentence is about.

The complete subject can be one word, or it can be more than one word. The complete subject is shown in red.

Iceland is an unusual land.

Many people call Iceland the Land of Frost and Fire.

B. Every complete subject has a simple subject.

The **simple subject** is the main word in the complete subject.

Many large volcanoes rise above the land.

(Volcanoes is the simple subject.)

If the complete subject has only one word, the simple subject and the complete subject are the same.

Ice covers much of the land.

Strategy

To find the simple subject of a sentence, first find the complete subject. It usually includes all the words before the verb. Then find the word that names whom or what the sentence is about.

Check Your Understanding

A. Write the letter of the complete subject.
  1. Lava flows from the volcanoes.
     a. Lava **b.** flows **c.** Lava flows **d.** from the
  2. Black smoke rises in the air.
     a. Black **b.** Black smoke **c.** smoke rises
     d. rises in

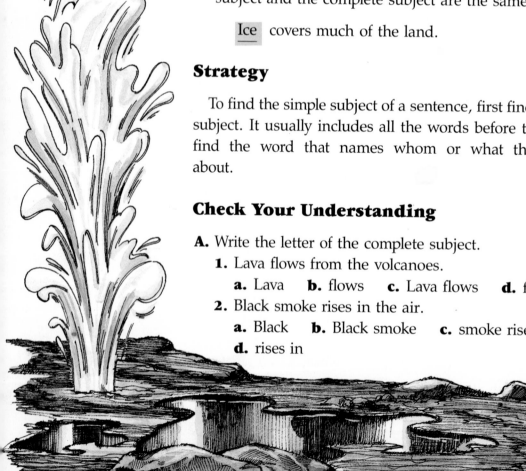

B. The complete subject is underlined. Write the letter of the simple subject.

> **3.** <u>Many scientists</u> study volcanoes.
>> **a.** many   **b.** many scientists   **c.** scientists

> **4.** <u>The bright sun</u> shines all day and night in June.
>> **a.** The   **b.** sun   **c.** bright sun

Practice

A. Write each sentence. Underline the complete subject.

> **5.** Water flows underground.
> **6.** Many hot springs gush from the ground.
> **7.** Springs heat some houses in the city.
> **8.** The strange springs interest many people.

B. Write each sentence. The complete subject is underlined. Underline the simple subject twice.

> **9.** <u>The blue ice</u> is very thick.
> **10.** <u>Snow</u> falls on the ice.
> **11.** <u>The thick ice</u> buries a volcano.
> **12.** <u>Heavy rain</u> falls over the crops.

C. Mixed Practice   Underline the complete subject once. Underline the simple subject twice.

> **13.** Some farmers raise sheep in Iceland.
> **14.** Teachers travel from farm to farm in some areas.
> **15.** The white snow melts slowly.
> **16.** Many beautiful waterfalls rush over cliffs.
> **17.** People live near volcanoes.
> **18.** Certain volcanoes are dangerous.
> **19.** The famous Mount Hekla exploded in 1948.
> **20.** Lava and rocks spread over the land.

Apply: Journal

Write five sentences in your journal about the area where you live. Use complete subjects that have only one word and some that have more than one word. Underline the complete subject in each sentence.

Compound Subjects

A sentence may have more than one simple subject. A **compound subject** is made up of two or more simple subjects that share the same predicate.

A. The two simple subjects in a compound subject are joined by the word *and*. The simple subjects are underlined below.

> Lizards and fish are colorful.

> Temperature and light change the color of some lizards.

B. Sometimes the complete subject contains other words besides the two simple subjects and the word *and*.

> Some lizards and certain fish disguise themselves.

> My book and that magazine tell about these animals.

Strategy

If you use a compound subject when you write, be especially careful to make the verb agree with the subject. Try replacing the complete subject with the word *they*. Then use the form of the verb you would use if the subject were *they*.

Birds and lizards (live, lives) in the forest.
They live in the forest.
Birds and lizards live in the forest.

Check Your Understanding

A. Write the letter of the two simple subjects in the compound subject.

1. Color and size protect many animals.
   a. color, size   **b.** many, animals   **c.** color, protect
2. Skin and scales change into different colors.
   a. Skin, and   **b.** Skin, scales   **c.** Skin, change

B. Follow the directions for Check Your Understanding A.

    3. Some colors and some patterns are beautiful.

        a. Some, colors   **b.** colors, patterns   **c.** some, some

    4. The shapes and dark colors blend into the trees.

        a. shapes, colors   **b.** shapes, dark   **c.** dark, colors

Practice

A. Write the sentence. Underline the two simple subjects in the compound subject.

    5. Color and patterns disguise an animal.

    6. Stonefish and rockfish look like rocks.

    7. Tigers and leopards have dark patterns on their skin.

    8. Stripes and spots help in the jungle.

B. Write each sentence. The complete subject is underlined. Underline each simple subject twice.

    9. The <u>light spots and dark stripes</u> look like shadows.

    10. <u>Fawns and young elk</u> are brown like many trees.

    11. <u>Many lizards and some fish</u> change their color.

    12. <u>Green frogs and small lizards</u> hide in plant leaves.

C. Mixed Practice Write the sentence. Underline the complete subject once. Underline each simple subject twice.

    13. Some butterflies and many moths look like bark.

    14. A few frogs and certain shrimp change color rapidly.

    15. Flounders and other fish blend into the background.

    16. Birds and insects hide in trees.

    17. The black shadows and dark water hide them.

    18. Walkingsticks and caterpillars look like twigs.

    19. Weasels, foxes, and hares grow white fur in winter.

    20. Frogs, toads and some birds blend in with plants.

Apply: Learning Log

What part of the lessons on simple and compound subjects did you find the hardest? Think of a way to help you name the complete and simple subjects of sentences. Write your method in your learning log.

Simple Predicates

A. You have learned that a sentence has two parts, a complete subject and a complete predicate.

The **complete predicate** of a sentence tells what the subject is or does.

The complete predicate can be one word or a group of words. The complete predicate is shown below in blue.

People see comets every year. The small light moves.

B. Every complete predicate includes a simple predicate.

The **simple predicate** is the main word in the complete predicate. The simple predicate is the verb.

The comet flies across the sky.

When the complete predicate is made up of just the verb, the simple predicate and the complete predicate are the same.

The comet spins.

The simple predicate can also be a linking verb such as *am, is, are, was,* or *were.*

A meteorite is like a large rock.

Strategy

To find the simple predicate of a sentence, first find the complete predicate. The simple predicate is usually the first word of the complete predicate. The simple predicate is the verb.

Check Your Understanding

A. Write the letter of the complete predicate.
1. A bright meteor appears in the sky.
   a. A bright meteor   **b.** appears in the sky
2. The flash of light disappears quickly.
   a. The flash of light   **b.** disappears quickly

344

B. Write the letter of the simple predicate. The complete predicate is underlined.

    3. A meteor <u>shines</u>.
        a. A   **b.** meteor   **c.** shines
    4. The trail of light <u>is very long</u>.
        a. trail   **b.** is   **c.** long

Practice

A. Write each sentence. Underline the complete predicate.

    5. Meteors move very quickly.
    6. They rush toward earth sometimes.
    7. Scientists collect meteorites.
    8. They place meteorites in museums.

B. Write each sentence. The complete predicate is underlined. Underline the simple predicate twice.

    9. The meteor <u>burns</u>.
    10. The large meteorite <u>was like a big piece of rock</u>.
    11. Some comets <u>are famous</u>.
    12. Edmond Halley <u>named the most famous comet</u>.

C. Mixed Practice Write each sentence. Underline the complete predicate once. Underline the simple predicate twice.

    13. The scientist saw the comet for the first time in 1682.
    14. The bright comet appears every 77 years.
    15. Halley's Comet appeared in 1986.
    16. People all over the world watched.
    17. Comets are very bright sometimes.
    18. The small meteor crumbles.
    19. It glows and leaves a trail of hot gasses.
    20. Many people had heard the crash of the meteorite.

Apply: Test a Partner

Imagine that you found a strange rock that fell from the sky. Write five sentences about it. Use some complete predicates with one word and some with more than one word. Trade papers with a partner. Underline each complete predicate once and each simple predicate twice. Check your partner's work.

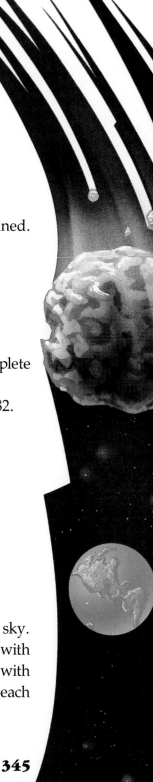

Compound Predicates

A sentence may have more than one simple predicate. A **compound predicate** is made up of two or more simple predicates that share the same subject.

A. The two simple predicates in a compound predicate are joined by the word *and*.

> An earthquake   begins and ends.
>
> The ground   shakes and cracks.

B. A complete predicate can include other words besides the two simple predicates and the word *and*.

> Scientists   test and study the earth carefully.
>
> The earthquake   shakes and damages buildings.

Strategy

When you write a sentence with a compound predicate, make sure both verbs are in the same tense.

> Incorrect: Ines researched and writes about earthquakes.
>   ↑ past tense   ↑ present tense
>
> Correct: Ines researched and wrote about earthquakes.
>   ↑ past tense   ↑ past tense
>
> Correct: Ines researches and writes about earthquakes.
>   ↑ present tense   ↑ present tense

Check Your Understanding

A. Write the letter of the two simple predicates in the underlined compound predicate.

   1. The ground moves and sways.

     a. ground, moves   **b.** moves, and   **c.** moves, sways

   2. Buildings tremble and fall.

     a. Buildings, tremble   **b.** tremble, fall   **c.** and, fall

B. Follow the directions for Check Your Understanding A.

   3. Rocks shift and loosen inside the earth.

      a. shift, and   **b.** shift, inside   **c.** shift, loosen

   4. The earth cracks and splits suddenly.

      a. earth, cracks   **b.** cracks, splits   **c.** and, splits

Practice

A. Write each sentence. Underline the two simple predicates in the compound predicate.

   5. The earth rises and falls.

   6. Weak bridges crumble and collapse.

   7. Scientists' instruments measure and record.

   8. Students read and learn.

B. Write each sentence. The complete predicate is underlined. Underline each simple predicate twice.

   9. An earthquake shocks and surprises people.

  10. Earthquakes frighten and worry us.

  11. An earthquake starts and grows stronger.

  12. Boulders slip and slide down mountains.

C. Mixed Practice Write each sentence. Underline the complete predicate once. Underline each simple predicate twice.

  13. The earthquake begins and travels underground.

  14. The earth bends and snaps at one point.

  15. The ground splits and quivers.

  16. Floors shake and move slightly in most earthquakes.

  17. Strong earthquakes damage and ruin important roads.

  18. Large windows shatter and explode.

  19. Some scientists observe and discuss animals' actions before an earthquake.

  20. Many earthquakes are harmless and never damage anything.

Apply: Work with a Partner

Imagine that there is a bad storm outside. Make a list of verbs that tell what happens during the storm. Work with your partner to write five sentences with compound predicates. Use the verbs from your list.

Compound Sentences

A **compound sentence** contains two simple sentences joined by the word *and*.

A. Read the compound sentence below.

Many animals | are fast , and | some animals | are strong.

simple sentence   simple sentence

Each simple sentence has a subject and a predicate and tells a complete thought. It could stand on its own as a sentence. The simple sentences have been combined to form a compound sentence.

B. Often two sentences tell about ideas that are similar. Two sentences with similar ideas can be combined to make a compound sentence by using a comma (,) and the word *and*.

Cheetahs | are big cats. | They | are very fast.

Cheetahs | are big cats | and | they | are very fast.

These two ideas are alike. Both are about cheetahs.

Strategy

It's easy to recognize a compound sentence. Look for two separate sentences joined by a comma and the word *and*. If each part has a subject and a predicate, the sentence is a compound sentence.

Check Your Understanding

A. Write the letter of the word that names each sentence.
1. Some animals run fast, and some animals fly high.
   a. simple   **b.** compound
2. A pigeon flies 60 miles an hour.
   a. simple   **b.** compound

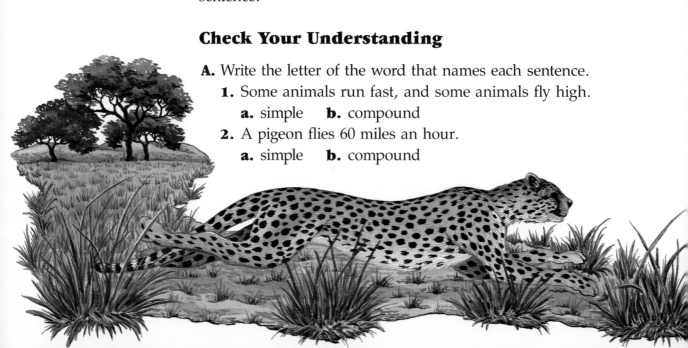

B. Write the letter of the correct compound sentence.

    3. a. The cheetah runs gracefully, and it runs fast.
       b. The cheetah runs gracefully, it runs fast.
    4. a. A horse is quick and, it runs long distances.
       b. A horse is quick, and it runs long distances.

Practice

A. Write each sentence. Then write *simple* or *compound* to name the sentence.
   5. The swift is a small bird.
   6. A swift is a fast bird, and a cheetah is a fast cat.
   7. The cheetah runs 70 miles an hour, and the swift flies over 100 miles an hour.
   8. A cheetah moves quickly.

B. Write compound sentences by combining each set of two sentences using a comma (,) and the word *and*.
   9. Antelopes run fast. They run far.
  10. Bees are very small. They fly quite fast.
  11. Whales dive deep. Flying fish jump into the air.
  12. The impala leaps high. It travels at fifty miles an hour.

C. Mixed Practice Write each sentence. Then write *simple* or *compound* to name each sentence. Underline the two simple sentences in each compound sentence.
  13. Turtles are slow, and snails are slower than turtles.
  14. The sloth moves at the same speed as a turtle.
  15. Hares run faster than turtles.
  16. Some athletes train hard, and they run quickly.
  17. Everyone runs at a different speed.
  18. A whale swims fast, and it is very large.
  19. A rabbit hops and leaps very quickly.
  20. Geese and terns fly high, and they fly for many hours.

Apply: Exploring Language

Write six sentences about animals in a jungle. Combine your sentences to make three compound sentences. Does each sentence make sense? Why or why not?

Reviewing Parts of Speech

The different kinds of words used in sentences are called the **parts of speech.** You have learned about five parts of speech.

A. Some words name things. Others name actions.

A **noun** is a word that names a person, place, or thing.

Mary Anning found the skeleton of a dinosaur.

A **pronoun** is a word that takes the place of a noun.

It was in the rocks in Lyme, England.

An **action verb** is a word that tells what someone or something does.

Mary found more skeletons.

A **linking verb** joins words in the subject with words in the predicate. It tells what the subject is or is like.

The skeleton was old.

B. Adjectives and adverbs tell more about other words.

An **adjective** is a word that tells more about a noun.

Scientists studied the odd skeleton.

An **adverb** is a word that tells more about an action.

Scientists examined it carefully.

Strategy

Each word in a sentence plays a role. It can act as a noun, a verb, or one of the other parts of speech. To tell what role a word plays in a sentence, remember the definitions in this lesson.

Check Your Understanding

A. Write the letter that names the part of speech of the underlined word.

    1. Old fossils are delicate.   **a.** noun   **b.** linking verb

    2. Animals lived long ago.   **a.** noun   **b.** action verb

B. Follow the directions for Check Your Understanding A.

    3. People find small bones.   **a.** adjective   **b.** adverb

    4. They dig slowly for bones.   **a.** adjective   **b.** adverb

Practice

A. Write each sentence. Write the part of speech that names the
underlined word.

    5. Some fossils are unusual.

    6. They are very famous.

    7. People collect fossils of plants and fish.

    8. Scientists learn about the earth of long ago.

B. Follow the directions for Practice A.

    9. Only hard objects become fossils.

   10. Frequently rocks preserve bones and teeth.

   11. Scientists look carefully at these pieces.

   12. They found many fossils in Colorado.

C. Mixed Practice Write each sentence. Write the part of speech
that names the underlined word.

   13. Roy Andrews found eggs of dinosaurs in China.

   14. He discovered them in 1923.

   15. These eggs are precious.

   16. The Chinese fossils were big.

   17. Scientists dig skillfully for bones.

   18. People find strange things in rocks.

   19. They have discovered unusual animals.

   20. You see the skeleton in a museum today.

Apply: Work with a Group

With your group, make a poster about the parts of speech you
have learned. Tell how each part of speech is used.

Homographs

Homographs are words that are spelled alike but have different meanings.

A. Many homographs sound alike.

> Waves crash upon the <u>rock</u>. (*Rock* is a piece of stone.)
> The ships <u>rock</u> back and forth. (*Rock* means to sway.)

The word *rock* sounds the same but has a different meaning in each sentence.

Some homographs do not sound alike.

> We live on a very <u>windy</u> road. (*Windy* means crooked.)
> Kites fly best on a <u>windy</u> day. (*Windy* means air in motion.)

B. You can tell what a homograph means by the way it is used in a sentence.

Read these sentences:

> Her dogs <u>bark</u> loudly every night.
> Indians made canoes from <u>bark</u>.

In the first sentence, the word *bark* means "the sound of a dog." What does *bark* mean in the second sentence?

Strategy

Homographs can be confusing when you read. If you don't know the meaning of the word or how the word sounds, look it up in the dictionary.

Check Your Understanding

A. Write the letter of the homographs in each pair of sentences.
  1. Maria saw a rainbow. Jose cuts wood with a saw.
   a. cuts   **b.** rainbow   **c.** saw   **d.** with
  2. Rain must fall first. Leaves turn color in the fall.
   a. rain   **b.** turn   **c.** first   **d.** fall

B. Write the letter of the meaning of the underlined word.

    3. Please <u>close</u> the window when it rains.

        a. near by   **b.** shut

    4. The colors of the rainbow appear in <u>rows</u>.

        a. a line; in order   **b.** uses oars

Practice

A. Write each pair of sentences. Underline the homographs.

    5. A rainbow has bands of color. The brass bands practice today.

    6. The sun's light causes rainbows. The feather felt light.

    7. Snow falls on a mountain top. The girl spins a top.

    8. Even the moon's light causes rainbows. The score was even after the game.

B. Write each sentence. Write the meaning of each underlined homograph. Choose from the meanings in parentheses.

    9. Birds <u>fly</u> over rainbows. (insect, move through the air)

    10. A <u>fly</u> buzzed around. (insect, move through the air)

    11. The rainbow appears in a <u>desert</u>. (dry region, leave)

    12. She will not <u>desert</u> them. (dry region, leave)

C. Mixed Practice Write each sentence and underline the pairs of homographs. Write the meaning of each homograph.

    13. Some rainbows disappear in a second. The second team won. (part of a minute, next after first)

    14. Rainbows present a colorful scene. She received a great present. (gift, to give or show)

    15. Many pencils are made of lead. They lead us to the rainbow. (type of metal, guide)

    16. One kind of scientist studies rainbows. The kind girl helped us. (friendly, type)

Apply: Work with a Partner

Think of a pair of homographs. Write a sentence with one of the homographs, and underline it. Trade papers with your partner. Write a new sentence using a homograph of the underlined word.

Giving an Oral Report

Your teacher gives you an assignment to make an oral report. You've written research reports before, but you've never given an oral report. What do you do?

An oral report is like a research report, only you don't write it all down. Instead, you tell the class what you learned. Here's what you do.

- ◆ Find a topic. If one is assigned to you, this step is easy. If not, pick a topic that interests you so that you will enjoy talking about it.
- ◆ Do research. Start off as if you were doing a written report. Find out all you can about the topic.
- ◆ Make notes. You can write them on a piece of paper, or you can use index cards. Write down what you want to talk about. These notes are only for you, so they don't have to be complete sentences. They are helpful to refer to when you give your report. Use a map or picture if it will help explain your subject.
- ◆ Give your report. Speak loudly and clearly. Make sure that everyone in the class can hear you. Remember, you're talking to your friends and classmates. There's no reason to be nervous.

Practice

On a separate piece of paper, answer these questions.
   1. What is the first thing you do to prepare an oral report?
   2. What is the purpose for your notes?
   3. When you are giving the report, how should you speak?

Apply

Give an oral report to your class. Pick any topic you like, or you may ask your teacher to suggest one. Research the topic, make notes, and present your report to the class.

TEST TAKING

Answering Test Questions with Sentences

Some test questions will have to be answered with several sentences. These are called **essay** questions. Follow these steps to help make answering essay questions easier.

- **Think About the Question** Before you begin to write, think about what is being asked. Look for key words such as *describe*, *explain*, *compare*, or *name*. These words will tell you what to do.

- **Write Your Answer** Turn the question or direction into a sentence as the beginning of your answer. For example:

   Question: Name some ways to save water.
   Statement: Some ways to save water are. . .

- **Check Your Answer** Reread each sentence, making sure that it answers the question and sticks to the topic.

- **Check for Complete Sentences** Check to see that all the sentences in your answer are complete. Begin each sentence with a capital letter and end it with a period.

Practice

Answer each question below.
1. What can you do to help you understand the question being asked?
2. What should you check for after writing your answer?
3. What should you check to make sure you have written a complete sentence?

Apply

Learning Log Decide what things from this lesson you found helpful. Write them in your learning log.

UNIT REVIEW

Research Reports   *(pages 317-319)*

1. Name three features of a research report.

Making an Outline   *(pages 328-329)*

2. Make an outline with the following main ideas and details.

I. Whales are mammals.

II. Whales are very big.

(1) Fin whales grow up to 80 feet long. (2) Whales are the largest animals in the world. (3) Like all mammals, whales breathe air, not water. (4) Blue whales grow up to 100 feet long. (5) Most mammals have four legs. (6) Whales' flippers are like front legs.

Combining Sentences and Proper Nouns, Titles, and Initials   *(pages 332-335)*

Combine each pair of sentences using the word *and*, *but*, or *or* and a comma.

3. Edith Hamilton could read Greek when she was seven.
She didn't write about Greece until she was 55.

4. She was a teacher.
She also wrote history books.

5. You can find her books in the library.
You can find them in a bookstore if you prefer.

Rewrite each sentence. Use capital letters and periods where needed.

6. mr j Cousteau explores the ocean.

7. His son, p Cousteau, does, too.

8. Whales live in the atlantic ocean.

9. Many americans hunted whales.

Simple and Compound Subjects   *(pages 340-343)*

Write each sentence. Underline the complete subject once. Underline each simple subject twice. Write *compound* if a sentence has a compound subject.

10. My friend and I signed up for the soccer team.

11. Mrs. Wilson coaches us.

12. The Tigers and the Bears play today at 3:00.

13. Some eager fans arrived by 2:30.

356

Simple and Compound Predicates *(pages 344-347)*

Write each sentence. Underline the complete predicate once. Underline each simple predicate twice. Write *compound* if a sentence has a compound predicate.

14. Class 4B wrote and published its own newspaper.

15. Reporters researched the articles.

16. Other students wrote and edited the stories.

17. The art staff cut and pasted the stories onto oaktag.

18. Everybody checked the spelling in each article.

19. Other classes in the school read and discussed the paper.

Compound Sentences *(pages 348-349)*

Write each sentence. Write *simple* if it is a simple sentence. Write *compound* if it is a compound sentence.

20. The wind blew, and the sky got dark.

21. The thunder roared, and the lightning crackled.

22. The campers ran for cover into their tents.

23. The rain started suddenly, and then it was over.

24. The sun peeked through the clouds, and the sky became blue.

25. The campers happily ran out of their tents.

Reviewing Parts of Speech *(pages 350-351)*

Write each sentence. Then write whether each underlined word is a *noun*, a *pronoun*, an *action verb*, a *linking verb*, an *adjective*, or an *adverb*.

26. A triangle is a shape with three sides.

27. Triangles are also musical instruments.

28. A musical triangle hangs on a string.

29. You hit it gently with a small metal bar.

30. The instrument sounds like a bell.

31. Children often play triangles in rhythm bands.

Homographs *(pages 352-353)*

Write each sentence and underline the pairs of homographs. Write the correct meaning of each homograph.

32. Can you see the stage?
   Please get a can of peas. (to be able to/metal container)

33. Duck before you hit your head.
   A duck is in the pond. (to bend down suddenly/a water bird)

34. The wind is very strong today.
   Did you wind your watch? (air in motion/to turn)

MAKING ALL THE
CONNECTIONS

You and several classmates will now write a short play together. What you have learned about writing a story will help you.

You will do the following in your play:

♦ Tell about **characters**—the people or animals in the story
♦ Describe the **setting**—the time and place of the story
♦ Create a **plot**—what happens in the story
♦ Include **dialogue**—what the characters say

Reading a Play

Read the following scene from a play about a curious way to prepare for a test. Notice the side notes that point out the features of a play. After discussing the scene, you and your classmates will write a short play together.

School cafeteria at lunchtime

The dialogue starts here. In the plot, a character faces a problem.

Sue: Tom, you look worried. What's wrong?
Tom: It's our health test this afternoon. I'm afraid I won't remember all the basic food groups.
Sue: But you have a *good* memory. You *always* remember jokes.
Tom: Jokes are easy for me. School work is different.
Sue: Well, stay calm in class. Don't be a chicken.
Tom: I guess I'm in the meat and poultry group.
Sue: Hey, I just got an idea. Why not remember the food groups by thinking of jokes? Does that sound *corny*?

In the plot, characters attempt to solve their problem.

Tom: *Corn*-y. That's the vegetable group. Sue, you're a *peach*! That's the fruit group.

Sue: Oh, you're just trying to *butter* me up.

Tom: That reminds me of the milk group.

Sue: And during the test, stay alert. Don't *loaf*!

Tom: The bread and cereal group. Sue, that's great!
Now I'll remember all the food groups for sure!

Speaking and Listening

Your teacher will assign you to a group. Choose a group leader. Talk about these questions.

1. In the play you read on page 356, who were the characters?

2. What was the setting of the play?

3. What problem did a character face in the play? Tell how the problem was solved.

4. What can you learn about the characters and setting of the play from the picture above?

Thinking

Brainstorming

Choose one person to be a note taker. Have the person take notes as you discuss these questions. Save your notes.

1. What funny or interesting problems have occurred in your school recently?

2. Exactly when and where did the problem occur? Tell which people were involved.

3. What did people say to each other during the incident?

4. What happened in the end?

5. What items would you need to act out the incident?

MAKING ALL THE CONNECTIONS

Organizing

When you prepare to write a play, it helps to put your details in a chart. Study the chart below. It shows details about the play on page 356.

Characters: Sue, a 4th-grader; Tom, her classmate			
Setting: a school lunchroom at noon			
Plot: Introduction	Problem	Solution attempts	Outcome
Sue and Tom are eating lunch together. Sue notices that Tom looks worried.	Tom is worried he will not re-member all the food groups for a test.	Sue and Tom make food jokes to re-mind Tom of the groups.	Tom is now confident he will do well on the test.

With the rest of your group, discuss a funny or interesting problem that occurred in school. Have one group member take notes and write them in a chart like the one above.

Writing a Play

Imagine that your school is having a Playfest. You will use the chart you made to help write a play for the Playfest.

Planning

- ◆ Review the chart your group made. Add any new details you may think of now.
- ◆ Talk about who the characters in the play will be.
- ◆ Talk about what the setting will be.
- ◆ Discuss the plot, including the problem that occurs and the outcome.
- ◆ Organize your details in an outline. First list your characters, then your setting, and then the plot.

Composing

- Work with your group to write your play. Choose one member to write down the first draft as everyone suggests ideas.
- First, list your characters and the setting.
- Next, write the exact dialogue that the characters will speak.

Revising

- As a group, read over your play line by line. Think of ways to make the dialogue sound more natural.
- Check that your plot has an introduction, a problem, solution attempts, and an outcome.

Proofreading

As a group, proofread your play. Choose one group member to make the changes on your draft. Answer these questions:

- Does every sentence have the correct end punctuation?
- Are compound subjects and predicates combined with *and*?
- Are compound sentences written correctly?
- Are all words spelled correctly?

Presenting

- Choose one group member to write a neat, final copy of your play.
- Perform the play for the rest of the class or school. Assign parts to group members. One group member may serve as the director. Prepare costumes or other items that will help you present the play on stage. If you wish, prepare a program for the audience to read.

Cumulative Review

A. Write the letter of the group of words that is a sentence. (*pages 40-41*)

   1. a. Waited for a plane.   **2. a.** The first jet.
      b. Many huge jets.   **b.** Jean boarded the plane.
      c. The plane landed.   **c.** A long line of people.

B. Write the letter of the word that names each sentence. (*pages 42-43*)

   3. Did Julie make that unusual bowl?
      a. exclamation   **b.** statement   **c.** command   **d.** question
   4. Mr. Lorca painted the decorations on this bowl.
      a. exclamation   **b.** statement   **c.** command   **d.** question
   5. This pottery has wonderful colors!
      a. exclamation   **b.** statement   **c.** command   **d.** question

C. Write the letter of the sentence with one line under the complete subject and two lines under the complete predicate. (*pages 44-47*)

   6. a. A cat hid in the grass.   **8. a.** Frogs sat in the pond.
      b. A bird flew past the cat.   **b.** A tree grew nearby.
      c. The cat watched the bird.   **c.** A leaf fell quietly.
   7. a. Yellow sunlight glowed.   **9. a.** A girl came to the field.
      b. Clouds gathered over-   **b.** The cat saw the girl.
       head.   **c.** The cat went to the girl.
      c. A cool wind blew.

D. Write the letter of the word that is a noun. (*pages 78-79*)

   10. The dog sleeps quietly.   **12.** A long snake crawls slowly.
      a. dog   **b.** quietly   **a.** long   **b.** snake
   11. The green frog jumps.   **13.** The animals hurry away.
      a. green   **b.** frog   **a.** animals   **b.** hurry

E. Write the letter of the correct plural noun. (*pages 80-81*)

   14. ox   **a.** oxes   **b.** oxen   **c.** oxs
   15. apple   **a.** appls   **b.** applees   **c.** apples
   16. peach   **a.** peaches   **b.** peachs   **c.** peachen
   17. tray   **a.** traies   **b.** trays   **c.** trayes

F. Write the letter of the correct possessive of each noun. (*pages 84-87*)

18. men   **a.** mens'   **b.** men's   **c.** mens's

19. tigers   **a.** tiger's   **b.** tigers'   **c.** tigers's

20. fox   **a.** fox'es   **b.** foxes'   **c.** fox's

G. Write the letter of the abbreviation that is written correctly. (*pages 82-83, 88-89*)

21. a. Mister. Tony Chee   **b.** Mrs. Wilma Alba   **c.** ms. ella rand

22. a. Sat., Feb. 4   **b.** Wednes., June 6   **c.** Fri Apr 7

23. a. 46 Spruce Rd   **b.** 7 Hay Blvd.   **c.** 56 Green st.

H. Write the letter of the word that names each verb. (*pages 126-129*)

24. Agatha Christie wrote many mysteries.

   a. action verb   **b.** linking verb

25. Miss Christie's mysteries are unusual.

   a. action verb   **b.** linking verb

26. Most of the stories have a real surprise at the end.

   a. action verb   **b.** linking verb

I. Write the letter of the correct tense of the verb. (*pages 130-131*)

27. Dad turned the channel to the weather report.

   a. present tense   **b.** past tense   **c.** future tense

28. The family watches the weather map on the TV screen.

   a. present tense   **b.** past tense   **c.** future tense

29. Tomorrow, clouds will bring showers to this area.

   a. present tense   **b.** past tense   **c.** future tense

J. Write the letter of the correct spelling for each underlined verb, using the tense in parentheses. (*pages 132-135*)

30. Sally stop Ms. Bueno in the hall. (past)

   a. stoped   **b.** stopped   **c.** stops

31. Sally ask a question about the science lab. (present)

   a. asks   **b.** askes   **c.** ask

32. The teacher reply with a smile. (past)

   a. replyed   **b.** replied   **c.** replyd

33. Sally hurry to the gym. (present)

   a. hurry   **b.** hurrys   **c.** hurries

34. Todd push the door open for Sally. (present)

   a. pushes   **b.** push   **c.** pushs

K. Write the letter of the correct main verb or helping verb. (*pages 160-161*)

35. Marilyn ____ building a model ship.
    a. is **b.** has **c.** had

36. Marilyn's brother had ____ model ships for years.
    a. collect **b.** collecting **c.** collected

37. Jim ____ filled two glass cases with beautiful ships.
    a. was **b.** is **c.** has

L. Write the letter of the correct past-tense verb. (*pages 162-165*)

38. The Pan American Games ____ in 1951.
    a. begin **b.** began **c.** begun

39. Athletes from many nations ____ to the Games.
    a. have go **b.** have went **c.** have gone

40. Many Olympic winners ____ in the 1987 Games.
    a. runned **b.** ran **c.** runs

41. The United States baseball team ____ well in the 1987 Games.
    a. did **b.** do **c.** done

M. Write the letter of the correct contraction. (*pages 166-167*)

42. were not
    a. were'nt **b.** weren't

43. is not
    a. isn't **b.** is'nt

44. had not
    a. hadn't **b.** had'nt

45. would not
    a. wouldn't **b.** won't

N. Write the letter of the correct subject or object pronoun to replace the underlined words. (*pages 212-215*)

46. Anna Kim visited the Asian kingdom of Bhutan.
    a. She **b.** We **c.** I

47. Ms. Kim saw the king.
    a. them **b.** us **c.** him

48. This man became king at the age of 18.
    a. They **b.** He **c.** She

49. Ms. Kim told Mom and me about the wonderful trip.
    a. us **b.** them **c.** her

O. Write the letter of the correct pronoun. (*pages 216-217*)

50. ____ work at a zoo.
    a. We **b.** Us

51. The animals watch ____.
    a. I **b.** me

52. Visitors ask ____ questions.
    a. we **b.** us

53. ____ enjoy this job.
    a. I **b.** Me

P. Write the letter of the possessive form of the pronoun that replaces each underlined possessive. (*pages 218-219*)

54. I heard about <u>Peg's</u> visit to Mount Rushmore.

    a. her   **b.** their   **c.** its

55. Peg admired the <u>Presidents'</u> faces on Mount Rushmore.

    a. his   **b.** its   **c.** their

56. Workers carved the four giant faces on <u>the cliff's</u> side.

    a. its   **b.** his   **c.** their

Q. Write the letter of the correct contraction. (*pages 220-221*)

57. we are

    a. we're   **b.** wer'e

58. they have

    a. they'ave   **b.** they've

R. Write the letter of the word that is an adjective. (*pages 250-251*)

59. A sweet smell came from the gardens.

    a. sweet   **b.** smell   **c.** gardens

60. Perfume makers use flowers in many perfumes.

    a. Perfume   **b.** flowers   **c.** many

S. Write the letter of the correct article. (*pages 252-253*)

61. Put milk in _____ blender.

    a. an   **b.** the

62. Add _____ egg and fruit.

    a. a   **b.** an

63. Add _____ ice cube.

    a. a   **b.** an

64. _____ drink tastes good.

    a. The   **b.** An

T. Write the letter of the correct adjective. (*pages 254-259*)

65. Australia is the _____ continent of all.

    a. smaller   **b.** smallest

66. Africa is _____ than South America.

    a. bigger   **b.** biggest

67. North America is _____ than Australia.

    a. more mountainous   **b.** most mountainous

68. Asia has the _____ cities of all.

    a. more ancient   **b.** most ancient

69. Europe's climate is _____ than Antarctica's climate.

    a. better   **b.** best

70. Antarctica has the _____ climate of all.

    a. worse   **b.** worst

U. Write the letter of the correctly punctuated sentence. (*pages 294-295*)

71. a. Al, please carry this bag for me.
    b. All right Karen I will.

72. a. I see apples pears, and grapes in this bag.
    b. They are for a surprise party, and the party is for you.

V. Write the letter of the word that is an adverb. (*pages 300-303*)

73. A balloon race started today in our town.
    a. started   **b.** today   **c.** town

74. Bright balloons floated overhead in the sky.
    a. bright   **b.** floated   **c.** overhead

75. The winner landed gently in a wide field.
    a. gently   **b.** wide   **c.** field.

W. Write the letter of the correct adverb. (*pages 304-305*)

76. Greyhounds run ____ than beagles.
    a. faster   **b.** more fast   **c.** fastest

77. Poodles learn tricks ____ of all.
    a. more easily   **b.** most easily   **c.** easiliest

78. Puppies eat ____ than adult dogs.
    a. more frequently   **b.** frequentliest   **c.** most frequent

X. Write the letter of the word that belongs in the sentence. (*pages 306-307*)

79. Mr. Ali is a ____ baker.
    a. good   **b.** well

80. He works ____ in his tidy kitchen.
    a. careful   **b.** carefully

81. His breads are ____ all over the city.
    a. popular   **b.** popularly

Y. Write the letter of the word that forms a sentence with one *no* word. (*pages 308-309*)

82. There is ____ name on this painting.
    a. no   **b.** any

83. Nobody ____ guess the name of the artist.
    a. could   **b.** couldn't

Z. Write the letter of the sentence with a compound subject. (*pages 340-343*)

84. a. Great inventions come from all over the world.

   b. Paper and printing began in China long ago.

   c. Chinese inventors made the first clocks too.

85. a. The steam engine and the bicycle came from England.

   b. French inventors flew the first passenger balloons.

   c. A Dutch scientist made the first telescope.

86. a. Many machines and useful tools are American inventions.

   b. Bell invented the first telephone in the United States.

   c. Americans developed many of the early computers.

AA. Write the letter of the sentence with a compound predicate. (*pages 344-347*)

87. a. Alex visited a Native American art museum.

   b. He saw many beautiful Pueblo baskets.

   c. The Pueblo people weave and dye bright rugs.

88. a. Northwest tribes carve and paint huge totem poles.

   b. A carver often uses an entire tree for the pole.

   c. The giant wooden canoes of the Northwest are famous.

89. a. Beads are important in Native American art.

   b. Native Americans have used shells for decoration too.

   c. Some groups make and wear silver jewelry.

BB. Write the letter of the words that name the sentence. (*pages 348-349*)

90. Margo played her new guitar for the class.

   a. simple sentence   **b.** compound sentence

91. She sang two songs, and Eli recorded them.

   a. simple sentence   **b.** compound sentence

CC. Write the letter that names the part of speech of each underlined word. (*pages 350-351*)

92. The <u>first</u> <u>films</u> <u>were</u> silent and black and white.

   a. noun, action verb, noun   **b.** adjective, noun, linking verb

93. <u>Today</u> <u>films</u> <u>have</u> color and sound.

   a. adverb, noun, linking verb   **b.** adverb, noun, action verb

Resources
Table of Contents

Here is your thesaurus it is like a dictionary. It lists words that are similar to one another. There is an entry for each main word. The main words are in heavy type and are listed in alphabetical order. Here is the entry for the word *give*:

part of speech

main word — **give** *verb* Give an apple to your friend.
Similar words: *grant* a favor, *offer* a new idea, *bestow* a gift, *donate* some old clothes, *furnish* the food for a party, *sacrifice* spare time to help a friend.
Opposite words: seize, **take**, hold.

another main entry word

Most entries contain the following information: the main word, its part of speech, a sentence using the main word, phrases suggesting similar words, and words that mean the opposite of the main word. Some entries give you other information. For example, the entry for *boat* lists kinds of boats.

The thesaurus can be very helpful when you are writing. Use it to find a different word to replace a word you have used several times. You can also use it to look for a word you can't remember. Look up a similar word. Maybe you will find the word you are thinking of.

It isn't a good idea to use a word from the thesaurus if you don't already know it. You might not use the word in exactly the right way. If you find a word you don't know, look it up in a dictionary.

Thesaurus

A a

above *adverb* The stars are above. *Similar words*: suitable for age two and *over*, the sky is *overhead*. *Opposite words*: **under, below**.

accident *noun* The cook had an accident with the eggs. *Similar words*: a **mistake** on the test, a *mishap* with the soup.

act *noun* He was caught in the act of wrapping presents. *Similar words*: the *action* of running, a hero's brave *deed*, a clever *feat*.

active *adjective* Owls are most active at night. *Similar words*: a *lively* dance, a *peppy* cheerleader, an *energetic* worker, a *frisky* horse, a *busy* bee. *Opposite words*: unmoving, idle, **lazy**, dull.

again *adverb* The window was broken again —for the fourth time! *Similar words*: birds returned *once more*, bells ringing *repeatedly*. *Opposite words*: never, once.

agree *verb* Do you agree that we should go? *Similar words*: *consent* to the plan, *accept* the decision, *acknowledge* that they are right. *Opposite words*: disagree, contradict.

angry *adjective* I was angry when my bike was broken. *Similar words*: *annoyed* at being late, *fuming* when the secret diary was read, *furious* at being forgotten, *gruff* words, *grumpy* because it's raining, *indignant* about the mistake, *irritated* at losing a pencil, ***mad*** as a wet hen, *outraged* that there was nothing to eat, *resentful* about losing the game, a *snarling* tiger, a *sulky* three-year-old baby, *upset* about burning the toast.

animal *noun* The panda is the most popular animal in the zoo. *Similar words*: a *beast* in the wild, a *creature* of nature, the *pest* that destroyed the crops, a family *pet*.

> Some animals are ant, bear, bird, cat, chicken, cow, dog, elephant, gerbil, horse, lion, mouse, monkey, pig, tiger, whale, and zebra.

> Some animal homes are barnyard, birdhouse, burrow, cage, den, doghouse, farm, hive, jungle, nest, pasture, perch, ranch, range, stable, stall, web, the wild, and zoo.

> Some animal sounds are bark, buzz, chirp, croak, crow, hiss, honk, hoot, howl, meow, moo, neigh, purr, quack, screech, squawk, and squeak.

answer *verb* A good student could answer that question. *Similar words*: to *respond* to a question, *retort* sharply.

argue *verb* The two of them argue and can't agree about anything. *Similar words*: *bicker* over who was at fault, *debate* the pros and cons, *quarrel* about whose turn it is.

artist *noun* The artist formed the clay into a graceful, delicate shape. *Similar words*: the *craftsperson* made a clay pot, the *creator* of a work of art.

> Some types of artists are actor, author, clown, composer, dancer, musician, painter, performer, photographer, poet, singer, and storyteller.

ashamed *adjective* He was ashamed about taking his brother's bike without asking. *Similar words*: a *sheepish* look, *embarrassed* at being discovered, *disgraced* for forgetting his report.

ask *verb* Please ask for help if you need it. *Similar words*: *quiz* the contestant, *beg* for mercy, *consult* with an expert, *demand* a meeting, *inquire* about their decision, *interview* the celebrity, *question* about the reasons, politely *request* more money.

attractive *adjective* The jar of jam was attractive to the bees and the bear. *Similar words*: an *appealing* puppy, a *magnetic* personality, an *alluring* perfume. *Opposite words*: repellent, disgusting.

awful *adjective* That rotten apple smells awful. *Similar words*: a *disgusting* movie, a *dreadful* painting, a *terrible* singing voice. *Opposite words*: **good**, excellent, **wonderful**.

B b

bad *adjective* She gave a bad performance full of mistakes. *Similar words*: an *awful* headache, an *evil* villain in the movie, did a *poor* job on the report, a *fake* message, a *worn-out* tool, a *nasty* surprise, a *terrible* dragon, *unfit* to eat, a *villainous* plot, *wicked* prince, a *naughty* child, a *nightmarish* experience, a *treacherous* climb, a *sinister* shadow. *Opposite words*: **good**, excellent, first-rate.

band *noun* The band played several marches. *Similar words*: many musicians in the *orchestra*, the conductor of the *symphony*, the four members of the *quartet*.

bang *verb* Use this hammer to bang the nail in. *Similar words*: *beat* the drum, *clang* the bell, pots and pans *clatter* in the kitchen, *knock* on the door, *slam* the door, *pound* on the table, *thump* on the piano.

beach *noun* I spent the day at the beach playing in the sand and the water. *Similar words*: a drive along the *coast*, swim close to *shore*, a fish market on the *waterfront*.

believe *verb* I believe your story is true. *Similar words*: *be of the opinion* that people are basically good, *trust* your friends.

below *adverb* The mountain climber looked at the valley below. *Similar words*: the submarine went **under**, someone digging *underneath*, the toys *underfoot*. *Opposite words*: **above**, overhead.

bend *verb* Bend at the waist to touch your toes. *Similar words*: *flex* a muscle, *crook* a finger at a friend, *fold* the pages back.

better *adjective* Water would be better for you than that drink full of sugar. *Similar words*: a good student with a *superior* test score, new and *improved* flavor.

big *adjective* There is much more shade under that big chestnut tree. *Similar words*: *giant* steps, *gigantic* skyscraper, *immense* body of water, *large*, filling meal, *enormous* crowd, **grand** spectacle, *huge* whale, *mighty* wrestler, *bulky* package, *mammoth* year-end sale, *massive* statue, *monumental* decision, *vast* planet. *Opposite words*: **small**, tiny, **little**.

bigger *adjective* I need a bigger box for all these supplies. *Similar words*: *expanded* balloon, an *increasing* group of people waiting for the star to arrive, an *enlarged* index, *multiplied* in numbers; a *larger* room. *Opposite words*: smaller, lesser.

bit *noun* Have a bit of this banana. *Similar words*: a *crumb* of bread, a *pinch* of cinnamon, a *speck* of dirt, a *flake* of snow, a *sliver* of wood, a *thimbleful* of water.

bite *verb* Bite into this crisp apple. *Similar words*: *nip* the sheep to herd them, *chew* some gum, *gnaw* on the chicken bone, *nibble* snacks.

black *adjective* The black cat disappeared into the night. *Similar words*: a fancy purse with *jet* beads, white and *ebony* piano keys.

boat *noun* The sailor had to row the boat. *Similar words*: sailing *ship*, sea-going *vessel*.

> Some types of boats are tug, canoe, rowboat, ferry, freighter, raft, sailboat, steamer, and clipper.

bother *verb* Running fingernails across a chalkboard can really bother me. *Similar words*: *annoy* me with that noise, *pester* me with so many questions, *nag* your sister, *upset* a friend.

brave *adjective* The brave girl rescued her kitten from the tree. *Similar words*: *bold* action, *courageous* firefighter, *daring* leap to safety, **heroic** rescue, *plucky* speech, *fearless* leader, *intrepid* explorer. *Opposite words*: cautious, timid, cowardly, wary.

break *verb* If you crawl out on that tree limb, it might break. *Similar words*: *smash* an egg, *snap* the twigs, *shatter* the glass, *chip* the bowl.

breathe *verb* Breathe deeply to relax. *Similar words*: *pant* like a dog, *puff* after running, *gasp* for breath, *yawn* during a boring meeting, *sigh* after a big meal, *inhale* and *exhale*.

bright *adjective* She paid for her lunch with bright new coins. *Similar words*: *brilliant* sunshine, *shiny* new car, *glittering* jewels, *fiery* diamonds, *luminous* watch, *sparkling* water, *radiant* glow, *twinkling* eyes, *dazzling* snow. *Opposite words*: dull, faded, pale.

bring *verb* Please bring some fruit to the picnic. *Similar words*: *fetch* the stick, **gather** your friends for a meeting, *carry* a meal to the table, *deliver* the mail.

building *noun* The doctor's office is located in that building. *Similar words*: built a *shelter* at the campsite, rooms in the *house*.

> Parts of a building are attic, ceiling, cellar, chimney, closet, courtyard, door, fireplace, gate, gutter, hallway, lobby, loft, platform, porch, office, rooms, sill, stairs, stairway, stoop, and window.

burn *verb* You'll burn the hot dog if it's that close to the fire. *Similar words*: the campfire *blazes*, coals that *smolder*, *kindle* a small flame.

C c

call *verb* Call my name if you need me. *Similar words*: **cry** out in surprise, **shout** at the top of your lungs, summon into the room.

calm *adjective* I want to spend a calm hour soaking in a warm bubble bath. *Similar words*: *soothing* music, *peaceful afternoon*, *even-tempered* boy. *Opposite words*: excited, restless.

carry *verb* Can you carry the groceries up those stairs? *Similar words*: *lug* the bowling ball, *haul* the trash away, *tote* the wood, *bear* a heavy load.

catch *verb* Learning how to run and catch a football is fun. *Similar words: trap* a fly, *net* some fish, *grasp* the ball, *hook* a trout. *Opposite words:* **throw**, release.

chair *noun* Find an empty chair. *Similar words:* park *bench*, best *seat* in the house, a queen on her *throne*, three-legged wooden *stool*, comfortable *armchair*.

change *verb* Change your clothes before we go out to dinner. *Similar words: adapt* to your surroundings, *alter* your bad behavior, *substitute* an ingredient, *transform* into a butterfly, *vary* what you eat each day.

choice *noun* I have a choice between chicken and beef. *Similar words:* faced with a difficult *dilemma*, the *vote* in the election, an *alternative* to watching television.

city *noun* More and more people live in the city each year. *Similar words:* friendly people in the small *town*, a sleepy little *village*, the state *capital*, a growing *settlement*, a busy *community*.

clean *verb* Clean your room before the guests arrive. *Similar words: bathe* the dog, *scrub* the tile, *scour* the greasy stove, *straighten* the messy closet, *wash* the socks.

clear *adjective* It was a clear day. *Similar words: pure* mountain stream, *cloudless* sky, *transparent* as glass.

climb *verb* It was hard work to climb that hill. *Similar words: ascend* the ladder, *mount* the horse, *scramble* up the cliff. *Opposite word:* descend.

cloth *noun* The cloth of this jacket is quite soft. *Similar words:* a stiff *fabric*, sew the *material*.

Types of cloth are lace, silk, velvet, wool, burlap, denim, and muslin.

---

clothes *noun* You'll need warm clothes for the coming winter. *Similar words:* a stylish *outfit*, a *costume* for the party, nurse's *uniform*, pile of dirty *laundry*.

cold *adjective* It's too cold outside to go swimming. *Similar words: cool* lemonade, *chilly* winter day, *icy* slopes, *frozen* lake, *wintry* weather, *unthawed* meat from the freezer. *Opposite words:* **hot**, heated.

color *noun* Your eyes are a lovely green color. *Similar words: dye* to color the cloth, *tint* in her hair, a reddish *hue*, a dark *shade* of green.

common *adjective* It's a common mistake made by many, many people. *Similar words:* the *usual* kind of shoes, just an *ordinary* dog, a *familiar* friend, a *standard* kind of car, a *regular* guest on the show, a *typical* apartment home. *Opposite words:* **special**, **rare**, **odd**, unusual.

complain *verb* The swan didn't complain that his neck was too long. *Similar words: protest* the assignment, always *grumble* and *whine* when I'm late, *mutter* unhappily about noise.

complete *adjective* They will read the complete works of Dr. Seuss—every book. *Similar words:* an *entire* meal, a *total* repair, the *whole* book.

compliment *verb* Let's compliment her on a job well done. *Similar words: congratulate* the winner, *applaud* the performance, *praise* the quick work. *Opposite words:* **complain**, criticize.

confused *adjective* He looked confused by the flashing lights. *Similar words*: *dazed* by the flash of light, *dizzy* from spinning, *bewildered* by the riddle, *baffled* by the magician's tricks, *flustered* by everyone yelling at once.

cook *verb* Let's cook a delicious feast. *Similar words*: *bake* bread, *barbecue* the hamburgers, *boil* the eggs, *prepare* a meal, *broil* the fish, *fry* some chicken, *steam* the vegetables, *stew* the meat in its juices, *heat* the soup, *roast* the potatoes in with the beef.

copy *verb* She will copy her report onto a clean sheet of paper. *Similar words*: *duplicate* her dress design, *imitate* the sound of his voice.

craft *noun* Sewing is a difficult craft, but fun to learn. *Similar words*: a useful *skill*, learn my aunt's *trade*, a *handicraft* like quiltmaking.

> Some of the people whose jobs are crafts are baker, barber, butcher, carpenter, cook, dressmaker, miller, potter, printer, shoemaker, smith, tailor, and weaver.

cry *verb* She started to cry when she fell off the wall. *Similar words*: *groan* because of sore muscles, *moan* with exhaustion, *sob* himself to sleep, *weep* for the loss, *whimper* and complain, *whine* like a tired child, *bawl* like a baby, *sniffle* into a handkerchief, *wail* loudly at the sad movie, wolves *howl* in the distance, *yell* angrily.

curious *adjective* We were all curious to see what was inside the box. *Similar words*: *inquisitive* cat in the cupboard, a *nosy* reporter, a *snooping* spy, a *probing* scientist.

cut *verb* The barber cut off all the baby's beautiful curls. *Similar words*: *carve* the turkey, *chip* the ice, *chop* the wood, *clip* the dog's nails, *crop* the bushes, *notch* the stick, *shred* the paper into strips, *slit* open the envelope, *snip* her bangs, *split* a log, *saw* a board, *slice* a lemon, *trim* the rosebush, *whittle* the soap, *shave* the beard, *shear* the sheep. *Opposite words*: **join**, fasten, connect.

D d

dangerous *adjective* Riding double on a bicycle is dangerous! *Similar words*: a *perilous* adventure, an *unsafe* toy, a *risky* dive into the shallow pool. *Opposite words*: safe, secure.

dark *adjective* Dark storm clouds gathered overhead. *Similar words*: it's hard, reading by *dim* light, a *dull* dress, *gloomy* gray day, *shadowy* hallway, *shady* side of the street. *Opposite words*: **light**, **bright**, lighted.

dead *adjective* Throw out that vase of dead flowers. *Similar words*: *extinct* volcano, *lifeless* performance. *Opposite words*: alive, existing.

different *adjective* You look quite different from your sister. *Similar words*: an **odd** group of characters, *various* things to see, *assorted* cheeses.

dig *verb* The tortoise will dig a hole to escape the heat. *Similar words*: *burrow* into the ground, *scoop* out the insides of the pumpkin, *plow* the field, *bore* through the rock, *unearth* an arrowhead, *excavate* an old city.

dinner *noun* She had a healthy dinner of grains and vegetables. *Similar words*: a late *supper* after the movie, a filling *meal* of pasta, a tremendous *feast* of Mexican food, a *banquet* for the wedding, a *buffet* where you can help yourself.

dirty *adjective* I can't see a thing through these dirty windows. *Similar words*: an *untidy* desk, *dusty* old furniture, *filthy* kitchen, *grubby* clothes, *messy* room, *hazy* city sky, *soiled* laundry, *sandy* floor of the beach house, *muddy* river bank, *murky* water, *grimy* stove, *sticky* fingers. *Opposite words*: neat, tidy, spotless, sparkling.

do *verb* Do your homework before dinner. *Similar words*: *accomplish* a great work, *achieve* your goals, *arrange* for things to happen, *conduct* business wisely, *perform* in a play, *carry out* a plan, *finish* a task. *Opposite words*: neglect, **ignore**.

drink *verb* Be sure to drink plenty of water when the weather is hot. *Similar words*: *sip* a glass of ice water slowly, *gulp* water from the canteen, *chug* a carton of milk.

duty *noun* It is a privilege and a duty to vote. *Similar words*: *responsibility* to obey the law, carry out your given *task*, have an *obligation* to complete.

E e

eager *adjective* The eager reader started the next book at once. *Similar words*: *enthusiastic* answer, *spirited* cheer. *Opposite words*: reluctant, unwilling.

early *adjective* The early show starts at six. *Similar words*: *primitive* spear, *premature* harvest.

eat *verb* I like to eat lunch with my friends. *Similar words*: **bite** into the sandwich, *devour* a whole plateful, *dine* at a fine restaurant, *feast* on a delicious meal, *nibble* a snack, *munch* on popcorn, *chew* carefully, quickly *gobble* the seeds, *graze* on the grassy hill.

edge *noun* The type ran off the edge of the paper. *Similar words*: *rim* of the bowl, *boundary* between the states, on the *verge* of a discovery, *threshold* of a new age, *brink* of a cliff, suburbs on the *outskirts* of the city.

empty *adjective* Put them in the empty vase. *Similar words*: *deserted* ghost town, *unoccupied* room.

episode *noun* The reporter witnessed the episode. *Similar words*: *incident* on the bus, special *occasion*, strange *occurrence*, a formal *affair*.

event *noun* The holiday parade was a big event in our tiny town. *Similar words*: birthday *celebration*, a serious *ceremony*, an important *occasion*, the rehearsal of the *program*, a *milestone* in our history, a live *performance* of the opera, an elaborate *spectacle*, a special *happening*.

excited *adjective* The children were excited to see their grandparents again. *Similar words*: **eager** for summer vacation, *enthusiastic* applause from the audience, *frantic* search for her lost pet, *frenzied* crowd at the football game, *thrilled* winner of the contest, *stimulated* by the excitement, *roused* to action. *Opposite words*: **calm**, **quiet**, bored.

explore *verb* Let's explore our new town. *Similar words*: *examine* a leaf, *search* the woods for wildflowers.

F f

fact *noun* He learned a new fact about nature. *Similar words: information* about elephants, *data* on the number of people who have taken up running.

fair *adjective* Taking turns is fair. *Similar words: honest* and true friend, *proper* order of things, umpire's *just* decision, an *accurate* summary. *Opposite words:* cheating, unjust, wrong, questionable.

fall *verb* Leaves fall from the trees. *Similar words: trip* on a crack in the sidewalk, *tumble* down the hill, *stumble* over the mess on the floor, the tall tower of blocks will soon *topple, drop* from the sky, sand castles *collapse* easily.

false *adjective* It is false that the moon is made of green cheese. *Similar words:* a *fake* cure, a *wrong* idea, a *phony* story. *Opposite words:* true, sincere, real.

famous *adjective* Everyone has heard of this famous poet. *Similar words:* the *well-known* politician, the *legendary* emperor.

far *adjective* School is *far* from my house. *Similar words:* the *distant* mountains, a *remote* village. *Opposite words:* **near**, close.

fast *adjective* Horses are fast runners. *Similar words: quick* as a bunny, *speedy* as a roadrunner, *swift* water in the river, *rapid* trains, the *rushing* stream, eat a *hasty* meal, *instant* oatmeal, *prompt* answer to her question, a *sudden* ending, the *hurried* people pushing and running. *Opposite words:* **slow**, delayed.

feel *verb* Feel how cold the snow is. *Similar words:* **touch** the dog, *stroke* its fur, *pat* its head, *handle* the tool, *fumble* with the keys, *finger* the cloth, *press* the button.

feeling *noun* I have a good feeling when I get a hug. *Similar words:* good and bad *mood*, rising **spirits**, a lion with a short *temper*, sunny *disposition*, artist known for *sensitivity, emotion* shows on their faces, the *sentiment* of the crowd.

fight *verb* Boxers fight in a ring. *Similar words: attack* the rival debating team, teams *battle* for first place, *struggle* to escape, the two sides always *argue*, donkeys *resist* being pulled, *quarrel* about who goes first, *wrestle* with a problem, push and *scuffle* with each other, *dispute* with him over the problem. *Opposite word:* **surrender**.

find *verb* Did you find the book you lost? *Similar words: discover* hidden treasure, *learn* the answer to a puzzle, *uncover* the reason, *come upon* a friend by chance. *Opposite words:* **lose**, misplace.

fix *verb* Can you fix the broken clock? *Similar words: mend* the hole in the screen door, *patch* the rip in my pants, *prepare* lunch, *repair* a broken toy, *replace* a light bulb, *sharpen* a pencil, *correct* a mistake, *rebuild* the tower of blocks, *overhaul* the car. *Opposite words:* **break**, shatter, demolish.

fly *verb* Airplanes fly above the clouds when they go across country. *Similar words:* gulls *soar* over the waves, little birds *flutter* about, hawks *swoop* down, *glide* in for a landing, startled pigeons *take wing*.

food *noun* Any food tastes good if you are hungry enough. *Similar words: refreshments* at a party, *provisions* on a camping trip, hearty *fare*, *edibles* in the garden.

forever *adverb* The movie seemed to go on forever. *Similar words*: I will be *eternally* grateful for your help, ocean tides move *endlessly*, *permanently* preserved, *constantly* on the move, *always* love someone.

free *adjective* Birds are free to fly anywhere. *Similar words*: the colonies declared they were *independent*, *at liberty* to do what you want.

friendly *adjective* A friendly neighbor looked after their house. *Similar words*: *amiable* shopkeeper, *kindly* librarian. *Opposite words*: hostile, gruff.

funny *adjective* The funny clown made us laugh. *Similar words*: *comical* movie, *amusing* joke, *droll* comedian, *silly* tongue twisters, *humorous* cartoon, *ridiculous* rubber nose. *Opposite words*: **sad**, serious, humorless.

G g

game *noun* Our team won the game today. *Similar words*: a *sport* anyone can play, an *activity* we all enjoy, just an *amusement* to you, the champions of the *tournament*, the *competition* began.

gather *verb* Gather all the eggs in the hen house. *Similar words*: *collect* the dirty dishes, *accumulate* used bottles and cans, *pile* the leaves in a basket, *heap* your clothes on the bed. *Opposite words*: scatter, spread out.

get *verb* I will get my coat. *Similar words*: *receive* the letter, *acquire* a tan at the beach, *win* a prize, **catch** a cold, *earn* a salary.

give *verb* Give an apple to your friend. *Similar words*: *grant* a favor, *offer* a new idea, *bestow* a gift, *donate* some old clothes, *furnish* the food for a party, *sacrifice* spare time to help a friend. *Opposite words*: seize, take, **hold**.

go *verb* We go to school every day. *Similar words*: *move* from place to place, *travel* by car, *advance* toward a goal, *leave* for vacation, *scat*, you cat, **leave** home at an early hour. *Opposite words*: **stop**, halt, come.

good *adjective* Good people often help others. *Similar words*: *excellent* report to read, water that is *pure* and safe to drink, *terrific* movie, *valuable* watch, *satisfactory* work, *dandy* outfit, *kind* deed, *respectable* job, *favorable* weather forecast, *wholesome* food, *reputable* used-car dealer.

grab *verb* She will grab the ball and run. *Similar words*: *seize* the box with both hands, *grasp* at straws.

grand *adjective* The queen looked grand in her crown. *Similar words*: *royal* robe, *noble* lion, *lordly* bearing, *splendid* palace, *majestic* mountain, *aristocratic* manners.

great *adjective* It is a great day for a party. *Similar words*: *glorious* morning, *fantastic* food at the party, *terrific* dancer, *superb* dinner, *important* achievement, *impressive* amount of money, *outstanding* grades, *spectacular* view. *Opposite words*: terrible, horrible, **awful**, **ordinary**.

group (of animals) *noun* Groups of animals are called different things. *Similar words*: a *herd* of cows or deer, a *flock* of chickens or sheep, a *pack* of wolves, a *swarm* of bees or wasps, a *school* of fish, a *pod* of whales or dolphins, a *pride* of lions.

377

Thesaurus

group (of things) *noun* What do you call a group of things? *Similar words*: a *set* of books, a *case* of cans, a first aid *kit*, a *collection* of bugs, *boxes* of belongings, a *cluster* of stars, a *fleet* of ships, a *batch* of muffins, a *network* of friends, a *bunch* of grapes, a *clutch* of eggs, a *bouquet* of flowers.

grow *verb* Many plants grow toward the light. *Similar words*: *thrive* on good care, *flourish* in rich soil.

grown-up *adjective* A grown-up colt is a horse. *Similar words*: an *adult* decision, *mature* fruit is ripe.

guide *verb* The leaders guide us through the forest. *Similar words*: *steer* around the rocks, *navigate* down the river, *pilot* the airplane, *show* the visitor around town, *escort* the famous person, *proceed* down the aisle, *maneuver* into the harbor, *lead* the team to victory.

H h

happen *verb* When did it happen? *Similar words*: *occur* later, *take place* at the beach.

happy *adjective* Everyone was happy to have a day off from school. *Similar words*: *glad* to hear that, *jolly* clown, *merry* party-goers, *joyful* song, *joyous* event, *overjoyed* expression on her face, singing and *rejoicing* voices, *cheerful* mood, *joking* storyteller, *contented* to read a good book, *gleeful* that the prank worked, *perky* after lunch, *frolicking* in the water. *Opposite words*: **sad**, gloomy.

hard (1) *adjective* The stale bread is hard. *Similar words*: *bony* fish, *crisp* crackers, *solid* ice, *sturdy* cardboard, *rugged* rocks, *rigid* pipe, *firm* vegetables, *stony* ground. *Opposite words*: **soft**, slack.

hard (2) *adjective* The test was very hard. *Similar words*: *difficult* words on the spelling test, *puzzling* clues, *confusing* messages. *Opposite words*: easy, **simple**, a cinch.

hate *verb* We hate to get up in the morning, and we hate to go to bed at night. *Similar words*: *dislike* spinach, *despise* boring films, *detest* the color pink. *Opposite words*: **like**, admire, honor, cherish, treasure, prize.

help *verb* I will help you carry that big box. *Similar words*: *assist* in reaching a goal, *aid* people in trouble, *enable* them to go to college.

heroic *adjective* She was a heroic astronaut. *Similar words*: *bold* sailor, *daring* acrobat, *adventurous* mountain climber, *gallant* knight, *fearless* explorer. *Opposite words*: afraid, timid, cowardly, fearful.

hill *noun* That green hill is not very high. *Similar words*: low *foothills*, *mountains* covered with pine trees, snowy *mount* too tall for trees, birds flying around the *peak*, sand *dunes* in windy places, erupting *volcano*, *butte* that looked like a rock table, steep *heights*, crumbling *cliff*, old burial *mound*. *Opposite words*: **valley**, **pit**, gully, crater, canyon, dale, glen.

hit *verb* You can hit the ball with that bat. *Similar words*: *paddle* the ping–pong ball, *pound* the clay out flat, *punch* the pillow, *whack* the ball, *stamp* on the floor, *drive* the nail into the board, *slap* the oar on the water, *strike* the gong.

hold *verb* Hold your arms up over your head. *Similar words*: *grip* the bar before you climb higher, **grab** the cat, *clasp* the child in your arms, *clench* the bone in its teeth, vines *cling* to the tree.

holiday *noun* On this holiday we eat turkey. *Similar words*: *vacation* at the beach, birthday *celebration*, *carnival* time in New Orleans, fun at the *festival*.

hot *adjective* I felt too hot by the bonfire. *Similar words*: the *warm* jacket, fireplace gave off *heated* air, *steaming* soup, *molten* lava, *sizzling* bacon. *Opposite words*: cold, frozen.

house *noun* People live in this house. *Similar words*: log *cabin* in the mountains, wooden *cottage* by the beach, *farmhouse* with a front porch, the *hut* made of palm leaves, round *hogan* with one door.

hungry *adjective* I am hungry for a big dinner. *Similar words*: *starving* for something to eat, am *empty* and could eat anything. *Opposite words*: fed, full.

hunt *verb* Go hunt for your missing sock. *Similar words*: *seek* a lost treasure, *look* for the right house, *search* for the missing map, *pursue* the prize, the cats that *chase* the mouse.

hurt (1) *verb* I hurt myself when I fell down. *Similar words*: *injure* his arm in the football game, harsh words *wound* my feelings, *cut* his finger on something sharp, stones *bruise* my foot, my feet *ache*, *scratch* myself on a thorn. *Opposite words*: heal, cure, soothe, **help**, comfort.

hurt (2) *verb* Cold weather will hurt the crops. *Similar words*: rain will *spoil* the picnic, ice can *harm* the trees, waves *destroy* the sand castle, winds *damage* the roof, those losses *ruin* the team's chances of victory. *Opposite words*: **fix**, repair.

I i

idea *noun* Whose idea was it to go for a ride? *Similar words*: a *theory* in science, *theme* of a story, a *scheme* to get rich quick, a false *notion*, a wild *speculation*.

ignore *verb* Ignore what those rude people are saying. *Similar words*: don't *neglect* your pet, *omit* the last three pages.

imagine *verb* Imagine what people did before television. *Similar words*: *pretend* to be a fish, *dream up* a new idea.

important *adjective* The most important thing is to use your time well. *Similar words*: **serious** mistake, *weighty* decision, a *major* new invention. *Opposite words*: unimportant, minor.

informed *adjective* An informed voter makes the best choices. *Similar words*: *educated* citizen, *knowledgeable* bookseller, *learned* professor.

interested *adjective* I am interested in collecting stamps. *Similar words*: *enchanted* by the view, *fascinated* by the kitten, *spellbound* by the music.

J j

job *noun* Most people make money doing a job. *Similar words*: *chore* of washing dishes, my *task* today, do office *work*, the **craft** of making rugs, a *career* may last a lifetime, using tools is a *skill*, put your heart into your **profession**.

Some types of jobs are **artist**,
astronaut, athlete, attendant, cleaner,
clerk, conductor, computer operator,
custodian, diver, driver, doctor,
editor, electrician, farmer, firefighter,
geologist, guide, housekeeper,
inspector, inventor, librarian,
manager, mechanic, merchant,
messenger, nurse, pilot, plumber,
police officer, rancher, reporter,
sailor, sales clerk, scientist, secretary,
shopkeeper, teacher, trader, trainer,
veterinarian, and zookeeper.

join *verb* The two friends *join* hands. *Similar words*: *attach* the papers with a paper clip, *braid* your hair, buttons that *fasten* shirts, *glue* the pieces back together, *knit* the yarn, *knot* your shoelaces, *sew* up the rip, *tape* the picture to the wall, *tie* with ribbon, *combine* the two liquids. *Opposite words*: untie, **cut**, separate.

jump *verb* The dog will jump the fence and run away. *Similar words*: *leap* to catch the ball, *hop* like a bunny, *skip* down the street, *hurdle* the gate, cats *pounce* on yarn, *dive* into the pool, *plunge* into the deep water.

K k

keep *verb* *Keep* this key in a safe place. *Similar words*: *preserve* the neighborhood's landmarks, *save* box tops to send in, *hold on to* the instructions for this game.

L l

laugh *verb* You will laugh at the clown. *Similar words*: *chuckle* about a funny story, start to *giggle*, *chortle* to yourself, *guffaw* loudly, *snicker* to yourself.

lazy *adjective* The lazy dog slept all day. *Similar words*: *shiftless* player, *drowsy* day, *slothful* study habits.

leave *verb* They will leave home when they are older. *Similar words*: *depart* on a trip, *evacuate* the airplane, *disembark* from the ocean liner.

leftovers *noun* We are eating leftovers from yesterday's turkey for dinner. *Similar words*: cold *ashes* in the fireplace, *scraps* of food, *remains* of an old car, *residue* of the party-goers, *remainder* of a bill.

level *adjective* If the table is level, the ball won't roll off. *Similar words*: *flat* surface collecting dust, *horizontal* lines of the long, low building. *Opposite words*: hilly, uneven, bumpy, vertical, **upright**.

lie *verb* Don't lie about your mistakes. *Similar words*: *bluff* your way out of trouble, *not tell the truth*, big talkers *exaggerate*, foxes *deceive* the chickens.

lift *verb* Lift the box onto the shelf, please. *Similar words*: *raise* your hat to say hello, *hoist* the heavy pipe into place.

light *adjective* Light yellow flowers look white in the sunshine. *Similar words*: **bright** stars, *candlelit* jack-o-lanterns, *gleaming* teeth, *glowing* coals in the fire, *moonlit* nights, *shiny* new pennies, *sunlit* gardens, *white* sheets hanging on the clothesline, *shining* sun on the water, a *pale* shade of green, *faded* blue jeans.

like *verb* I like to have new friends. *Similar words*: *enjoy* the movie, *fancy* some new shoes, *care about* your best friend, *be fond* *of* grandmother, *prefer* peaches to apples, *appreciate* a gift.

line *noun* The teacher drew a line across the board. *Similar words*: a skunk has a *stripe* down its back, there is a *streak* of red in the painting, the children stood in single *file*.

limp *verb* I limp because I have a sore foot. *Similar words*: *shuffle* in big shoes, *hobble* along with the help of a cane.

little *adjective* The little mouse ran under the door. *Similar words*: **small** helping of peas, *dainty* china cup, *tiny* baby. *Opposite words*: **big**, large.

load *noun* A mule can carry a heavy load. *Similar words*: bearing a *burden*, ship's *cargo*.

look *verb* I look both ways before I cross the street. *Similar words*: *watch* for the green light, *peek* around a corner, *stare* at the television, *gaze* in the toy store window, *glance* at the mirror, *peer* into the dark, *examine* the bug, *search* for the right answer.

lose *verb* You will lose your money if you don't put it away. *Similar words*: *misplace* a pencil, *be defeated* in a game, *miss* the point of a joke, *Opposite words*: win, **find**.

lot *noun* I have a lot of toys. *Similar words*: did *much* to help, a **group** of singers, a *number* of people, *plenty* of food, a *great deal* of time spent watching television.

M m

mad *adjective* I am mad at the person who took my pencil. *Similar words*: **angry** at losing the game, *cross* because your feelings got hurt, *upset* and yelling, *grumpy* and frowning, *furious* with yourself, *irritated* by the ending of the book, a *snarling* wild animal, **sulky** and full of tears, *annoyed* by a fly, *huffy* at being ignored, *fuming* over the broken glass, *sullen* and sad, *outraged* and loud, *resentful* about waiting.

make (1) *verb* The children make paper airplanes. *Similar words*: *build* a doghouse, *form* a statue out of clay, *invent* a new machine, *compose* a song.

make (2) *verb* You can't make me change my mind. *Similar words*: *cause* an accident, *force* someone to agree, *persuade* her to come with us.

make-believe *adjective* The story takes place in a make-believe country. *Similar words*: *imaginary* friend, a *magic* fairy, the *legendary* hero, a dragon is a *mythical* beast, a *fabulous* castle with golden towers.

many *adjective* There were many people at the parade. *Similar words*: *several* people on the bus, *countless* grains of sand, *numerous* choices, *considerable* effort, *much* excitement. *Opposite word*: few.

mark *noun* There is a mark on the table where the bleach was spilled. *Similar words*: The report had a *smudge* from her dirty fingers, the dog had a brown *spot* on his ear, he has a *birthmark* on his chin, the apple has a *bruise* from when it fell off the tree.

maybe *adverb* Maybe we can play after we finish the work. *Similar words*: *perhaps* it will rain today, she said she would do it, *possibly*, he thinks it will *probably* happen.

meal *noun* We ate a meal at the restaurant. *Similar words*: fancy food at the *banquet*, *feast* fit for a king and a queen, a *picnic* in the park, milk and crackers for a *snack*.

mean *adjective* A mean person took my lunch. *Similar words*: taking more than your part is *unfair*, a *low* trick, the *spiteful* cat scratched the chair, stepping on the bug was *cruel*, the *savage* lion, *menacing* cat chasing the bird, a *selfish* child took it all, the *stingy* person did not share. *Opposite words*: generous, grateful, good-natured, merciful.

medicine *noun* The doctor used a new medicine to treat the disease. *Similar words*: a *cure* for chicken pox, a *remedy* for the cold.

meeting *noun* Who was at the meeting? *Similar words*: a *conference* about pollution, an *appointment* with a doctor.

messy *adjective* The messy house took hours to clean. *Similar words*: the attic was *dusty*; test the *polluted* air; paper blowing in the *littered* street, an *untidy* room; *grubby* hands that need to be washed, it is a *sloppy* sandwich, *jumbled* clothes and shoes. *Opposite words*: neat, **tidy**.

mistake *noun* By mistake, they used salt instead of baking soda. *Similar words*: *slip* of the tongue, catcher made a *goof*, a math *error*, a terrible *blunder*.

money *noun* Put the money in the bank. *Similar words*: two dollars in *cash*, a handful of *coins*, great *wealth*, a fabulous *fortune*, the *riches* of Midas, *treasure* of gold and jewels, an *income* from stocks, enjoying *prosperity*.

more *adjective* You can have more dinner. *Similar words*: *additional* work, *extra* effort, *greater* skill.

move *verb* I will move the chair into the other room. *Similar words*: **push** the swing, **pull** the wagon, *pass* the jelly, rivers *flow* to the ocean, children *rush* to school, *scatter* seeds in the garden, birds *migrate* south, the plane will *depart* soon, the mule would not *budge*, *shift* the books from the table to the shelf, brooms *whisk* away dust, the wagon will **hit** the curb, lines *progress* into the movie, cattle *mill* about in the stockyard.

N n

natural *adjective* It is natural to drink water when you are thirsty. *Similar words*: *normal* for water to run downhill, an *instinctive* talent for music.

near *adjective* The store is near my school. *Similar words*: the *nearby* library, the *neighboring* town, a *close* relative. *Opposite words*: **far**, distant.

new *adjective* I have shiny new shoes. *Similar words*: rockets are *modern* inventions, a *young* cow is called a calf, replaced with an *unused* part. *Opposite words*: **old**, ancient, antique, used, second-hand.

news *noun* Did you hear the latest news on the radio? *Similar words*: the club's *bulletin*, *tidings* of a long-lost friend, a magazine *article*, get *information* about the event, a *report* from the White House.

next *adjective* You are the next one in line to get a ticket. *Similar word*: each *succeeding* person gets a turn. *Opposite words*: previous, former.

nice *adjective* It is nice to have a good friend. *Similar words*: *agreeable* about taking turns, *pleasant* to have warm milk, *cozy* kitchen, *charming* kitten, *delightful* day at the beach, *amiable* friends agree on everything, her *gracious* greeting made me feel welcome, *pleasing* manners, *likable* person. *Opposite words*: naughty, **awful**, dreadful, ghastly, horrid, hateful, fierce.

noise *noun* The plane's engine made a loud noise. *Similar words*: a terrible *racket*, an *uproar* over the unfair decision, the *blare* of the radio, *bustle* of the city, *jangle* of metal, *din* of the lunchroom, *commotion* in the halls.

noisy *adjective* The noisy children didn't hear the teacher. *Similar words*: *loud* music that hurts my ears, *deafening* jet plane, *shrill* sirens, *roaring* engine, *booming* drums, *crashing* cymbals, *blaring* television, *earsplitting* howl, *thunderous* clapping, *resounding* echoes. *Opposite words*: **quiet**, **calm**, **peaceful**.

now *adverb* I have to go to the store now. *Similar words*: come here *immediately*, do it *this instant*, we must cross the street *this moment*, *presto*! and a rabbit appears. *Opposite words*: later, earlier, in the future, in the past.

O o

odd *adjective* The kitten looked odd among the puppies. *Similar words*: a **different** kind of string bean, a strange pen, an *unusual* purple bird, *unlikely* to win a

million dollars, *eerie* houses, *weird* sounds from the dark house, *unexpected* knock, *peculiar* smell in the closet, *unfamiliar* place. *Opposite words*: usual, **ordinary**, everyday, **common**.

often *adverb* We often play together. *Similar words*: babies cry *frequently*, I *usually* eat at noon.

old *adjective* The old house had no paint on the walls. *Similar words*: the *aged* book was torn and faded, *ancient* times, a *traditional* method, *quaint* gingerbread house, *antique* furniture. *Opposite words*: modern, **new**.

ooze *verb* The slime will ooze out of the box. *Similar words*: smells *emanate*, oils *seep* through.

open *verb* Please open the door and let me in. *Similar words*: *unlock* the box, *unfold* the letter, *unwrap* the gift.

order *verb* Order them to stop! *Similar words*: *command* the dog to speak, *bid* the class to stand up, *tell* the students to study. *Opposite words*: **ask**, obey.

ordinary *adjective* It was an ordinary school day. *Similar words*: *standard* way of doing things, *routine* check for homework, *customary* greeting, *regular* route to school, an uninteresting, rather *pedestrian* painting. *Opposite words*: **odd**, strange, unusual.

outdoors *noun* The outdoors is beautiful. *Similar words*: bears in the *wilderness*, watching the *scenery* from the train, walking in the *countryside*, animals in *nature*. *Opposite words*: indoors, interior.

P p

part *noun* Please, could I have part of your sandwich? *Similar words*: a **piece** of the puzzle, a backpack with an inner *compartment*, main *ingredient* in homemade soup, a *fraction* of the total output, a *portion* of the display, one *element* in the compound.

peaceful *adjective* The quiet garden was peaceful. *Similar words*: the *smooth*, *calm* bay, *safe* in mother's arms, a *friendly* agreement, a *secure* way of life. *Opposite words*: **noisy**, **dangerous**.

person *noun* The person walked down the street. *Similar words*: a *human being* talks and thinks, the *character* in the movie, each *individual*, a Greek myth about a god and a *mortal*.

picture *noun* The picture was hanging on the wall. *Similar words*: crayon *drawing* of a house and flowers, *doodle* of lines and circles, a *photograph* of my grandma, the T-shirt *design*, *portrait* that looked just like her, a *diagram* of how things fit together, an *illustration* in the book, a framed *etching*, a *painting* of some beautiful flowers.

piece *noun* I would like a piece of paper. *Similar words*: a *shred* of cloth, a *slice* of bread, a *patch* to cover the small hole, a *strip* of tape, a *scrap* of metal, a *lump* of butter, a *fragment* of a poem, a *morsel* of food, a *hunk* of meat, a *quantity* of water. *Opposite words*: whole, unity, total.

pit *noun* They dug a pit to bury the treasure. *Similar words*: bats from the *cave*, an underground *cavern*, the *crevice* in the snow field, a giant meteor *crater*, a *well* for water, a trench for protection.

place *noun* I know a place to go. *Similar words*: a *point* in space, a local *area*, the player's *position*, the *scene* of the big event, the historic *landmark*, the house's *location*, a gold-mining *region*.

plan *noun* What is the plan for today? *Similar words*: *arrangements* for a vacation, *design* of a toy, *strategy* for winning a game. *Opposite words*: impulse, improvisation.

plane *noun* The plane is taking off from the runway. *Similar words*: a *jet* flies high, the blast of the *rocket*, the old-timers' *flying machine*.

plant *noun* I watered the tomato plant. *Similar words*: trim the *shrub*, acorns grow on an oak *tree*, a rose *bush*, a green *shoot*, tulips are one kind of *flower*, ivy is a *vine*, *weeds* grow everywhere.

> Some plant parts are bloom, branch, bud, bulb, flower, fruit, leaf, petal, root, seed, stalk, stem, and twig.

> Some places where plants grow are forest, garden, **swamp**, jungle, lawn, meadow, prairie, yard, grove, nursery, orchard, and underbrush.

plod *verb* We plod down the long, long road. *Similar words*: *slouch* down the alley, bears that *lumber* through the forest, ducklings that *straggle* after their mother, *shuffle* along the big shoes, *trudge* through the deep snowdrifts.

police officer *noun* The police officer directs the traffic. *Similar words*: the *detective* searches for clues, the *guard* watches the gate, the *state trooper* stopped the speeding car.

praise *verb* The teacher will praise my good work. *Similar words*: kind words *flatter* me, *congratulate* me on those high grades, we *cheer* the team.

pretty *adjective* It is a pretty flower. *Similar words*: *cute* puppy, *beautiful* rose, the *elegant* swans, *glamorous* movie stars. *Opposite words*: plain, **ugly**.

profession *noun* She wants to enter the medical profession. *Similar words*: He has a *job* as an editor, her *work* takes her all over the country, he has been in this *business* for many years, nursing is a wonderful *career*.

> Some professions are architect, dentist, doctor, engineer, librarian, nurse, professor, and teacher.

promise *verb* I promise to do a good job. *Similar words*: *swear* to tell the truth, *vow* to do all my work, *assure* the scared child that everything will be fine, *pledge* to repay the money.

proud *adjective* She is the proud owner of a new bicycle. *Similar words*: the *dignified* judge, *majestic* kings sat on their thrones. *Opposite words*: humble, apologetic, modest.

public *adjective* There are public meetings at city hall. *Similar words*: a stage *exposed* to the weather, *open* hearings, *well–known* person, *advertised* in the paper. *Opposite words*: **secret**, hidden, under cover, mysterious, private, enclosed.

pull *verb* The horses pull the wagon. *Similar words*: *drag* out that old rug, *jerk* on the handle, *pluck* the flower, *yank* his hair, the car will *tow* the trailer. *Opposite words*: **push**, shove.

push *verb* You push a baby buggy. *Similar words*: *bump* your head against the wall, *pump* air into the tire, *press* hard with your hand, *pack* the sand tightly in the pail, *thrust* the sword through the curtain, *nudge* it with your toe, *wedge* the doorstop under the door, can't *shove* people in the line, motors *propel* the boats, *poke* with your finger, *jar* the books off the shelf. *Opposite word*: **pull**.

Q q

quiet *adjective* With all the children gone, the house was quiet. *Similar words*: as *silent* as a mouse, speaking in *hushed* tones, *muffled* voices through the closed door, *placid* cow, *subdued* child on a chair, *mute* radio, *speechless* with surprise, *noiseless* empty room. *Opposite words*: **noisy**, loud.

quit *verb* Did he quit his job? *Similar words*: *resign* from office, **stop** moving around, *end* the game, *cease* making noise. *Opposite words*: start, begin, continue.

R r

rain *noun* The rain fell from dark clouds. *Similar words*: a fine *mist*, a brief *shower*, *cloudburst* after the thunder, there was a light *drizzle*. *Opposite words*: drought, dry spell.

rare *adjective* This blue parrot is a rare bird. *Similar words*: *unusual* events, the *unexpected* surprise, *uncommon* amount of rain, a **special** treat. *Opposite words*: usual, **common**, **ordinary**.

red *adjective* The red fire engine raced through the town. *Similar word*: cheeks that were *rosy* from the cold.

Some shades of red are pink, scarlet, magenta, ruby, cherry, cardinal, carmine, crimson, and beet-red.

---

refuse *verb* I refuse to go out in the rain. *Similar words*: *turn down* a second helping, *decline* a cup of soup. *Opposite words*: **agree**, accept.

road *noun* The road goes right by my house. *Similar words*: a winding country *lane*, the *alley* between the tall buildings, *zoom* along the *highway*, the main *route* across the country, the *trail* in the woods, the *course* for the race, the *path* by the side of the river, busy *avenue* full of cars, a busy *street*.

rock *noun* A rock lay in the path. *Similar words*: the heavy *stone*, a lot of little *pebbles*, on top of the big *boulder*, *gravel* crunching under our feet, a rock made of a shiny *mineral*, flat sides of a *crystal*, we found a *meteorite* that fell from space.

round *adjective* Columbus said the earth was round. *Similar words*: the toy train ran on a *circular* track, the marble is *spherical*, the road isn't straight but *curved*, the football is *oval*, some squash are *egg-shaped*.

rule *verb* Wise leaders rule the country. *Similar words*: *govern* the city, *direct* the band, *control* the team of horses, *lead* an army, *head* the team, *command* the troops. *Opposite words*: obey, follow.

run *verb* I like to run on the beach. *Similar words*: *jog* around the block, *dash* for the bus, hummingbirds *dart* to the feeder, the horse will *gallop* across the field, then slow to a *canter*, cars *race* around the track, rockets *zoom* into space, scared animals *bolt* from the forest fire, the mice *scurry* to their holes, cattle *stampede* across the range, ponies *trot* in front of the cart, rivers *rampage* during floods, bears *lope* into the forest, *flee* from danger, bunnies *scamper* in the garden, crabs *scuttle* across the beach, runners *sprint* down the hill.

S s

sad *adjective* The boy was sad when a good friend moved away. *Similar words*: *gloomy* players lost a game, *unhappy* with a report card, *miserable* moving to a new school, *discouraged* while learning to ride a bicycle, *disappointed* when I couldn't go to the zoo, *mournful* music, *sorrowful* dog, *lonely* without my best friend, *wistful* look at the toy, *regretful* of the wasted day, *inconsolable* over the loss.

said *verb* I said, "No!" see **say**.

save *verb* I like to save stamps. *Similar words*: *protect* the wild animals, *rescue* the whales, *defend* your country from attack, **keep** these instructions in a safe place.

say *verb* Did you say you like school? *Similar words*: *cry* in a loud voice, **ask** a question, **complain** about the test grade, **whisper** softly, *announce* to the audience, *declare* a state of emergency, *demand* quiet in the theater, *discuss* the weather, **tell** a story to the class, *pronounce* each sound carefully, *boast* of high grades.

saying *noun* "The early bird gets the worm," as the old saying goes. *Similar words*: an advertising *slogan*, a college's *motto*, the *moral* of the story.

scared *adjective* Scared by the monsters, I left the movie. *Similar words*: *afraid* of the dark, *fearful* of the large dog, *frightened* by a grizzly bear, *nervous* about a spelling test, *startled* by a sudden loud noise, *timid* speaking in front of the class, *horrified* faces in the audience, *cowardly* about trying new things, *awed* by the thunder and lightning, *dreading* to see my report card, **worried** about sickness, *uneasy* thinking about earthquakes, *tense* as I heard a noise, *terrified* by the roller coaster ride, a *panicked* crowd, a *petrified* mouse in the corner. *Opposite words:* **brave**, courageous.

search *verb* I search for the lost book. *Similar words:* *look for* clues to solve the mystery, *examine* the room for a secret entrance, *ransack* the room to find the lost letter. *Opposite words:* **find**, discover.

secret *adjective* The secret trap door is hidden under the rug. *Similar words:* *buried* treasure, *hidden* presents for a surprise party, *private* papers in the safe, *mysterious* symbol on the map, *puzzling* code, *undiscovered* gold in the hills, *concealed* entrance, *masked* actor, *veiled* stranger, *disguised* face, *undercover* detective, *stealthy* actions of a cat, *confidential* information. *Opposite words:* **public**, frank, above-board, exposed, advertised.

see *verb* I can see the ocean from my room. *Similar words:* *notice* the sentences on the chalkboard, *sight* an airplane, hunters *spot* deer, *observe* animals at the zoo, *view* a movie, *recognize* animal tracks, **understand** what they are trying to say, *comprehend* the plan.

sell *verb* Stores sell things. *Similar words:* *peddle* vegetables door-to-door, *vend* your wares, *merchandise* a new product.

send *verb* We send letters to our friends. *Similar words:* *shoo* the chickens off the porch, *give off* a pleasant scent, *broadcast* a radio program, **throw** the ball to third base, *dismiss* someone from the room, *deliver* an important message, *mail* a package.

sense *verb* I sense a growing interest in health. *Similar words:* *detect* a breeze, **feel** a person's mood, *be aware of* danger, *be sensitive to* their feelings.

serious *adjective* He read a serious book about President Abraham Lincoln. *Similar words:* a *grave* mistake, a *solemn* promise, an *earnest* plea for help, a *sober* decision.

shake *verb* The ground shakes during an earthquake. *Similar words:* *shiver* from the cold, *vibrate* like a violin string, **wiggle** your foot, *wobble* before they fall over, flowers *sway* in the breeze, *waver* between the two choices, *quiver* like a leaf in a breeze, *totter* across the street, *tremble* with excitement.

shout *verb* People shout at the ball game. *Similar words:* **call** for help, *cheer* the team, *exclaim* in excitement, *scream* in danger, *yell* in anger. *Opposite words:* **whisper**, mutter.

show *verb* Show me how to bake bread. *Similar words:* *point out* how it works, *indicate* the correct answer, *reveal* the secret, *display* the jewelry.

shy *adjective* Shy animals are easily frightened. *Similar words:* *timid* at my first party, *bashful* among adults, *modest* about receiving the award, *uneasy* in front of an audience. *Opposite words:* confident, boastful.

Thesaurus

sick *adjective* I was sick and stayed home. *Similar words: ill* after eating too much, *feverish* with the flu, an *aching* tooth, *itchy* mosquito bite, a *diseased* plant, *ailing* for a long time, *stricken* with a virus. *Opposite words:* healthy, **strong**, vigorous, well.

simple *adjective* She wrote a simple letter of thanks. *Similar words: plain* blue jeans, *basic* design, *elementary* words, *unadorned* clothing, *natural* beauty. *Opposite words:* fancy, fussy, elaborate.

sleep *verb* Do you sleep well at night? *Similar words: doze off* after dinner, *slumber* all night, *nap* in the afternoon, *snooze* for a short time.

slide *verb* We began to slide on the ice. *Similar words: glide* across the dance floor, *slip* on a banana peel, *slither* through the weeds, *lunge* toward an opponent, *skid* on gravel.

slow *adjective* He was slow at the start of the race and almost lost. *Similar words: gradual* rise in temperature, an *unhurried* trip, a *sluggish* snake. *Opposite words:* rapid, quick, speedy, **fast**.

small *adjective* A new baby is very small. *Similar words:* **little** rock by the big boulder, *narrow* pass between the mountains, *short* stem on the apple, *slim* chance, *thin* sheet of paper, *tiny* seed, a *dainty* glove, *miniature* model cars, *skinny* stray dog, *slender* dancers, *slight* change in the weather, *wee* drop of flavoring. *Opposite words:* **big**, huge, giant, enormous.

smaller *adjective* The smaller basket was easier to hold. *Similar words: dwindling* supply of paper, *ebbing* tide, *reduced* price, *finer* print, *waning* moon, *diminished* fame.

Opposite words: **bigger**, increasing, expanding.

smart *adjective* The smart student reads many books. *Similar words: brainy* answers on the quiz show, *clever* detective solved the mystery, *gifted* student of art and music, an *intelligent* dog following commands, *thoughtful* teacher, *wise* students who do their homework, *cunning* foxes, Einstein's *genius-level* mind, *shrewd* traders.

smell *noun* The smell of a pine forest is pleasant. *Similar words: perfume* of flowers, *scent* of the sea, *odor* of bread baking.

smile *noun* What a friendly smile! *Similar words:* a delighted *grin*, a *beam* of pleasure. *Opposite words:* frown, wince.

snow *noun* Snow fell until the ground was covered with white. *Similar words: snowflakes* floated through the air, a *blizzard* stopped all traffic, a four-foot *drift* buried cars.

soak *verb* Soak your tired feet in the warm water. *Similar words: seep* through the ground, heavy rains *drench* the garden, *douse* the campfire.

soft *adjective* The rabbit's fur was soft. *Similar words: velvety* flowers, *slack* muscles. *Opposite words:* **hard**, firm, unyielding.

some *adjective* Some people are waiting for the bus. *Similar words:* a *few* drops of rain, *several* pages of words, a *handful* of raisins, a *number* of people.

song *noun* My favorite song is about animals. *Similar words:* sing the *music*, play a *tune* on the piano, to whistle a *melody*, beat out the *rhythm*, singing a *carol*, a *chant* sung over and over, *lullaby* for a baby, repeated *refrain*.

special *adjective* As a special treat, we got to stay up late. *Similar words*: **rare** stamp collection, *choice* seats at the theater, *unusual* party for my birthday, *precious* diamond ring. *Opposite words*: **ordinary**, everyday.

spirit *noun* The school spirit was heard in the loud cheers. *Similar words*: the horse's *temper*, a cheerful *disposition*, an outgoing *personality*.

stoop *verb* Stoop down and pick it up. *Similar words*: *kneel* before the king and queen, *squat* down to peer through the keyhole, *slump* in the chair, *slouch* under the branch, *crouch* behind the sofa, **bend** to find the coin.

stop *verb* Stop at the corner. *Similar words*: *brake* the car at a stop sign, *halt* the march for a rest, *pause* for a drink of water, *hesitate* before writing the answer, **quit** making the same mistake, cars may *stall* on a steep hill, *end* the performance, *cease* making a noise, *interrupt* the program, *prevent* tooth decay. *Opposite words*: start, begin.

strict *adjective* Our town has strict laws against littering. *Similar words*: *harsh* rules, *stern* commands of the leader, a *severe* expression.

string *noun* Tie the package with a piece of string. *Similar words*: the *cord* that pulls the curtains, tie the box with *twine*, wool *yarn*, sewing *thread*, a cowboy's *rope*.

strong *adjective* Exercise builds strong muscles. *Similar words*: a *hardy* plant, *powerful* horses, an *athletic* build, a *mightly* effort, a *sturdy* building, a *muscular* athlete. *Opposite words*: feeble, fragile, vulnerable, weak.

stupid *adjective* The stupid act caused a wreck. *Similar words*: a *pointless* joke, *dull* book with no pictures, a *foolish* decision, a *silly* idea, *idiotic* phrase.

sulky *adjective* The sulky person refused to smile. *Similar words*: a *sullen* crew ready to jump ship, a *resentful* loser, a *huffy* customer.

sure *adjective* Are you sure you've done the best you know how to do? *Similar words*: *certain* to get the job, *determined* runner in the race, *resolved* to keep the promise, *firm* ground, *safe* plan.

surprised *adjective* Surprised by the start of the story, I read it all. *Similar words*: *amazed* contest winner, *astonished* audience, *shocked* expression, *startled* rabbit.

surprising *adjective* The taste of the new food was surprising. *Similar words*: the *unforeseen* result, an *unexpected* visitor, the *unpredicted* storm.

surrender *verb* The losing team will surrender to the winners. *Similar word*: *submit* a story to the editor.

swamp *noun* Cypress trees may grow in a swamp. *Similar words*: cranberry *bog*, birds in the *marsh*, a *mud flat* near the ocean.

swim *verb* It is fun to swim in the ocean. *Similar words*: *paddle* across the pool, *float* on an inner tube, *bob* up and down in the pool, *wade* in the shallow water, *tread water*.

Thesaurus

T t

talk *verb* He likes to talk with children about their hobbies. *Similar words*: my friend and I *chat* before class, *chatter* without listening, *gossip* about the neighbors, *speak* a few words, *recite* poetry out loud, *lecture* about grizzly bears, *babble* like a baby, **whisper** so no one else can hear.

tasty *adjective* That was a tasty sandwich. *Similar words*: *delicious* homemade bread, *flavorful* salad, *yummy* pizza. *Opposite words*: bitter, stale.

tease *verb* The cartoon mice tease the cat. *Similar words*: *mock* the villain in the story, the crows *taunt* the scarecrow, the clowns who *jeer* at one another, *sneer* at the new invention.

tell *verb* The teacher could tell interesting stories. *Similar words*: *report* the news, **say** what you mean, *express* your ideas, *recite* a story.

thankful *adjective* The farmer was thankful for a good harvest. *Similar word: grateful* for help with homework.

thing *noun* What is that thing that you found in the attic? *Similar words*: that strange *object*, kitchen *utensil* for cooking, *artifact* in a museum, *article* of clothing, an *item* for sale, *device* for finding metal, fine *specimen* of diamond, a cold, heavy *substance*, their very own *possessions*, his personal *belongings*.

throw *verb* The pitcher will throw the ball to the catcher. *Similar words*: *toss* me an apple, *pitch* the baseball, *chuck* a log into the fireplace, *lob* a tennis ball, *fling* a handful of pebbles.

tired *adjective* The runners are tired after a race. *Similar words*: *worn out* by the swim, *exhausted* after a hike, *weary* after work, *frazzled* from trying to do too much. *Opposite words*: brisk, frisky.

together *adverb* We saluted the flag together. *Similar words*: *united* in marriage, sing in *unison*.

tool *noun* A drill is a handy tool for making holes. *Similar words*: *equipment* used by carpenters, *machine* for making lenses, *gear* to move machinery, *instrument* to measure distance, a *device* to make work easier, science *apparatus*.

touch *verb* The runner did not touch base. *Similar words*: *brush* close to another person, *rub* a sore back, *pat* on the head, *tag* to put out of a game, *tap* on the shoulder to interrupt, *tickle* to make laugh, *handle* a snake, *stroke* a purring kitten, *nudge* with your elbow.

trick *verb* The fence will trick the dogs into staying in the yard. *Similar words*: *outwit* other players, riddles *puzzle* you.

trip *noun* We took a trip to the mountains. *Similar words*: a slow *journey* across the desert, an early morning *flight* in the plane, a *tour* of the city, a *voyage* across the ocean, a *cruise* up the river, an *expedition* to the far north.

try *verb* Try to do your best work. *Similar words*: *attempt* to read a hard book, *aim* to please, *seek* to win the game, *strain* to reach the mountain top, *strive* to get good grades.

turn *verb* Turn to look behind you. *Similar words*: *twirl* around and around, *crank* the wheel to start the motor, the earth *revolves* around the sun and *rotates* on its axis, *twist* the dial, *spin* the top, *whirl* overhead, *wring* the water out of your socks, *coil* the rope.

two *adjective* Use two hands to hold on. *Similar words*: *Both* animals are running in the field, *twin* sheep were born, this egg has a *double* yolk, a *double-decker* bus.

U u

ugly *adjective* The ugly building was unpainted and ready to fall down. *Similar words*: a *bad-looking* cut on a finger, the *hideous* beast. *Opposite words*: handsome, **pretty**.

under *adverb* The divers went under. *Similar words*: the river flows **below**, lift the lid and look *beneath*, found it *underneath*. *Opposite words*: **above**, over, overhead.

understand *verb* I can understand French but not German. *Similar words*: *comprehend* fractions, *realize* that what goes up must come down, *fathom* the reasons.

V v

vain *adjective* Vain people admire themselves all the time. *Similar word*: *conceited* people bragging about what they do.

valley *noun* The valley was between two mountains. *Similar words*: steep *canyon*, washed-out *gully*, wild *gorge*, a dry *arroyo*, trees and bushes in the tangled *ravine*.

very *adverb* A whale is very big. *Similar words*: a *truly* good player, *extremely* happy, *especially* strong, *deeply* embarrassed, *terribly* shy.

W w

wait *verb* I will wait for the next bus. *Similar words*: *stand in line*, *rest* in the chair, *be still* and listen, *perch* on the fence, *settle* in for the winter, *remain* at your desk.

walk *verb* Let's walk, not drive, to the park. *Similar words*: soldiers *march* in step, *strut* like a proud peacock, dress up and *parade* around the room, tigers *pace* back and forth, babies *crawl*, *creep* under the bushes, **limp** with a sore foot, **plod** along at the end of the day, *tiptoe* quietly, *hike* for three miles, horses *prance* about, kittens *skitter* across the floor, *tread* heavily, *stride* with long steps, *sidle* unnoticed across the dance floor.

wander *verb* Did the child wander into the street without looking? *Similar words*: *drift* without plan or purpose, *roam* across the open spaces, *stray* away from home, *dawdle* behind the other children, *stroll* around the neighborhood, *amble* down the street in no hurry.

want *verb* Do you want to check a book out of the library? *Similar words*: *desire* a long and happy life, *hope* for a new bicycle, *long* for vacation to be here, *yearn* for a bedroom of my own. *Opposite words*: do not care about, couldn't care less about, have no interest in.

water *noun* I drank a glass of water. *Similar words*: the *flood* destroying the bridge, **rain** showered the earth, **snow** on my mittens, *steam* out of the hot teakettle, *tides* coming in and going out, *waves* on the *ocean*, only a *trickle* out of the broken faucet, *stream* flowing to the *lake*.

wet *adjective* The wet dog shook himself. *Similar words*: mist making my clothes *damp*, *melting* snow and ice, *moist* from the fog, rain on *slippery* streets, the garden *muddy* from the rain. *Opposite words*: dry, waterproof.

whisper *verb* I will whisper a secret in your ear. *Similar words*: *mumble* the answer, *mutter* to myself, the brook *murmurs*. *Opposite words*: **shout**, yell, scream, roar.

white *adjective* Puffy white clouds floated in the sky. *Similar words*: *ivory* keys on the piano, *pearly* teeth.

wiggle *verb* They will wiggle their toes in the water. *Similar words*: *squirm* in your seat, *wriggle* out of wet clothes.

wind *noun* The leaves were scattered by the blowing wind. *Similar words*: a gentle *breeze* that cooled me, sudden *gust* blowing the hat off, *twister* destroying many homes, *whirlwind* uprooting the tree, *cyclone* carrying off the roof.

winning *adjective* We cheered the winning team. *Similar words*: the *successful* student, hail the *conquering* hero, the *victorious* team, the *triumphant* band marching proudly. *Opposite words*: beaten, failing, defeated, losing.

wipe *verb* Wipe up the milk spilled on the desk. *Similar words*: *shine* your shoes with a brush, *polish* silver with a soft cloth, *mop* the floor.

wonderful *adjective* There was a wonderful dinosaur exhibit at the museum. *Similar words*: *marvelous* time at the zoo, *fantastic* concert, an *excellent* book.

wood *noun* It is fun to make a box out of wood. *Similar words*: wide *beam* of the roof, sawed a *board* for the picnic table, the *bark* of an oak tree, *logs* floating down the river to the sawmill, a round *peg* in the hole, tall telephone *pole*, a fence *post*, a slender *branch*.

worried *adjective* The child was worried about losing lunch money. *Similar words*: *concerned* citizens, *alarmed* children crying, *anxious* to get test results, *dismayed* about the smashed bike, *distressed* by news reports, *fretful* babies. *Opposite words*: relieved, carefree.

wrap *verb* Wrap the birthday presents. *Similar words*: *drape* the table with a cloth, *encase* the gems in a velvet box, *enclose* the money in a card, *bundle* yourself in a warm coat, *bind* a stack of newspapers.

writing *noun* The writing was done with purple ink. *Similar words*: the *prose* of the story, *verses* of poetry, hasty *scribbles*, well-formed *script*, *scrawls* on the wall, an *inscription* carved in marble.

Type of Writing: Personal Narrative

A **personal narrative** has the following features:

- ◆ It tells about an event that involved the writer, and usually tells how the writer felt about the event.
- ◆ It can be funny or serious.
- ◆ It mentions the characters, time, and place of the event.
- ◆ The parts of the event are listed in time order.

Telling a story about the events in daily life and putting the events in time order creates a narrative. A narrative paragraph usually gives one overall impression. It can be a true story or it can be imaginary. A narrative paragraph tells the reader what happened, when it happened, and to whom it happened. The details a writer chooses will affect how the reader feels about a narrative.

Writing About Personal Narratives

1. Your days at school may be filled with ideas for stories. When you hear the phrase "good times," what events at school do you think of? Give two examples that would make interesting narrative paragraphs. When you hear the word "adventure," what events at school do you think of? Give two examples.

2. When you write a narrative paragraph, you may try to give the reader one overall feeling about the event. Feelings you might aim to express are happiness, sadness, surprise, or excitement. If you were to write a narrative paragraph about each of the following topics, what overall feeling might you aim for? Why?

   a. a two-year old at a friend's birthday party

   b. a fourth-grade boy or girl who is asked to lead the Fourth of July parade

   c. a shopper who drops and breaks a big jar of apple juice that breaks on the floor of the supermarket

3. The ability to write events in order is important in writing a narrative paragraph. Practice this skill by listing, in order, the things you did today from the time you woke up until you ate lunch. Try to list the most important events of your day.

4. When you look at yourself in a mirror, you see an image of yourself. Suppose the image were able to step out of the mirror and join you for a day. In a few sentences, tell what the day would be like for you and your image. Use your imagination to tell this story.

Reading More Personal Narratives

All children feel both joy and sadness. It does not matter where or how they live. When you read about other boys and girls, you often learn things about yourself.

Blue Willow by Doris Gates
Janey, daughter of migrant workers in California, and her family had to move often so that her father could find work. Janey very much wanted a permanent home and friends. When she met Lupe, she found a best friend.

First Snow by Helen Coutant
When a Vietnamese family settles in New England, there is much happiness and excitement for their son, Lien. He sees the beauty of snow for the first time. The changes, however, also bring him sadness.

The Comeback Dog by Jane Resh Thomas
Daniel lives on a farm. After losing his own dog, he finds an injured dog, Lady, and nurses her back to health. Lady, however, is not friendly. Daniel wonders if she will ever trust him. Finally, he lets Lady off the leash so she can be free. Do you think Lady will return?

Type of Writing: Directions

Directions should have these features:

- They begin with the starting point and include the destination.
- They are divided into simple steps.
- The steps are arranged in the order in which they will be followed.
- Whenever possible, they include landmarks to make them easy to follow. A landmark is something familiar or easy to see, such as a red house or a flagpole.

When giving directions, using sequence words such as "first," "next," "after that," and "then" helps the reader or listener follow the directions.

Writing About Directions

1. In the directions below, the underlined words are not very clear. Copy the directions, making them more exact. Create imaginary landmarks.

   Go straight until you see the sign. Turn right and walk until you see this big place. Turn left. My house is the big one.

2. When giving directions, is it better to use the terms, "Go right, then left," or "Go north, then west"? Write what you think and why.

Reading About Directions

Maps and Globes by Jack Knowlton
   The author tells about the history of mapmaking and the importance of maps in exploration. Maps and globes are compared to show the advantage of each.

Mapmaking by Karin Mango
   This book tells how to use a map and compass—important for finding the way in the woods.

Type of Writing: Tall Tale

A **tall tale** is a story that has these features:

♦ It has a larger-than-life, or superhuman, main character with a specific job.
♦ There is a humorous situation, or a problem that is solved in a funny way.
♦ Exaggerated details that describe things as greater than they are or could be.
♦ It has characters who use everyday language.

Tall tales were once told about workers from all over America. Today, writers of tall tales use modern-day heroes. Tall tales are told or written to amuse the audience. The heroes are always at their best—stronger, braver, smarter, or more honest than anyone else. Because the heroes have amazing abilities, the reader can imagine what it would be like to have these abilities, too. That is why it is fun to make up a hero and write a tall tale.

Writing About Tall Tales

1. Today many of our heroes come from sports. Make up a sports hero for a tall tale, and describe the special and amazing things he or she can do. For example, "She can swim faster than a speeding boat," or "He can hit a ball so hard that it blasts a hole through the outfield fence." Tell what sport or sports your hero plays. Then, in a few sentences, describe what he or she can do.

2. Think about all the amazing things you have read about the heroes in tall tales. If someone wrote a tall tale about you, what unbelievable things would you like to be able to do? Write one sentence to describe what you would like to do in each of the following situations.

   a. on the sports field   **c.** in the kitchen
   b. in your studies   **d.** in front of an audience

3. Animals in tall tales are able to do things that are almost as amazing as the things heroes do. Pick an animal that is not in any of the tall tales you have read. For example, you might pick a California condor. In a few sentences, describe what you would have your animal do if it were in a tall tale.

4. When people think about the American frontier, they think of bison, wide open spaces, and settlers taming the Wild West. Why do you suppose so many tall tales take place on the American frontier? Write your answer in one or two complete sentences.

Reading More Tall Tales

Books of tall tales, legends, fairy tales, and folklore are often found together in the same section in school or public libraries. Their Dewey decimal number is 398.2.

Daniel Boone's Echo by William O. Steele

Daniel Boone tries to persuade the pioneers to move with him to Kentucky. The state is beautiful, but wild and filled with dangerous animals. Of all the pioneers, only young Aaron agrees to go. This book is the story of their journey, during which Daniel takes Aaron's mind off his fears by telling him tall tales.

Joe Magarac and His U.S.A. Citizenship Papers by Irwin Shapiro

Joe works in a Pennsylvania steel mill. He is so strong that he can bend steel rails with his bare hands. The story and drawings are exciting and action filled.

Witcracks: Jokes and Jests from American Folklore by Alvin Schwartz

If you like riddles, shaggy dog stories, and knock-knock jokes, you'll like this book. Explanations of how and where they were first told are also included.

Type of Writing: Letters

A **friendly letter** has these features:

◆ It contains news, and helps you stay in touch with a friend or relative.
◆ It responds to news or questions the other person has sent you.
◆ It is written in everyday language.
◆ It has five parts: a heading, a greeting, a body, a closing, and a signature.

A friendly letter is a written conversation between the writer and the reader. In a friendly letter, the writer can share experiences, and ideas. A well-written letter is like a gift, because the writer has taken the time to include lively and interesting details.

Writing About Letters

1. Why is getting a letter from friends or relatives who are far away like having a "visit" with them? Explain your answer in a few complete sentences.
2. Suppose you are away from home. You are writing a friendly letter to your family and they already know where you are. In a few sentences, explain why you should still include the return address on both the letter and the envelope.

Reading More Letters

My Dad Lives in a Downtown Hotel by Peggy Mann
   Joey's father doesn't live with his mother and him anymore. Joey thinks it must be his fault. He writes his father a letter asking him to come home.

The Muppet Guide to Magnificent Manners: Featuring Jim Henderson's Muppets by James Howe
   Kermit the Frog tells you the correct way to write letters. There are also hints on holding interesting conversations and introducing your friends.

Type of Writing: Descriptive Writing

A descriptive paragraph has these features:

♦ It tells about a particular person, place, or thing.
♦ It uses sensory words to describe. Sensory words tell how the subject looks, sounds, feels, tastes, or smells.
♦ It paints a picture with colorful words.

A descriptive paragraph contains the writer's observations and impressions. Description is used in other types of writing, such as short stories, tall tales, and narrative writing.

Writing About Descriptive Writing

1. Descriptive writers are good observers. Look around the room you are sitting in right now. Do not get up to touch or feel anything. Make four columns on a sheet of paper: rough, smooth, sharp, soft. List each thing you see in the room under the word that best describes it.
2. Good descriptions sometimes include unexpected details. Imagine you are at the beach. Think of five details that describe how a beach tastes (not necessarily the sand, what do you eat at the beach?) or smells. Now, think of a bakery. List five details that tell how a bakery sounds and feels.

Reading More Descriptive Writing

The King's Flower by Mitsumasa Anno
   Everything the king owns has to be the biggest and the best. When he tells his gardeners that he wants the biggest and best flower in the world, he learns an important lesson.

The Philharmonic Gets Dressed by Karla Kuskin
   When you go to a concert, all the musicians—105 of them—are on the stage. This book describes what is involved in their getting ready and getting to the hall.

Type of Writing: Book Report

A book report has these features:

- ◆ It gives the title and author of the book.
- ◆ It tells where and when the story takes place.
- ◆ It describes the main characters.
- ◆ The first part tells about events in the book without giving away the ending.
- ◆ The second part explains why the book is or is not interesting or worth reading.

A book report is one way to let other readers know about books they might want to read. People read book reviews to help them decide what is interesting to read.

Writing About Book Reports

1. Some books can be read and enjoyed by anyone, no matter what the person's age. Suppose an adult you know asked you to recommend a book you have read. What book would you recommend and why?
2. What kind of endings do you like in the books you read? Do you prefer happy endings, surprise endings, sad endings, endings that solve a mystery, or some other type of ending? Explain your answer in a paragraph.

Reading for a Book Report

The Borrowers by Mary Norton
   Report on this story about a special family if you like fantasy books.

Little House on the Prairie by Laura Ingalls Wilder
   If you enjoy stories about pioneer, you might like to do a book report on this adventure book. You could also read other books in the series, including *Little House in the Big Woods* and *Farmer Boy*.

Type of Writing: Story

A **story** has these features:

- It has **characters**, people or animals who do things.
- It has a **setting**, the time and place of the events.
- It has a **plot**, the series of events that happen.
- The plot starts with the **introduction**, which describes the characters and the setting.
- The **problem** tells what difficulty a character faces.
- The **solution attempts** tell how the characters try to solve the problem.
- The **outcome** tells the result of the problem and the solution attempts.

People of all ages love stories. There are shelves in every bookstore and library with hundreds of stories to read. The writer of a story has the opportunity to let his or her imagination run free. The writer can make up wonderful tales about unusual places, interesting people, and exciting situations. Writers use all their descriptive and narrative skills to write a good story.

Writing About the Story

1. Some writers like to use a pseudonym. A *pseudonym* is a made-up name. Writers sometimes use a different pseudonym for each type of story they write. Sometimes a man will use a woman's name, or a woman will use a man's name. For each type of story below, make up a pseudonym for yourself that seems to fit the story type.
   Example: a science fiction story—Rob Robot
   a. a mystery story
   b. an adventure story
   c. an animal story
2. Think of a favorite story you have read. Why is it one of your favorites? Think about how the writer made it so good. Write a few sentences about why you liked the story.

3. In writing a story, you may want to have people, animals, or objects talking. The dialogue can add interest. However, if you keep using, "he said, . . . she said, . . . they said, . . ." you will tire the reader. List four different ways to say "he said" or "she said." You may want to refer to the thesaurus at the end of this book (p. 369).

4. If a story took place at sea, you would not be surprised if one of the characters were a sailor. For each setting below, describe a character who would fit the story.

a. an abandoned farm **c.** an office building
b. a rocket ship going to Mars **d.** a school playground

Reading More Stories

In addition to books such as those listed below, magazines like *Cricket*, *Children's Digest*, and *Penny Power* also contain stories. You can borrow these magazines from the library or have them sent to your home.

Encyclopedia Brown Takes the Cake! by Donald J. Sobol
Leroy Brown earned his nickname, "Encyclopedia Brown," by always being well informed. He applies his knowledge to solving mysteries. In this book, he solves seven puzzling mysteries.

Mortimer Says Nothing by Joan Aiken
Here are four stories about Arabel and her clever pet raven, Mortimer. You'll laugh as Mortimer gets the best of a bird researcher who bothers him, and you'll be delighted when he takes Arabel's side against her nasty cousin, Annie.

Summer Fun by Carolyn Haywood
The ten short stories in this collection are about Betsy, Eddie, Billy, and Patricia, as well as some new friends. You can follow their adventures on the beach, at the lake, at camp, and in their neighborhood.

Type of Writing: Research Report

A **research report** has these features:

◆ It gives information on a topic.
◆ It requires research because it must include information you found out for the report.
◆ The topic may be divided into several main ideas.
◆ Each main idea is supported with facts.
◆ The information in the report is true. It does not contain opinions.

A writer doing a research report is like a detective looking for information. The writer uses a variety of sources, such as magazines, encyclopedias, books, and pamphlets to answer questions about a topic. In addition, the writer may interview experts on the subject.

Writing About Research Reports

1. To get information for a research report, you consult many sources, including books, magazine articles, and entries in encyclopedias. You may have to copy a lot of information so that you can remember it. Then you must write the research report in your *own* words. In a few sentences, explain why you benefit from writing a report in your own words.

2. Where would you get information if you had a question about each subject listed below? If you cannot think of a written source, whom could you ask for information? Tell why you would choose that person.
   a. Egyptian history
   b. Siamese cats
   c. Native American cooking
   d. word history
   e. skateboards and surfboards
   f. twentieth-century inventions

3. Imagine someone is writing a research report about you. Where could they get information if they couldn't talk to you? Explain your answer in a few sentences.

4. Many researchers do surveys to get information. They may call people on the telephone or stop them on the street to get facts about their topic. Pretend you are doing a survey. You are going to interview people and ask them what they think about Saturday morning cartoons on television. Write five questions you would ask.

Reading for Research Reports

Almost anything that interests you can be the subject of a research report: the way your heart works, the life of a football player, different kinds of trucks. Books on these topics will give you the information you need.

Heartbeats: Your Body, Your Heart by Alvin Silverstein
This book explains how the heart works. It also tells what doctors do when the heart doesn't work properly. It explains the different treatments available for people who have heart diseases. The full-color diagrams of the heart identify its different parts and are easy to understand.

The Juice: Football's Superstar O.J. Simpson by Dick Belsky
O.J. Simpson's childhood in the city, his college football years, and his record-breaking professional career explain why he is considered a superstar.

Monster Trucks and Other Machines on Wheels by Jerry Bushey
Wonderful illustrations with great detail are included in this book on extra large vehicles. You'll enjoy reading about and looking at pictures of gigantic snowblowers, tree crushers, front-end loaders that have tires 12-feet tall, and trucks that can hold 34 elephants!

Steps of Writing: When Time Matters

Usually, you have lots of time for the steps of writing. Sometimes, you have to write with a time limit. You still use the steps, but you spend less time on each step.

Planning Your Time

Be sure to find out how much time you have. Spend about five minutes thinking about the writing topic and planning what to write. Next, do your writing. This will take most of your time. Save about five minutes to revise and proofread.

Understanding Directions

First, read the writing topic *very* carefully. Look for words that tell you what kind of writing to do. Notice words and phrases such as, "Describe," "Tell about," and, "Give directions for." If you may write on the paper, underline the important words.

Planning

First, brainstorm for ideas to use. Try making a story map, writing word clusters, or making lists of phrases. Organize your ideas. If you cannot make notes, think silently about the ideas you want to include in your writing.

Composing

As you write, keep your purpose and your audience in mind. Have a clear beginning so the reader knows you understand the writing topic. The middle should support your ideas. Use exact details and give good reasons. The conclusion should let the reader know that you have finished your topic. Try to write without taking a break. Look at your notes for ideas if you are stuck.

Proofreading

Read your paper. Ask yourself, "Do all my sentences make sense?" Add or remove words or phrases if something is unclear. Because of your time limit, do not try to make major changes. Check your paper and correct punctuation, capitalization, and spelling errors.

Practice

A. Write a story in 30 minutes. First read the directions below. Then follow the steps described.

Directions: Think about something embarrassing or funny or silly that happened to you or someone you know. Write a story for your classmates. Include important details.

1. Notice the important words in the directions. They are "story," "important details," "classmates," "embarrassing or funny or silly," and "you or someone you know."

2. Brainstorm the details you remember. What happened? Was it embarrassing or funny or silly? What did the person do? How does the story end? Put the details in order.

3. Write your story. Use the ideas you wrote down in the brainstorming step. Include lively, interesting details.

4. Spend the last few minutes reading your paper. Does the story make sense? If you need to, make quick changes and corrections.

B. *Directions*: Your shoes will do a lot of traveling before they get thrown away. Pretend you are your shoes. Think about what they see and do in one day. In a narrative paragraph, tell your classmates a story about what happens to your shoes during that day. Write the paragraph in 30 minutes.

C. *Directions*: Most people have a favorite room in their home. They may go there to relax, to eat, or to think. What room is your favorite? Write a description of the room for your classmates.

What does it look like? What do you do there? Explain why the room is special to you. Do your writing in 30 minutes.

Steps of Writing: When You Use a Computer

Writing on a computer is special and fun. It is different from writing with a pencil, but the steps of writing are still important.

Planning

It is a good idea to brainstorm your ideas before you begin your first draft. A computer works well for this step. The words you write show up quickly on the screen. You see your ideas immediately. You can concentrate on your ideas instead of worrying about your handwriting. As you brainstorm, you may want to organize your ideas by putting them on different parts of the screen. Then, you may want to print out what you wrote.

Composing

When you do your first draft, write sentences as your thoughts come. You may want to use your notes for ideas and details. If you make a mistake or want to change something, you can fix things easily with the computer.

Revising and Proofreading

Revise your work. You may want to have a classmate read your draft to help make sure you have said what you mean. You can do this on the screen or on printout. Make any changes that you need on the computer. Correct any spelling, punctuation, and capitalization errors. Now your finished paper is ready to print.

Letter Forms

Friendly Letters

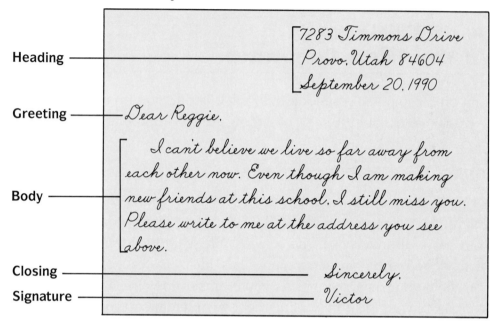

Heading

7283 Timmons Drive
Provo, Utah 84604
September 20, 1990

Greeting

Dear Reggie,

Body

I can't believe we live so far away from each other now. Even though I am making new friends at this school, I still miss you. Please write to me at the address you see above.

Closing

Sincerely,

Signature

Victor

A **friendly letter** has these features:

- The **heading** gives the writer's address and the date. There is a comma between the city and state and between the day and the year.
- The **greeting** is the word *Dear* and the name of the person receiving the letter. The greeting begins with a capital letter and ends with a comma.
- The **body** of the letter contains the writer's message. Each paragraph of the body is indented.
- The **closing** finishes the letter. The closing begins with a capital letter and ends with a comma.
- The **signature** is the writer's signed name.

Practice: Copy the friendly letter above. Circle the commas and the capital letters. Draw two lines under the greeting. Draw an arrow where the body is indented. Make a box around the closing. Underline the signature.

Envelopes

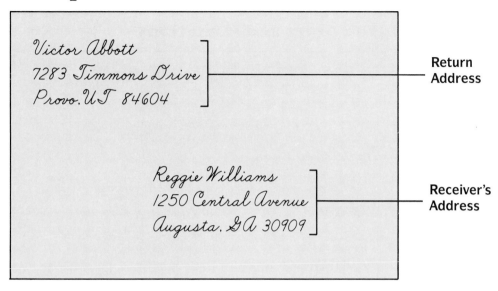

Victor Abbott
7283 Timmons Drive
Provo, UT 84604 — **Return Address**

Reggie Williams
1250 Central Avenue
Augusta, GA 30909 — **Receiver's Address**

An **addressed envelope** has these features:

* The **return address** gives the writer's name and address. The return address appears in the upper left-hand corner.
* The **receiver's address** gives the name and address of the person who is receiving the letter. The receiver's address appears in the middle of the envelope.
* Postal abbreviations of states' names can be used in each address. These abbreviations are written with two capital letters and without periods (p. 149).

Practice: Draw two envelopes on your paper. Find the mistakes in the information below. Use the corrected information to address each envelope.

1. *Receiver's address:*
   miss julie epstein
   345 cornwall Avenue
   norwalk, ct 06854

   Return address:
   mrs. Louise stephenson
   207 155th Street
   new york, NY 10034

2. *Return address:*
   jeff Carlson
   308 Orchard circle
   Manchester, NH 03102

   Receiver's address:
   Marcus washington
   12 regents road
   Chicago, il 60614

Letter Forms

Thank-You Notes and Invitations

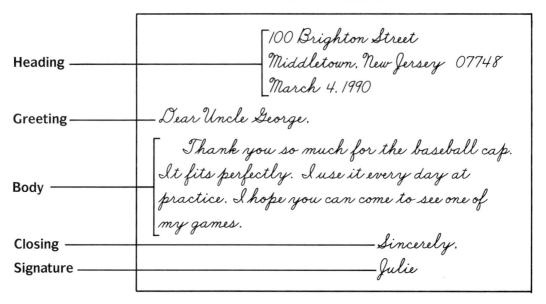

Heading
> 100 Brighton Street
> Middletown, New Jersey 07748
> March 4, 1990

Greeting — Dear Uncle George,

Body —
> Thank you so much for the baseball cap. It fits perfectly. I use it every day at practice. I hope you can come to see one of my games.

Closing — Sincerely,
Signature — Julie

A **thank-you note** has the same features as a friendly letter: heading, greeting, body, closing, and signature.

Practice: Imagine you have received a gift or favor you have always wanted. Write a thank-you note for that gift or favor.

You're invited to: _A Barbecue_
At: _125 Rigby Lane_
Date and Time: _July 4th, 1 p.m._
From: _Chris Henley_

An **invitation** is a letter, form, or note inviting someone to an event. It should include this information: the type of event, the time and place the event will be held, and the name of the sender.

Practice: Write yourself an invitation to an event that you would like to attend. Show who sent the invitation.

Spelling Strategies

1. Check in a dictionary if you are unsure how to spell a word. First look up the spelling you think is correct. If it is not listed, try another spelling.

2. There are a few ways to learn spelling. Find the way that works best for you.

   ◆ Look at the word. Picture the letters in your mind.
   ◆ Say the word aloud. Listen to the sounds.
   ◆ Write the word. Practice making the letters.

3. Some words share the same letter pattern. Knowing a letter pattern can help you spell many words.

   ◆ These words contain the *ack* letter pattern:
   rack   snack   track
   ◆ These words contain the *ide* letter pattern:
   divide   slide   wide

4. Some words can be broken into word parts. Knowing a word part can help you spell an entire word.

   ◆ These words start with the word part *im*:
   immobile   impatient   impossible
   ◆ These words end with the word part *less*:
   aimless   blameless   homeless

5. Many words can be broken into syllables. If a long word is hard for you to spell, break it into syllables. The spelling may then become easier.

   composition $\longrightarrow$ com po si tion

6. You may have trouble remembering whether a word ends in *-able* or *-ible*. If so, say the word while stressing the syllable that gives you difficulty.

   say ador*a*ble ("ador **AY** ble")   say flex*i*ble ("flex **IH** ble")

7. Sometimes a memory hint can help you spell a word.

Which spelling is correct, *friend* or *freind*?
Memory hint: I'll be your fri<u>end</u> till the <u>end</u>.

Invent a memory hint to help you spell a difficult word.

Commonly Misspelled Words

1. above	26. honey	51. soup
2. across	27. hospital	52. sure
3. against	28. language	53. swing
4. almost	29. learn	54. tear
5. answer	30. library	55. their
6. breath	31. loose	56. though
7. brought	32. lose	57. threw
8. build	33. machine	58. through
9. busy	34. marry	59. tomorrow
10. chief	35. meant	60. touch
11. country	36. measure	61. toward
12. course	37. minute	62. trouble
13. cover	38. mirror	63. truth
14. early	39. neighbor	64. two
15. eight	40. none	65. wear
16. either	41. ocean	66. weather
17. every	42. often	67. Wednesday
18. field	43. once	68. whole
19. flood	44. oven	69. wolf
20. front	45. piece	70. woman
21. garage	46. pour	71. world
22. ghost	47. prove	72. worry
23. half	48. quiet	73. worth
24. heard	49. rough	74. you're
25. heavy	50. some	75. young

Handwriting Models

When you write to someone, it is important for them to be able to understand and enjoy what you say. This handwriting is clear and neat. It's a good model for your own writing.

Grammar Definitions and Practice

Sentences I

♦ A **sentence** is a group of words that tells a complete thought. It must start with a capital letter and end with an end mark. (*page 40*)

The class takes a field trip to the aquarium.

A. Practice Write *sentence* or *not a sentence* for each group of words.
1. A tour guide greets the bus.
2. Shows the children around the aquarium.
3. The children walk up the steps.
4. Julie, Lamar, and the other children.
5. The shallow pools of ocean water.
6. The tour starts at these shallow pools.
7. Plant and animal life.
8. The guide points to a starfish.
9. Many cities have public aquariums.
10. One aquarium in Holland began in 1882.

B. Practice Write each group of words that is a complete sentence. Add a capital letter and an end mark.
11. people made the first flags long ago
12. the red and white flag of Japan
13. many countries use the colors red, white, and blue
14. people in Canada put a maple leaf on their flag
15. have stars on their flags
16. many flags have stripes
17. the flags of Australia and Britain
18. each state has a flag
19. sent messages with signal flags
20. ship companies have their own flags
21. stood for our first thirteen states
22. the very first flags

♦ A **statement** is a sentence that tells something. Put a period at the end of a statement. (*page 42*)

   The students are very eager about this trip.

♦ A **question** is a sentence that asks something. Put a question mark at the end of a question. (*page 42*)

   Will we see the first car of all?

♦ A **command** is a sentence that gives an order or an instruction. Put a period at the end of a command. (*page 42*)

   Frank, don't eat your lunch on the bus.

♦ An **exclamation** is a sentence that shows strong feeling or surprise. Put an exclamation mark at the end of an exclamation. (*page 42*)

   Wow, look at those cars!

A. Practice Write each sentence. Tell if it is a *statement*, a *question*, a *command*, or an *exclamation*.

   1. The children visit a car museum.
   2. Have you seen cars like this before?
   3. One old car runs on steam.
   4. Tell me about this early car.
   5. It looks so different from modern cars!
   6. The first Model-T car appeared in 1908.
   7. Did Henry Ford invent this car?
   8. Help us find the oldest car in the museum.
   9. These cars went so slowly!
   10. What an interesting museum this is!

B. Practice Write each sentence. Use the correct end mark. Then write if it is a *statement*, a *question*, a *command*, or an *exclamation*.

   11. France has a lot of car museums
   12. Which French cities have car museums
   13. Take my picture next to this car
   14. The first cars had no roofs
   15. Where is the engine in this car

16. Wow, this car looks so strange

17. Tell me about the inventor of this car

18. Please find this car in the guidebook

19. What wonderful wheels this car has

20. How do you steer this car

21. Have you visited many car museums

22. Maria went to a car museum in Michigan

♦ The **complete subject** of a sentence tells whom or what the sentence is about. (*page 44*)

A clock tells time.

A. Practice Write each sentence. Draw a line under the complete subject.

1. People told time by the sun long ago.

2. The Aztecs built a calendar stone.

3. A sundial told time with the sun and shadows.

4. Hourglasses told time with sand.

5. The sand flowed from the top glass to the bottom one.

6. The ancient Romans used water or oil in clocks.

7. A European inventor made a clock with gears and wheels.

8. An English clock started with a key.

9. Artists decorated many old clocks.

10. The artists painted beautiful pictures on the clocks.

11. The gold clock fits in the palm of her hand.

12. Many people wear wristwatches.

13. Mr. Ratner carries a pocket watch on a chain.

14. Computers tell time exactly.

B. Practice Write each sentence. Draw a line under the complete subject.

15. Roger plays the flute.

16. Mr. Rodriguez gives Roger music lessons.

17. The first lesson begins at four o'clock.

18. Many musicians teach music in schools and homes.

19. Some musicians direct singing groups.
20. The children play in a concert.
21. One young girl steps onto the stage.
22. The girl sits at the piano.
23. Thomas beats the drums loudly.
24. The music ends with three fast notes.

♦ The **complete predicate** of a sentence tells what the subject is or does. (*page 46*)

Miss Chan works at a television station.

A. Practice Write each sentence. Draw a line under the complete predicate.
1. Miss Chan reports the weather on television.
2. The weather map shows the whole country.
3. A snowstorm travels across the Rocky Mountains.
4. Miss Chan points to the Atlantic Ocean.
5. Rain falls on the coast.
6. A strong wind blows.
7. The sun shines over the Northwest.
8. Miss Chan predicts cloudy weather.
9. The weather changes.
10. Maps show the new weather patterns.

B. Practice Write each sentence. Draw one line under the complete subject. Draw two lines under the complete predicate.
11. Bears eat many foods.
12. Some bears enjoy blueberries.
13. Polar bears live in Alaska and Canada.
14. Bats have wings.
15. These strange animals fly very well.
16. Many bats hang by their feet in caves.
17. Those large bats fly at night.
18. Many wildcats live in North America.
19. The cougar hunts in parts of Florida.
20. Furry bobcats live in many forests in the north.

Nouns

◆ A **noun** is a word that names a person, place, or thing. (*page 78*)
   The boy has a garden behind the house.
   A rosebush grows by the wall.

A. Practice Write each sentence. Draw a line under each noun.
   1. The students order seeds from a catalog.
   2. The children choose flowers and vegetables.
   3. A garden needs sun and water.
   4. The girl sprays water on the flowers.
   5. The boy digs a hole in the ground with a shovel.
   6. A child grows carrots by the garage.
   7. The people in that house grow tomatoes and beans.
   8. The children eat the spinach from the garden.
   9. Friends admire the roses and the other flowers.
   10. A student wins a prize for tulips and daffodils.
   11. Plants grow on every street in the town.
   12. The mayor praises the students and the teachers.

◆ A **singular** noun names one person, place, or thing. A **plural** noun names more than one person, place, or thing. (*page 80*)
   A large bird lives in the maple tree.
   Many birds live in those trees.

◆ Add *s* to form the plural of most singular nouns. (*pages 80-81*)
   book $\longrightarrow$ books   table $\longrightarrow$ tables

◆ Add *es* to form the plural of nouns that end in *s, ss, x, z, ch,* or *sh*. (*page 80*)
   class $\longrightarrow$ classes   box $\longrightarrow$ boxes   peach $\longrightarrow$ peaches

◆ If a noun ends in a consonant and *y*, change the *y* to *i* and add *es* to form the plural. (*page 80*)
   sky $\longrightarrow$ skies   berry $\longrightarrow$ berries

◆ If a noun ends in a vowel and *y*, add *s* to form the plural. (*page 80*)
   tray $\longrightarrow$ trays   boy $\longrightarrow$ boys

418

◆ Some nouns have special plural forms. (*page 80*)

man → men   child → children   goose → geese

A. Practice Write the plural form for each singular noun.

1. dish	**6.** poppy	**11.** shovel
2. firefly	**7.** sash	**12.** hose
3. lunch	**8.** dress	**13.** way
4. daisy	**9.** woman	**14.** beet
5. donkey	**10.** blueberry	**15.** foot

B. Practice Write each sentence. Use the plural form of the noun in parentheses.

16. Many people have gardens in _____. (city)

17. Gardeners grow plants in window _____. (box)

18. Often, the _____ look like small farms. (roof)

19. _____ grow in containers. (Strawberry)

20. Some city gardens even have _____. (rosebush)

21. Some lucky _____ have backyards. (family)

22. People put chairs and _____ in the yard. (bench)

23. Children can play with _____ outside. (toy)

◆ A **common noun** names any person, place, or thing. (*page 82*)
An <u>inventor</u> thinks up new <u>machines</u>.

◆ A **proper noun** names a particular person, place, or thing. A proper noun always begins with a capital letter. Some proper nouns have more than one word. (*page 82*)
In <u>France</u>, <u>Robert Fulton</u> invented a submarine.

A. Practice Write each sentence. Underline the common nouns. Capitalize the proper nouns.

1. robert fulton developed many inventions.

2. This inventor was also a painter.

3. fulton invented a steamboat and a submarine.

4. The submarine was called the nautilus.

5. The nautilus was made of iron.

6. Two men steered the submarine.

7. The steamboat traveled along the hudson river.

8. The boat went from albany to other cities.

B. Practice Write each sentence. Underline the common nouns. Capitalize the proper nouns.

9. eli whitney was an inventor from massachusetts.

10. whitney lived on a farm as a boy.

11. eli whitney went to yale college in connecticut.

12. This inventor built a machine for farmers.

13. The machine separated seeds from cotton.

14. Another inventor was john roebling.

15. roebling designed bridges all over the country.

16. In 1883, roebling finished the brooklyn bridge.

17. This is a famous bridge in new york city.

18. Many bridges cross the rivers of this large city.

♦ A **possessive** is a word that tells who or what owns or has something. Add an apostrophe (') and an *s* to make most singular nouns possessive. (*page 84*)

The girl has a baseball.   the girl's baseball

A. Practice Write the noun that has or owns something. Then write that word as a possessive.

1. The game had a score.	**6.** Elizabeth owns a mitt.
2. The catcher had a mask.	**7.** The child has a bat.
3. The player owns shoes.	**8.** The cap had a brim.
4. Jake has a cap.	**9.** The coach had a chair.
5. Kate owns a medal.	**10.** The winner had a prize.

♦ A **plural possessive** shows that more than one person, place, or thing owns something. If a plural noun ends in *s*, add an apostrophe (') to form the possessive. If a plural does not end in *s*, add an apostrophe (') to form the possessive. If a plural does not end in *s*, add an apostrophe and *s* to form a possessive. (*page 86*)

the boys' house   the women's plans

A. Practice Write the noun in parentheses as a possessive.

1. The (children) game began on time.
2. The (players) uniforms had numbers on the back.
3. The (parents) group raised money for the uniforms.
4. The (pitcher) curve ball flew over the base.
5. The (batters) helmets prevented injuries.
6. Everyone clapped for (Angela) home run.
7. The ball slipped from the (fielder) glove.
8. The (men) cheers were very loud.
9. People booed the (umpire) call.

B. Practice Write the noun in parentheses as a possessive.

10. The family read (Mom) letter.
11. The letter told about the (women) visit to Victoria.
12. Mom enjoyed the trip through (Canada) countryside.
13. The women saw the (farmers) fields from the train.
14. The tourists enjoyed the (city) gardens.
15. The (visitors) hotel had a huge indoor garden.
16. Mom watched the (boys) soccer game in the park.
17. Everyone enjoyed the (museums) displays.
18. Mrs. Egle loved the (park) totem poles.

◆ An **abbreviation** is a shortened form of a word. Many abbreviations begin with a capital letter and end with a period. (*page 88*)

St. Rd. Blvd. Ave.

Jan. Feb. Mar. Apr. Aug. Sept. Oct. Nov. Dec.

Sun. Mon. Tues. Wed. Thurs. Fri. Sat.

Mrs. Dr. Ms. Mrs. Miss

A. Practice Write each name, date, or title in abbreviated form. Use capital letters and periods where needed.

1. Doctor Gina B. Mays
2. 36 Marshall Road
3. Thursday, February 24
4. 358 Maple Boulevard
5. (a married woman) Jo Reed
6. Wednesday, December 9
7. 47 Apple Street
8. Tuesday, March 8
9. Friday, April 27
10. (a married man) Roger Hall

Verbs I

♦ An **action verb** is a word that tells what someone or something does. (*page 126*)

The boy runs easily.

♦ Some action verbs tell about actions we cannot see. They tell about who or what owns something. (*page 126*)

The men have new sneakers.

A. Practice Write each sentence. Underline the action verb.
1. Kate trains for a race.
2. Joe has a big meal the night before the race.
3. Kate jogs in place on the day of the race.
4. The runners have numbers on their shirts.
5. People run slowly at first.
6. The crowds cheer for the runners.
7. Most runners sprint toward the finish line.
8. Kate beats Joe in the race.
9. Kate wins the race.
10. Joe congratulates Kate.
11. The winners walk in a parade through town.
12. Television reporters interview the winners.

B. Practice Write each sentence. Underline the action verb.
13. Bicycle riders rush around the track.
14. The bicycles travel at 50 miles an hour.
15. The riders pedal hard.
16. The winner has a gold medal.
17. Sailboats compete in races, too.
18. Many sailors enter the America's Cup races.
19. Americans won the America's Cup races almost every time.
20. Australia finished first in 1983.
21. A fast sailboat travels at 40 miles an hour.
22. Sailboats use the wind for power.

♦ A **linking verb** joins the subject of a sentence with a word or words in the predicate. A linking verb usually tells what the subject *is* or *is like*. Most linking verbs are forms of the verb *be*. (*page 128*)

Mary Johnson is the race director.

A. Practice Write each sentence. Underline the linking verb.
1. Mark Spitz was a famous swimmer.
2. Spitz's seven gold medals are an Olympic record.
3. Mark Spitz was in the 1972 Olympics.
4. Many fast swimmers were in the Olympics that year.
5. Shane Gould was the winner in three women's races.
6. Shane Gould is from Australia.
7. Johnny Weissmuller is another famous swimmer.
8. Weissmuller was the winner of many gold medals.
9. Weissmuller was in the Olympics in 1924 and 1928.
10. Later, Weissmuller was an actor in films.
11. Swimmers are excellent athletes.
12. Swimmers' muscles are strong.

B. Practice Write each sentence. Underline the action verbs once and the linking verbs twice.
13. The Wharf to Wharf is a race in California.
14. The race covers five miles.
15. The two friends ran in the race.
16. Lisa had orange juice for breakfast that day.
17. Jacob wore purple shorts and a yellow shirt.
18. This was Lisa's second big race.
19. Large crowds watched the race.
20. The day was very hot.
21. People squirted water at the runners along the way.
22. Jacob and Lisa were happy after the race.
23. The friends had lunch together afterwards.
24. Jacob's picture was in the newspaper the next day.
25. Lisa ran well all through the race.
26. Jacob finished just behind the winners.

♦ The **tense** of a verb tells when something happens. A verb in the **present tense** tells about something that is happening now. (*page 130*)

 Ed Khan <u>paints</u> posters.

♦ A verb in the **past tense** tells about something that already happened. Past tense verbs often end in *ed*. (*pages 130-131*)

 Ed <u>painted</u> the posters for the race.

♦ A verb in the **future tense** tells about something that will happen in the future. The word *will* is part of each future tense verb. (*page 130*)

 Next week, Ed <u>will display</u> the posters.

A. Practice Write each sentence. If the underlined verb is in the present tense, write *present*. If the verb is in the past tense, write *past*.

 1. Our class <u>paints</u> posters for the race.
 2. Sharon <u>snapped</u> pictures of the race's route.
 3. The class <u>used</u> the snapshots for poster ideas.
 4. Mrs. Card <u>handed</u> materials to each child.
 5. The students <u>practiced</u> on scratch paper.
 6. Carol <u>uses</u> bright green and yellow crayons.
 7. Paul's picture <u>shows</u> all the houses along the route.

B. Practice Write each sentence. Underline the verb. Write *present*, *past*, or *future* to show the tense.

 8. Soon the class will learn long division.
 9. The lesson will begin tomorrow.
 10. Last year the students learned multiplication tables.
 11. Jim remembers all of the tables.
 12. Mrs. Davis will talk about fractions tomorrow.
 13. Some students solved problems with calculators.
 14. Batteries supply the calculators with power.
 15. Some calculators use solar energy.
 16. The class worked without calculators on the test.
 17. The students will learn about computers soon.

♦ The subject and the verb in the present tense must work together in a sentence. When they work together, they **agree**. For most singular nouns and *he*, *she*, or *it*, a verb in the present tense ends in *s*. For most plural nouns and *I*, *you*, *we*, or *they*, a verb in the present tense does not end in *s*. (*page 132*)

The astronaut explores.   The astronauts explore.

A. Practice Write each sentence with the correct form of the verb.

1. An astronaut ____ for long hours. (train, trains)
2. Astronauts ____ many difficult tests. (pass, passes)
3. Many astronauts ____ in Houston, Texas. (live, lives)
4. Space flights often ____ in the desert. (land, lands)
5. Astronauts ____ special food in space. (eat, eats)
6. Juan ____ forward to astronaut school. (look, looks)
7. He ____ hard at math and science. (work, works)
8. Ellen ____ books about space. (read, reads)
9. She ____ films on space travel. (watch, watches)
10. They ____ of space. (dream, dreams)
11. Scientists ____ a spaceship. (launch, launches)
12. The spaceship ____ toward Neptune. (travel, travels)

♦ To write the present tense form of a verb that goes with a singular subject, add *s* to most verbs. (*page 134*)

talk ⟶ talks   run ⟶ runs

♦ Add *es* to verbs ending with *s*, *ss*, *ch*, *sh*, *x*, or *z*. (*page 134*)

push ⟶ pushes   hiss ⟶ hisses

♦ If a verb ends in a consonant and *y*, change the *y* to *i* and add *es*. (*page 134*)

fly ⟶ flies   marry ⟶ marries

♦ To write the past tense form of most verbs, add *ed*. (*page 134*)

visit ⟶ visited   greet ⟶ greeted

♦ If a verb ends in *e*, drop the final *e* and add *ed*. (*page 134*)

tie ⟶ tied   paste ⟶ pasted

♦ If a verb ends in a consonant and *y*, change the *y* to *i* and add *ed*. (*page 134*)

worry ⟶ worried   try ⟶ tried

♦ For a verb of one syllable that ends with consonant-vowel-consonant, double the final consonant and add *ed*. (*page 134*)

chop ⟶ chopped   pet ⟶ petted

A. Practice Write each sentence, using the correct form of the verb in the present tense.

1. The boy (want) some bread.
2. Amos (mix) the batter.
3. Amos (carry) the pan to the oven.
4. The bread (rise) in the oven.
5. The oven timer (ring) after thirty minutes.
6. Amos (rush) to the oven.

B. Practice Write each sentence, using the correct form of the verb in the past tense.

7. Something unusual (happen) at the children's zoo.
8. The goat (open) all the animal pens.
9. Calves and sheep (scurry) out of the pens.
10. Zookeepers (dash) after the beasts.
11. At last the zookeepers (stop) the escape.
12. Visitors to the zoo (clap) for the goat.

C. Practice Write each sentence. Write the underlined verb, using the tense in parentheses.

13. An eagle fly high above. (present)
14. The robin carry twigs for a nest. (present)
15. The bluebird spot the insect. (past)
16. The egg hatch in the nest. (present)
17. A sparrow pass the tree. (present)
18. The hawk drop through the clouds. (past)
19. An owl's wings flap silently in the night. (past)
20. A photographer snap the birds' pictures. (past)
21. The sun rise over the forest. (present)

♦ The verb part of a sentence can have more than one verb. A **main verb** is the most important verb in the sentence. A **helping verb** helps the main verb tell about an action. Most helping verbs are forms of the verbs *be* and *have*. A main verb usually ends in *ed* or *ing*. (*page 160*)

Bob is reading a book.
Ruth has studied for a long time.
Carlos was starting his work.
Meg had read that book already.

A. Practice Write each sentence. Underline the helping verb once. Underline the main verb twice.

1. Sally is searching for a book for her book report.
2. She has looked in two libraries.
3. Jeff is reading *Treasure Island*.
4. Marcia has finished *Prince Caspian*.
5. The teacher had suggested many books.
6. The school librarian has discussed nonfiction books.
7. Gina and Annie are planning a report on reptiles.
8. The girls have read several books about snakes.
9. Olga and Miguel are writing reports on sports.
10. Olga is gathering information about soccer.

B. Practice Write each sentence, using the correct main or helping verb in parentheses.

11. The boys were _____ a good movie. (watching, watched)
12. Mac _____ discovered the movie. (is, had)
13. Julie Andrews _____ playing the lead role. (is, has)
14. *Mary Poppins* had _____ as a book. (starting, started)
15. Doug is _____ the movie. (enjoying, enjoyed)
16. The movie makers _____ added songs. (have, were)
17. Mary Poppins _____ dancing. (is, has)
18. The children _____ riding a merry-go-round. (is, are)
19. The cartoon horses _____ galloped away. (have, are)
20. Travis is _____ for the book. (looking, looked)

◆ **Irregular verbs** do not form the past tense by adding *ed*.
(*pages 162, 164*)

Present	Past	Present	Past with have, has, or had
begin	began	begin	begun
bring	brought	bring	brought
come	came	come	come
do	did	do	done
fly	flew	fly	flown
go	went	go	gone
grow	grew	grow	grown
ride	rode	ride	ridden
run	ran	run	run
say	said	say	said
see	saw	see	seen
take	took	take	taken
throw	threw	throw	thrown
write	wrote	write	written

A. Practice Write each sentence, using the correct past tense form of the verb in parentheses.

    1. Ed Young has ____ drawings for many books. (do)

    2. Young ____ pictures for *Eyes of the Dragon*. (do)

    3. Margaret Leaf ____ the book. (write)

    4. The writer ____ the idea from a fairy tale. (take)

    5. The story ____ in a village in China. (begin)

    6. A picture of a dragon has ____ to life. (come)

    7. Irene ____ the book in the library. (see)

    8. Irene ____ the book to class. (bring)

B. Practice Write each sentence, using the correct past tense form in parentheses.

    9. A boys' chorus ____ to Boston. (come)

    10. The group ____ here from Europe. (fly)

    11. People in Boston have ____ the chorus before. (see)

12. The boys have ____ some new music this time. (bring)
13. The concert had ____ at 2:00 p.m. (begin)
14. First the chorus leader ____ a few words. (say)
15. The singers ____ many beautiful songs. (do)
16. At the end, people ____ flowers onstage. (throw)
17. The boys have ____ the train to New York. (take)
18. A television crew has ____ with the boys. (ride)

◆ A contraction is a shortened form of two words. An apostrophe (') takes the place of the missing letters. (*page 166*)

| is not → isn't | has not → hasn't |
| have not → haven't | could not → couldn't |

A. Practice Write the contraction for each pair of words.

1. were not	**4.** has not	**7.** is not
2. should not	**5.** does not	**8.** had not
3. are not	**6.** do not	**9.** could not

B. Practice Write each sentence, using a contraction for the underlined words.
10. Thomas Jefferson was not the first President.
11. Benjamin Franklin did not become President.
12. People should not forget the Presidents' names.
13. A President has not traveled in space yet.
14. Jerry could not name the tenth President.
15. Coolidge would not run for another term as President.
16. Alexander Hamilton is not on the list of Presidents.
17. John Adams and his son were not two-term Presidents.

C. Practice Write each sentence, using a contraction for the underlined words.
18. Paul Revere did not get much sleep on April 18, 1775.
19. The people of Concord were not awake.
20. The Redcoats should not find them asleep.
21. Paul did not have much time.
22. Paul was not riding slowly.
23. Paul Revere did not stop for anything.
24. The British could not stop Paul.
25. Americans have not forgotten Paul Revere.

Pronouns

♦ A **pronoun** is a word that replaces a noun or nouns. A **subject pronoun** is used in place of a noun in the subject part of a sentence. *I, you, he, she, it, we,* and *they* are subject pronouns. (*page 212*)

The class drew cartoons. They used pencils.

A. Practice Write each sentence. Write a subject pronoun to replace the underlined word or words.

1. Harry and I draw a comic strip for the class project.
2. Susannah draws a comic strip about a cat.
3. Jim and Paul write the words for the strip.
4. Robert has a good idea for a comic strip.
5. The comic strip stars an elephant.
6. Teri and Robert are making comic books.
7. The books tell long stories.
8. Miguel and I like Robert's comic book.
9. Mrs. Rossi also praises Robert's work.
10. The school has a display of all the comic strips.
11. Parents like the display.
12. Dad laughs at the jokes in the comic strips.

B. Practice Write each sentence. Write a subject pronoun to replace each underlined word or words.

13. Doctors do important jobs.
14. Elizabeth Blackwell became a famous doctor.
15. Dr. Blackwell was born in England.
16. Family members moved to the United States in 1832.
17. Doctors were all men in those days.
18. Elizabeth Blackwell changed that.
19. Emily Blackwell also became a doctor.
20. Elizabeth and Emily Blackwell opened a doctor's office.
21. The office soon did well.
22. Hospitals owe a lot to these brave women.

♦ An **object pronoun** is used in place of a noun that follows an action verb. It is found in the predicate part of the sentence. *Me, you, him, her, it, us,* and *them* are object pronouns. (*page 214*)

Regina met Mrs. Velasquez.   Regina met her.

A. Practice Write each sentence. Use an object pronoun in place of the underlined words.

1. The reporter photographed Andrew Chin.
2. He interviewed Mrs. Hadley.
3. The announcer presented Stella and me.
4. The picture showed Mr. and Mrs. Diaz in the audience.
5. The audience cheered the winners.

B. Practice Write each sentence. Write an object pronoun for the underlined word or words.

6. My parents took Rita and me on a camping trip.
7. Dad drove the car to a state park.
8. Mom took Rita on a plant hunt.
9. Dad called Mom and Rita for lunch.
10. We cooked potatoes on a campfire.
11. Rita spotted a butterfly near the trees.
12. I photographed Dad by the tent.
13. At night we watched the stars.

C. Practice Write each sentence. Write an object pronoun for the underlined word or words.

14. Tim asked the students for names of famous people.
15. Ellie named Alfred Nobel.
16. Alfred Nobel began the Nobel Prizes in the late 1800s.
17. Sweden awards the prizes in many fields.
18. A committee picked Marie Curie for two science prizes.
19. Several American Presidents won the Nobel Peace Prize.
20. Sometimes several scientists share a prize.
21. Mom told Ellie and me about Pearl Buck.
22. This American author won the Nobel Prize.
23. I asked Mom for names of other prizewinners.

♦ *I* and *we* are **subject pronouns**. Use *I* and *we* in the subject part of a sentence. *Me* and *us* are **object pronouns**. Use *me* and *us* in the predicate part of a sentence. (*page 216*)

    I helped Tim.   Tim helped me.

    We cheered the teacher.   The teacher cheered us.

A. Practice Write each sentence. Write the correct pronoun.

  1. Megan and ____ collect postcards. (I, me)

  2. ____ have cards from many countries. (We, Us)

  3. People often ask ____ about this hobby. (I, me)

  4. ____ have over 300 postcards. (I, Me)

  5. They teach Megan and ____ about other lands. (I, me)

  6. Megan and ____ also collect very old cards. (I, me)

  7. ____ have postcards from the year 1907. (We, Us)

  8. A friend from Alaska visited ____. (we, us)

  9. She told ____ about her stamp collection. (we, us)

  10. ____ collect stamps too—on the postcards! (We, Us)

♦ **Possessive forms** of pronouns tell who or what owns or has something. The possessive forms of pronouns are *my, your, her, his, its, our,* and *their.* (*page 218*)

    Jill's kitten is gray.   Her kitten is gray.

A. Practice Write each sentence. Underline the possessive pronoun.

  1. My new kitten Patsy is hiding in that shoebox.

  2. Her fur is soft and white.

  3. Joe named his black cat Midnight.

  4. Both Patsy and Midnight keep their fur clean.

  5. Beth calls her cat Tabby.

  6. The kitten snuggles against his mother.

  7. Your cat looks like the cat on television.

  8. I play with my kitten every day.

  9. Their whiskers are still very short.

  10. Our kittens have learned many funny tricks.

B. Practice Write each sentence. Replace the possessive with the correct possessive form of the pronoun.

11. The big cats at the zoo are <u>Lisa's</u> favorite animals.
12. The zookeeper told us the <u>lions'</u> names.
13. The <u>zookeeper's</u> name is Miss Gray.
14. She answered <u>the children's</u> questions.
15. The <u>zoo's</u> snack bar doesn't sell snacks for the lions!
16. This zoo is <u>New York's</u> biggest zoo.
17. <u>Andy's</u> mother was the class mother on the trip.
18. <u>Mrs. Stein's</u> purse contained the list of students.
19. <u>The children's</u> parents gave permission for the trip.
20. We ate lunch in <u>Tommy's and my</u> favorite spot.

♦ A **contraction** is a shortened form of two words that are combined together. An apostrophe (') takes the place of the missing letter or letters. Pronouns can be combined with the verbs *am, is,* or *are* to form contractions. (*page 220*)

I am → I'm	I will → I'll	you are → you're
it is → it's	we are → we're	you have → you've

A. Practice Write each sentence. Use the correct contraction for the underlined words.

1. <u>I am</u> planning a Round the World party.
2. <u>It is</u> on Saturday afternoon.
3. <u>You are</u> invited to the party.
4. <u>They will</u> bring food from Japan and Mexico.
5. <u>We have</u> planned party games from many countries.
6. <u>He is</u> practicing music from Greece.
7. <u>She will</u> teach us a song from Africa.
8. <u>I have</u> cooked a soup from China.
9. <u>He will</u> set the table with special plates.
10. <u>We are</u> making our own puppets.
11. <u>They are</u> wearing costumes to the party.
12. <u>I will</u> need a pineapple for the dessert.
13. <u>They have</u> brought paper cups.
14. <u>We will</u> eat after the songs and games.

433

Adjectives

◆ An **adjective** is a word that tells about a noun. (*page 250*)

a <u>yellow</u> rose   a <u>loud</u> noise   <u>some</u> crops

◆ Many adjectives tell *what kind*. (*page 250*)

The United States is a <u>big</u> country.

◆ Other adjectives tell *how many* there are. (*page 250*)

We visited <u>three</u> states and <u>several</u> cities.

A. Practice Write each sentence. Underline each adjective twice. Underline the noun it tells about once.

1. People in Britain built many castles.
2. Stone walls rise around the castles.
3. A wooden bridge leads to Grosmont Castle.
4. They built round towers at Conway Castle.
5. The castles have narrow windows.
6. Thick walls protect them.
7. Many people visit the castles.
8. They are old buildings.
9. Bolton Castle has tall towers.
10. Several buildings are inside the walls.
11. Windsor Castle has five towers.
12. The tall castle stands on a hill.
13. A king began the huge castle.
14. Many rulers added sections to it.

◆ The words *a*, *an*, and *the* are special adjectives called **articles**. *A* and *an* are used before singular nouns only. *The* is used before singular or plural nouns. (*page 252*)

Meredith ate <u>a</u> sandwich and <u>an</u> egg.
<u>The</u> man carried <u>the</u> suitcases.

◆ Use *a* before a noun that begins with a consonant sound. Use *an* before a noun that begins with a vowel sound. (*page 252*)

<u>a</u> pin   <u>a</u> holiday   <u>an</u> apple   <u>an</u> hour

A. Practice Write each sentence, using the correct article.

1. Louise has a mind like (a, an) encyclopedia.
2. She knows (a, the) names of some unusual things.
3. The tall parts of a bridge are (an, the) towers.
4. The part with the road is (an, the) span.
5. A hot air balloon's outer cover is (a, an) envelope.
6. (An, The) skirt is the bottom part of the envelope.
7. On a zipper, (an, the) slide moves up and down.
8. You hold the pulltab of (an, the) zipper.
9. The bottom of a safety pin is (a, an) coil.
10. The guard is the part at (a, the) end.

♦ Adjectives can be used to compare two or more nouns. Add *er* to an adjective to compare two people, places, or things. (*page 254*)

    Boulder is a small city.
    Cheyenne is smaller than Boulder.

♦ Add *est* to an adjective to compare three or more people, places, or things. (*page 254*)

    Boulder is a small city.
    Cheyenne is smaller than Boulder.
    Sitka is the smallest city of the three cities.
    Sitka is the smallest city of all.

♦ You must spell some adjectives differently when you add *er* or *est*. When an adjective ends with *e*, drop the final *e* before adding *er* or *est*. (*page 254*)

    cute $\longrightarrow$ cuter $\longrightarrow$ cutest

♦ When an adjective ends with a consonant followed by *y*, change the *y* to *i* before adding *er* or *est*. (*page 254*)

    sorry $\longrightarrow$ sorrier $\longrightarrow$ sorriest

♦ When a one-syllable adjective ends in a vowel followed by a consonant, double the final consonant before adding *er* or *est*. (*page 254*)

    flat $\longrightarrow$ flatter $\longrightarrow$ flattest

A. Practice Write each sentence, using the correct form of the adjective in parentheses.
1. Which student's project was the (fine) of all?
2. Wendy's map is the (large) of all.
3. Dirk's map has (bright) colors than Jon's map.
4. Bob's paintbrush is (thin) than Shelley's brush.
5. The green map is (clear) than the red map.
6. Barry's report is the (tidy) of all.

B. Practice Write each sentence, using the correct form of the adjective in parentheses.
7. New York is (noisy) than Portland.
8. Fairbanks is the (cold) city of the three cities.
9. Denver is (new) than San Antonio.
10. Boston is (old) than Cleveland.
11. Buffalo's snowfall was the (heavy) snowfall of all.
12. Phoenix was the (hot) city of all.
13. Chicago was (windy) than New Haven.
14. Tampa's weather is (warm) than Detroit's weather.

♦ For many adjectives with two or more syllables, use *more* before the adjective instead of adding *er*. (*page 256*)
    Ed's guitar is beautiful.
    Fran's guitar is more beautiful than Ed's guitar.

♦ For many adjectives with two or more syllables, use *most* before the adjective instead of adding *est*. (*page 256*)
    Ed's guitar is beautiful.
    Fran's guitar is more beautiful than Ed's guitar.
    Paco's guitar is the most beautiful guitar of all.

A. Practice Write each sentence, using the correct form of the adjective in parentheses.
1. The drum is the (ancient) instrument of all.
2. Harp music is the (beautiful) music of all.
3. A bagpipe is (unusual) than a flute.
4. The violin is (difficult) than the tuba.

436

5. The piano is the (popular) instrument of all.
6. The trumpet is (famous) than the trombone.
7. The harmonica is the (practical) instrument of all.
8. A horn is (useful) than a piano in a parade.

B. Practice Write each sentence, using the correct form of the adjective in parentheses.

9. Hook shots are the (difficult) basketball shots of all.
10. Will is the (popular) player of all.
11. Jerry is a (eager) player than Paul.
12. Ms. Barnes is the (helpful) coach of all.
13. Frank is the (valuable) player on the team.
14. Mr. Crawford is the (loyal) fan of all.
15. Basketball is a (difficult) game than volleyball.
16. Tomas is (careful) than Cammie with his shots.

♦ The adjectives *good* and *bad* have special forms for comparing two or more nouns. To compare with *good*, use *better* and *best*. (*page 258*)

Tin is a good metal.
Iron is a better metal than tin.
Gold is the best metal of all.

♦ To compare with *bad*, use *worse* and *worst*. (*page 258*)

Silver is a bad metal for boats.
Iron is worse than silver for boats.
Lead is the worst metal of all for boats.

A. Practice Write each sentence, using the correct form of the adjective in parentheses.

1. Stone is (good) than wood for strong walls.
2. Straw is the (bad) material of all for walls.
3. Glass is the (good) material of all for windows.
4. Wool is (good) than cotton for warm coats.
5. Silk is the (bad) cloth of all for play clothes.
6. Wood is (bad) than leather for boots.
7. Gold is (good) than tin for rings.
8. Plastic is (bad) than steel for locks.

Adverbs

◆ An **adverb** is a word that tells more about an action. Many adverbs that tell *how* an action is done end in *ly*. (*page 300*)

The train traveled <u>swiftly</u>.

A. Practice Write each sentence. Look at the underlined verb. Draw two lines under the adverb that tells *how*.

1. The people <u>walked</u> eagerly to the station.
2. They got quickly onto the train.
3. A whistle blew loudly.
4. The train pulled slowly out of the station.
5. The wheels turned smoothly.
6. Passengers glanced happily out the windows.
7. The train traveled quickly through the valley.
8. It sped noisily into a tunnel.
9. Lights glowed dimly in the tunnel.
10. People walked unsteadily through the train.
11. The train rolled rapidly toward the town.
12. It stopped completely beside the platform.

B. Practice Write each sentence. Look at the underlined verb. Draw two lines under the adverb that tells *how*.

13. Dr. Zixx <u>looked</u> proudly at his baseball machine.
14. He <u>pressed</u> hard on the start button.
15. The machine <u>sat</u> silently on the table.
16. Dr. Zixx <u>tapped</u> impatiently on the machine.
17. Lights and dials <u>twinkled</u> brightly.
18. Gears <u>whirled</u> unevenly all over the machine.
19. Baseballs <u>flew</u> wildly into the air.
20. Dr. Zixx <u>pushed</u> desperately at all the buttons.
21. The doctor <u>sat</u> wearily in his chair.
22. Real baseball players <u>throw</u> expertly without machines.

◆ Some adverbs tell *where* an action is done. (*page 302*)

A tree grew <u>here</u>.

♦ Some adverbs tell *when* an action is done. (*page 302*)

    Yesterday we planted another tree.

A. Practice Write each sentence. Look at the underlined verb. Underline the adverb twice. Write what the adverb tells about the verb.

  1. Plant seeds occur everywhere.
  2. Seeds blow around in the wind.
  3. Sometimes birds carry seeds in their mouths.
  4. Many seeds fall down from trees.
  5. These seeds land nearby.
  6. Their roots grow underground.
  7. Later, new little seedlings sprout.
  8. Finally, seedlings grow into trees.
  9. Once forests covered large parts of this country.
 10. Today, farmland replaces many old forests.
 11. Many plants grow indoors.
 12. Often people raise flowers in greenhouses.

B. Practice Write each sentence. Look at the underlined verb. Underline the adverb twice. Write what the adverb tells about the verb.

 13. Yesterday Pete cleaned his room.
 14. First he made the bed.
 15. He looked underneath for stray toys and clothes.
 16. Next Pete cleaned the desk.
 17. The cat ran out in disgust.
 18. Later Pete swept the floor.
 19. Today Pete wakes in his clean room.
 20. First he goes to the closet.
 21. He soon finds one sneaker.
 22. Pete looks everywhere for the other sneaker.
 23. Still he has one shoe and one bare foot.
 24. Sometimes a clean room causes problems.

♦ An adverb can be used to compare two or more actions. Add *er* or *est* to adverbs of one syllable. (*page 304*)

> fast → faster → fastest

♦ Add *more* or *most* before most adverbs ending with *ly*. (*page 304*)

> quickly → more quickly → most quickly

A. Practice Write each sentence, using the correct form of the adverb.

1. A steamship travels (more quickly, most quickly) than a sailboat.
2. A jet flies (higher, highest) of all.
3. People ride (more comfortably, most comfortably) of all on an ocean liner.
4. A balloon flies (more slowly, most slowly) than a jet.
5. The Metroliner travels (faster, fastest) of all trains.
6. Jet engines rumble (more loudly, most loudly) of all.
7. Buses depart (more frequently, most frequently) than trains from this city.
8. The car's front lights shine (more brightly, most brightly) than its back lights.
9. Bruce got on the bus (earlier, earliest) than Greg did.
10. The train arrived (more promptly, most promptly) of all.
11. The car trip lasted (longer, longest) of all.

♦ An adverb can tell *how, where,* or *when* about a verb. An adjective can tell *what kind* or *how many* about a noun. (*page 306*)

> The game ended <u>quickly</u>.　　Lena is a <u>quick</u> runner.

♦ *Good* is an adjective. Use it to tell about a noun. *Well* is an adverb. Use it to tell about a verb. (*page 306*)

> She has a <u>good</u> voice.　　She sings <u>well</u>.

♦ Sometimes *well* is used to mean *in good health*. When it is used this way, *well* is an adjective. (*page 306*)

> He feels <u>well</u> today.

A. Practice Write each sentence, using the correct word. Then write whether the word is an *adjective* or an *adverb*.

1. Cheetahs run (good, well).
2. (Powerful, Powerfully) eagles soar above tall trees.
3. Hawks fly (swift, swiftly) through the clouds.
4. Frogs breathe through (damp, damply) skin.
5. Monkeys climb (easy, easily) up trees and vines.
6. Deer run (timid, timidly) from strange noises.
7. Grain is a (good, well) food for many wild birds.
8. Some birds sing (beautiful, beautifully).
9. Snakes slither (smooth, smoothly) over rocks.
10. A prairie dog digs a (deep, deeply) hole for a home.
11. A tiger's fur has (bright, brightly) stripes.
12. Goats leap (graceful, gracefully) along high cliffs.

♦ *Not* is an adverb that makes a sentence mean *no*. A contraction ending with *n't* also makes a sentence mean *no*. Words such as *never*, *nowhere*, *no*, *nobody*, and *nothing* also make a sentence mean *no*. Use only one *no* word in a sentence. (*page 308*)

> Incorrect: Good cooks don't never work carelessly.
> Correct: Good cooks don't work carelessly.
> Correct: Good cooks never work carelessly.

A. Practice Write each sentence. Choose the word that will form a sentence with one *no* word.

1. Magnets (do, don't) work on tin.
2. A magnet can't attract (any, no) gold or silver.
3. (Anybody, Nobody) can use a magnet on lead.
4. Gold doesn't (ever, never) rust.
5. You can't mine plastic (anywhere, nowhere).
6. Miners (do, don't) dig for pearls in the ground.
7. A needle (will, won't) scratch a diamond.
8. No factory (can, can't) make steel from silver.
9. Ancient people knew (anything, nothing) about steel.
10. They couldn't make (any, no) metal stronger than bronze.

Sentences II

- The **complete subject** tells who or what the sentence is about. (*page 340*)

   This little book tells about life long ago.

- The **simple subject** is the main word in the complete subject. (*page 340*)

   My favorite <u>chapter</u> tells about Egypt.

A. Practice Write each sentence. Underline the complete subject once. Underline the simple subject twice.

1. Early people lived very simply.
2. Many ancient people made stone tools.
3. The first towns began thousands of years ago.
4. Some early cities rose along trade routes.
5. One famous old city is Jericho.
6. Strong animals were the main form of transportation.
7. Straw roofs kept homes dry.
8. Clay pots held water or grain.
9. The people stored food for the winter.
10. The first kingdoms were in Asia and Africa.
11. Rich soil helped farmers in ancient Egypt.
12. Many crops grew near the Nile River.
13. This powerful kingdom lasted for many centuries.
14. Another ancient country was China.
15. Some beautiful art remains in China from long ago.
16. Many museums show art from ancient kingdoms.

- A sentence may have more than one simple subject. A **compound subject** is made up of two or more simple subjects that share the same predicate. The two simple subjects in a compound subject are joined by *and*. (*page 342*)

   Many <u>cities</u> and <u>towns</u> are full of tall buildings.

A. Practice Write each sentence. Underline the complete subject once. Underline each simple subject twice.

1. Architects and engineers built many things.
2. Bridges and tunnels are important to every city.
3. Many cars and trucks travel on bridges.
4. Small roads and large highways lead to the bridges.
5. Many trains and buses travel by tunnel under rivers.
6. Homes and tall offices fill many cities.
7. Bricks and glass are good material for buildings.
8. Heavy machines and shovels clear the land.
9. Carpenters and bricklayers work on the building.
10. The floors and the walls go up first.
11. Museums and libraries are useful buildings, too.
12. Designers and architects develop the plans.

♦ The **complete predicate** of a sentence tells what the subject is or does. (*page 344*)

Anna studies math every night.

♦ The **simple predicate** is the main word in the complete predicate. (*page 344*)

Anna studies hard.　　　She is a good student.

A. Practice Write each sentence. Underline the complete predicate once. Underline the simple predicate twice.

1. Mathematics is a useful subject.
2. People use mathematics in many careers.
3. Clerks keep a record of costs.
4. Geologists measure the size of rocks.
5. Athletes compare their scores.
6. Math helps the designers of buildings.
7. Architects plan the size of a building.
8. Carpenters follow their directions.
9. Space scientists develop new rocket fuels.
10. Storekeepers give the correct change.
11. Grocers weigh many foods.
12. Computers require a knowledge of mathematics.

♦ A sentence may have more than one simple predicate. A **compound predicate** is made up of two or more simple predicates that share the same subject. The two simple predicates are joined by *and*. *(page 346)*

The Town Theater Group   rehearses and gives plays.

A. Practice Write each sentence. Underline the complete predicate once. Underline each simple predicate twice.

1. The community planned and wrote a play.
2. The play celebrated and honored the town's founders.
3. One committee fitted and sewed the costumes.
4. Mrs. Gomez chose and worked with the actors.
5. The stars studied and memorized their parts.
6. A local company designed and printed the programs.
7. A dozen workers built and painted scenery.
8. Audience members talked and whispered in the seats.
9. The lights flickered and faded.
10. Two actors entered and faced the audience.
11. The town's children sang and danced with the stars.
12. One person talked and told jokes.
13. Three clowns leaped and danced in a circle.
14. The audience clapped and cheered for the players.
15. The players smiled and bowed in front of the curtain.

♦ A **compound sentence** contains two simple sentences joined by the word *and*. *(page 348)*

Mike is an author , and Jean is a scientist.

A. Practice Write each sentence. Then write *simple* or *compound* to name each sentence. Underline the two simple sentences in each compound sentence.

1. Many jobs and careers are popular.
2. Conductors direct orchestras and choruses.
3. Authors write books, and publishers print them.
4. Police officers and firefighters often save lives.
5. Actors can work in film, and they can work on stage.

6. Nurses treat sick people, and they prevent sickness, too.
7. Letter carriers deliver letters and packages.
8. Computer operators work in many different businesses.
9. City planners design the cities of tomorrow.
10. Some pilots fly jets, and other pilots fly helicopters.
11. Engineers build bridges and tall buildings.
12. Lawyers work in courts, and doctors work in hospitals.
13. Teachers work with children and adults.
14. Grocers sell food, and chefs prepare meals.

◆ The different kinds of words used in sentences are called the
parts of speech. Parts of speech include *nouns, pronouns, action*
and *linking verbs, adjectives,* and *adverbs.* (*page 350*)

The boys hurried quickly to their swim club.
(noun, action verb, adverb)
They are excellent swimmers.
(pronoun, linking verb, adjective)

A. Practice Write each sentence. Write whether each underlined
word is a *noun, pronoun, action verb, linking verb, adjective,* or
adverb.
1. Many children enjoy unusual activities after school.
2. Pam is a dancer.
3. She practices hard every day.
4. Pam attends a special school in the afternoon.
5. The school teaches dance.
6. The students study there for two hours.
7. They learn many kinds of dance.
8. Soon the students will put on a performance.
9. Pam and her friends rehearse frequently.
10. Eli is a volunteer at the town's park.
11. He works there with other volunteers.
12. The volunteers plant many bushes and flowers.
13. Sometimes they sweep the paths and the playgrounds.
14. The proud volunteers work eagerly at their jobs.
15. The park is a beautiful place because of them.

445

Mechanics Rules and Practice

Capitalization and End Punctuation

Capitalize the following	
the first letter of each sentence *(page 34)*	The tulip is yellow.
each word in a proper noun, such as people's names and titles and specific places or things *(pages 82, 88, 154, 334)*	Miss Julie Ling *(pages 88, 334)* Kansas City *(pages 82, 154)* Golden Gate Bridge *(pages 83, 334)*
each word in the greeting of a friendly letter, except the word *and (page 154)*	Dear Jean, Dear Ana and Jose
the first word only in the closing of a letter *(page 154)*	Your friend, Sincerely yours,
Use this end punctuation	
a period at the end of a declarative sentence *(pages 34, 42)*	The bridge is narrow.
a period at the end of an imperative sentence *(pages 34, 42)*	Pick up that rake.
a question mark at the end of an interogative sentence *(pages 34, 42)*	Is he your brother?
an exclamation mark at the end of an exclamatory sentence *(pages 34, 42)*	Wow, what a great movie!

A. Practice   Write each sentence. Correct the capitalization and the end punctuation.

1. our flag is red, white, and blue
2. Are there other countries with a flag those colors
3. there is France, Belgium, Luxembourg, Great Britain, Australia, New Zealand, and many others
4. wow, you named a lot of countries
5. can you name any others
6. yes, I think I can
7. quick, name three more
8. there is Costa Rica, Liberia, and Thailand

B. Practice   Write each sentence. Correct the capitalization.

  9. South of the equator, it is summer in december.

 10. It is winter there in july and august.

 11. They can swim outdoors in november.

 12. Where I live, leaves fall from the trees in october.

 13. There are many office buildings on wall street.

 14. Cable cars still run on hyde street.

 15. Our president lives on pennsylvania avenue.

 16. You can see the elevated train on wabash avenue.

 17. The capital of vermont is montpelier.

 18. In florida, the capital is tallahassee.

 19. The capital of california is sacramento.

 20. Did you know that topeka was the capital of kansas?

 21. The grand canyon was formed by erosion.

 22. The sears tower was built by people.

 23. The mississippi river is the longest in our country.

 24. The george washington bridge crosses the hudson river.

 25. Many people visit the lincoln memorial each year.

 26. Have you read any books by laura ingalls wilder?

 27. No, but last week I read a book by mark twain.

 28. When I was younger, I loved books by dr. seuss.

 29. My favorite books are the ones about doctor doolittle.

 30. They were written by hugh lofting.

C. Practice   Write the letters. Use correct capitalization.

31. dear laurie,
    I'll see you at the soft-ball game.
                your friend,
                Yvonne

32. dear uncle louis,
    Thank you for the poster you sent.
                love,
                James

33. dear miguel,
    We hope you'll feel better soon.
                best wishes,
                Your Class

34. dear nana and papa,
    I'm glad you came to my birthday party.
                love,
                Sara

Commas

Use a comma	
to set off the name of a person spoken to use two commas if the name is in the middle of a sentence *(page 294)*	Peter, please open your book. Please close the door, Maria. Please, Jim, don't shout.
after *yes, no,* and *well* when they begin a sentence *(page 294)*	Yes, I am the oldest.
to separate three or more items in a series *(page 294)*	I need milk, eggs, and bread.
before the word *and* in a compound sentence when joining two complete thoughts *(pages 294, 348)*	I went to the circus, and I saw the clowns.
between the city and the state in an address *(page 154)*	Boulder, Colorado
between the day and the year in a date *(page 154)*	December 31, 1990
after the greeting in a friendly letter *(page 154)*	Dear Samuel,
after the closing in a letter *(page 154)*	Love, Your friend,

A. Practice   Write each sentence adding needed commas.

1. Juana here is your book.
2. You can keep it if you'd like Peter.
3. Rachel I like the vase you made.
4. Yours is nice, too Aretha.
5. I should tell you Darryl your bicycle tires look flat.
6. Thanks Phil I'm glad you told me.
7. Yes today is the coldest day of the year.
8. Yes I have my mittens and my scarf.
9. No I don't have my earmuffs.
10. Well maybe it would be a good idea.
11. No I don't know what the temperature is exactly.
12. Well it certainly is cold.
13. Fish shellfish and dolphins live in the sea.
14. My bathing suit is green blue and white.
15. At the beach, we swim splash and shout.
16. We bring towels pails and shovels to the beach.
17. The seagulls are white black and gray.
18. We feed them bread popcorn and seeds.
19. I like the beach in winter spring summer and fall.

B. Practice   Write each sentence adding needed commas.

20. America has many national parks and they are very beautiful.
21. Yellowstone Park is the oldest and it is famous.
22. There are steaming hot springs to see in Yellowstone Park and you can see bear and buffalo too.
23. Old Faithful is a geyser and people love to see it.
24. The park has a petrified forest and there is also a canyon with two waterfalls.
25. It is a wonderful place to visit and I am glad it is a national park.
26. Mt. Rushmore is also a national park and it is in South Dakota.
27. There are four faces carved on it and they are all of American Presidents.
28. Gutzon Borglum designed the monument and his son Lincoln finished it.

C. Practice   Write each letter. Add commas where necessary.

29.   321 Oak Street
        Boise Idaho 83707
        July 18 1990
    Dear Cherise
        Thank you for the great birthday gift.
            Your friend
                Ray

31.   6 Francis Road
        Glen Cove NY 11542
        May 5 1990
    Dear Yukiko,
        I can't wait to see you this summer.
            Love
                Tai

30.   14 Sacajawea Rd.
        Cheyenne WY 82001
        May 5 1990
    Dear Paco
        I hope you can visit me in Wyoming.
            Your friend
                David

33.   5 Peach St.
        Atlanta GA 30301
        November 11 1990
    Dear Grandma
        Here is a picture of Billy and me.
            Love
                Dionne

449

Apostrophes, Abbreviations, and Initials

Use an apostrophe	
followed by the letter *s* to form the possessive of a singular noun or a plural noun that does not end in *s (pages 84, 86, 200)*	Regan's book *(pages 84, 200)* Susan's apple *(pages 84, 200)* the children's shouts *(pages 86, 200)*
alone to form the possessive of a plural noun that ends in *s (pages 86, 200)*	the girls' books the boys' paints
to show where a letter or letters have been left out of a contraction *(pages 166, 200, 220)*	do not don't *(pages 166,200)* they will they'll *(pages 200, 220)*
When writing an abbreviation	
capitalize the first letter of a proper noun in abbreviations *(pages 72, 88, 334)*	Ms. Smith *(pages 88, 334)* Park Rd. *(pages 72, 88)* Feb., Mon. *(pages 72, 88)*
there is usually a period at the end *(pages 72, 88)*	Dr., Ave., Tues.
for the initials in a person's name, use capital letters followed by periods *(page 334)*	P.G. Wodehouse R.L. Stevenson
for an ordinal number, write the numeral and an ending, but no period. *(page 72)*	1st, 2nd, 3rd 18th, 25th, 81st
for time, use periods, but not capital letters *(page 88)*	7 a.m. 10 p.m.

A. Practice   Write each underlined possessive correctly.

1. Montanas state tree is the Ponderosa.
2. The capitals dome is 165 feet high.
3. The governors home is on a hill.
4. The states resources include gold and silver.
5. Glacier Parks peaks are often snow covered.
6. The childrens cheeks were red from the cold.
7. The mens hands were dirty.
8. The mices tails were long.
9. All roses thorns are sharp.
10. All tulips colors are bright.
11. All crocuses leaves are striped.
12. All lilies stems are tall.

B. Practice   Write each underlined word correctly.

13. He isnt on the softball team.
14. She doesnt like lemons.
15. We wouldnt swim there.
16. Ill learn to ski next year.
17. I hope youll learn, too.
18. Theyll be at the party.
19. I hope Im strong enough.
20. I'm sure shes tall enough.
21. I know were a good team.
22. He knows Ive seen that movie before.
23. Theyve finished already.

C. Practice   Write each underlined word or initial correctly.

24. Mr and mrs Chan live on Maple strt in my town.
25. I think ms Brown lives on Pine rd, near me.
26. Go see dctr Wallace on Grand avn, near the school.
27. Did you know that miss Gonzalez lives on Elm bvd, next door to me?
28. The science fair is next weds at City Hall.
29. Every mond I have a piano lesson.
30. In sept, we go back to school.
31. In jany and febr, it is very cold.
32. Do you know the book *From the Mixed-Up Files of Mrs. Basil e Frankweiler* by e l Konigsburg?
33. Do you know any books by e b White?
34. The President after j f Kennedy was l b Johnson.

D. Practice   Abbreviate each underlined word.

35. George Washington was our first President.
36. Abraham Lincoln was the sixteenth President.
37. D. D. Eisenhower was our thirty-fourth President.
38. The library is open from 9 in the morning to 6 in the evening on school days.
39. It is open from 10 in the morning to 4 in the afternoon on weekends.

Writing Titles and Conversation

To write titles of works	
Capitalize the first word, the last word, and all important words *(page 244)*	*Green Eggs and Ham* *The Long Winter*
Don't capitalize unimportant words unless they start or end the title *(page 244)*	*The Wheel on the School* *On the Skateboard*
Underline book titles *(page 244)*	The Wolves of Willoughby Chase
Put story, poem, and song titles in quotation marks *(page 244)*	story: "The Journey Home" poem: "Travel" song: "This Land is Your Land"

To write conversation	
Put spoken words in quotation marks *(page 120)*	Kato said, "Nice to meet you."
Capitalize the first letter of the quote *(page 120)*	Gina replied, "Nice to meet you, too."
Separate a quote from the rest of the sentence with one or more commas *(page 120)*	I said, "Come in." "I am Li," he said. He said, "It's warm," opening the window.
If the quotation is a question or an exclamation, end it with a question mark or an exclamation mark instead of a comma *(page 120)*	"Shall I close the window?" he asked. "Oh no, it's so hot!" we answered.
If a quoted statement ends a sentence put the period inside the quote marks *(page 120)*	Mr. Li said, "Let's turn the heat off."

A. Practice   Write each title correctly.

1. book: the tale of timmy tiptoes
2. book: beasts by the bunches
3. book: the monkey and the crocodile
4. story: and maggie makes three
5. story: the gray whales
6. story: clara joins the circus
7. poem: little tree
8. poem: africa dream
9. poem: the edge of the world

10. song: gold and silver

11. song: home on the range

12. song: down by the bay

B. Practice   Write each sentence. Correct the capitalization, and add quotation marks wherever necessary.

13. The guard said, the museum is closing soon.

14. Let's hurry to the Egyptian room, I said.

15. My brother answered, no, let's see the lions.

16. just make it snappy, the guard said.

17. My sister said, we could look at the knights' armor.

18. no, we saw that last time, I said.

19. The guard said, the museum is closed.

C. Practice   Write each sentence adding needed commas.

20. "Look at this big leaf" Karen said.

21. "Let's look it up in our book" her mother replied.

22. Dad said "I don't see it in the book."

23. "I've never seen one like it before" Mom said.

24. Karen said "We know this one" picking up a leaf.

25. She said "It looks like the Canadian flag" holding up a maple leaf.

D. Practice   Write each sentence. Add correct punctuation.

26. The announcer said, "I think it will be a double"

27. "Oh wow, it's a triple" he yelled.

28. He announced, "The next batter will be Sandy Reed"

29. "Will he hit another home run" he asked.

30. "Fantastic, what a long home run" he shouted.

E. Practice   Write each sentence. Add proper capitalization and punctuation.

31. Oh, a wolf the little boy shouted.

32. Everyone came and asked where is the wolf.

33. The boy said I guess it's gone and apologized.

34. He did it again his father complained.

35. The boy shouted help, help, a wolf.

36. Why isn't anyone coming he cried.

37. Everyone said we're tired of his jokes.

Troublesome Words

◆ Homophones are words that sound alike but have different spellings and different meanings. This chart shows some homophones that are easy to confuse.

Word	Meaning	Example
their	belonging to them	Dogs wag their tails.
there	in or at that place	Put your hat there in the hall.
they're	they are	They're my best friends.
to	in the direction of	The train goes to Chicago.
too	also;	It stops in Detroit, too.
	more than enough	The ticket costs too much.
two	the number 2	The trip takes two hours.
who's	who is	Who's your gym teacher?
whose	belonging to whom	Whose shoes are these?
your	belonging to you	Do you have your money?
you're	you are	You're late for breakfast.

A. Practice   Write each sentence, using the correct word.

    1. We walk _____ the auditorium. (to, too, two)

    2. Our class practices the play _____. (there, their)

    3. Is this _____ hat? (your, you're)

    4. _____ costume needs buttons? (Who's, Whose)

    5. The red shirt is _____ big for me. (to, too, two)

    6. _____ in charge of the scripts. (Your, You're)

    7. We need _____ copies of it. (to, too, two)

B. Practice   Follow the directions for Practice A.

    8. We went _____ Jim and Tina's house. (to, too, two)

    9. We saw _____ pictures of Utah. (their, there, they're)

    10. Bryce Canyon is located _____. (their, there, they're)

    11. We saw Joline's pictures, _____. (to, too, two)

    12. Did _____ family ever visit Utah? (your, you're)

    13. _____ camera did you use? (Who's, Whose)

    14. _____ a good photographer. (Your, You're)

♦ This chart shows other words that are easy to confuse. Study the chart to help you use the words correctly.

Word	Meaning	Example
its	belonging to it	I borrowed Len's bike. Its tire is flat.
it's	it is	It's time to fix the tire.
are	form of the verb *be*	The books are on the shelf.
our	belonging to us	We put away our books.
good	adjective; tells about nouns	We ate a good lunch.
well	adverb; tells about verbs	Dora plays the piano well.

A. Practice Write each sentence, using the correct word in parentheses.

1. Ms. Chen took _____ class to the post office. (are, our)

2. _____ a very busy place. (Its, It's)

3. The post office opens _____ doors early. (its, it's)

4. Clerks give customers _____ service. (good, well)

5. Letter sorters work _____ as a team. (good, well)

6. Some stamps _____ colorful. (are, our)

7. Letter carriers know our area _____. (good, well)

8. A mail truck carries _____ load. (its, it's)

9. We had a _____ time. (good, well)

10. Now we know about _____ post office. (are, our)

B. Practice Follow the directions for Practice A.

11. Terry gave _____ family a kitten. (are, our)

12. I found a _____ box for its bed. (good, well)

13. _____ time for the kitten's dinner. (Its, It's)

14. _____ dinner tonight is tuna fish. (Its, It's)

15. The kitten licked _____ whiskers. (its, it's)

16. Then it slept _____. (good, well)

17. We feed the kitten _____. (good, well)

18. A kitten makes a _____ pet. (good, well)

19. There _____ several pets in _____ house. (are, our)

20. A _____ cat cleans itself _____. (good, well)

Index

Illustrations: Howard Berelson, 40–41, 162–163; Marie De John, 287; Nancy Didion, 104–105, 230; Len Ebert, 97, 99, 175, 357, 359; Judy Ann Griffith, 28–29, 34, 226–227, 242–243, 329; John Killgrew, 112–113, 254; David Rickman, 45, 136–137, 206–207, 314–315; Carol Schwartz, 25, 40–41, 58–59, 64–65, 68, 71, 80–81, 88, 142–143, 161, 168, 192–193, 213–215, 252–253, 259, 310, 312–313, 318, 348, 353; Steven Schindler, 39, 77, 125, 159, 211, 249, 298, 339; Karen Schmidt, 195, 200, 205; Robert Shore, 83, 114–115, 120–121; Gary Torrisi, 67, 74, 127, 129, 132, 149, 188–189, 241, 300–301, 305, 325, 340–341, 345; Fred Winkowski, 228–229, 238–239; Lane Yerkes, 18–22, 60–63, 106–111, 123, 154–155, 276–277, 279–280, 283–285.

Photographs: 27 John Lei/Omni-Photo Communications, Inc.; **43** John Lei/Omni-Photo Communications, Inc.; **46–47** Ken Karp/Omni-Photo Communications, Inc.; **72** Ken Karp/Omni-Photo Communications, Inc.; **78–79** John Lei/Omni-Photo Communications, Inc.; **87** John Lei/Omni-Photo Communications, Inc.; **90** John Lei/Omni-Photo Communications, Inc.; **119** Ken Karp/Omni-Photo Communications, Inc.; **131** John Lei/Omni-Photo Communications, Inc.; **144–145** John Lei/Omni-Photo Communications, Inc.; **151** Ken Karp/Omni-Photo Communications, Inc.; **157** Ken Karp/Omni-Photo Communications, Inc.; **167** Ken Karp/Omni-Photo Communications, Inc.; **184–185** John Lei/Omni-Photo Communications, Inc.; **191** Ken Karp/Omni-Photo Communications, Inc.; **196–197** Ken Karp/Omni-Photo Communications, Inc.; **217** Ken Karp/Omni-Photo Communications, Inc.; **236–237** John Lei/Omni-Photo Communications, Inc.; **250–251** Ken Karp/Omni-Photo Communications, Inc.; **260–261** John Lei/Omni-Photo Communications, Inc.; **290–291** John Lei/Omni-Photo Communications, Inc.; **294–295** John Lei/Omni-Photo Communications, Inc.; **302–303** Ken Karp/Omni-Photo Communications, Inc.; **308** Ken Karp/Omni-Photo Communications, Inc.; **317** Ken Karp/Omni-Photo Communications, Inc.; **319** The Granger Collection. Montage by Ken Karp/Omni-Photo Communications, Inc.; **327** Ken Karp/Omni-Photo Communications, Inc. **330–331** Ken Karp/Omni-Photo Communications, Inc.; **342** John Lei/Omni-Photo Communications, Inc.; **350** John Lei/Omni-Photo Communications, Inc.

Acknowledgments

For permission to adapt and reprint copyrighted materials, grateful acknowledgment is made to the following publishers, authors, and other copyright holders:

Atheneum Publishers for "Time" from *The Apple Vendor's Fair* by Patricia Hubbell. Copyright © 1963 by Patricia Hubbell. Used by permission of Atheneum Publishers.

Doubleday & Company, Inc., for "The Ceiling" from *The Collected Poems of Theodore Roethke* by Theodore Roethke. Copyright © 1932, 1961 by Theodore Roethke. Copyright © 1937, 1966 by Beatrice Roethke as Administratix of the Estate of Theodore Roethke. Used by permission of Doubleday & Company, Inc.

Farrar, Straus & Giroux for "bell" from *still more small poems* by Valerie Worth. Copyright © 1976, 1977, 1978 by Valerie Worth. Reprinted by permission of Farrar, Straus & Giroux.

Greenwillow Books (A Division of William Morrow) for "Bulgy Bunne" from *The New Kid on the Block* by Jack Prelutsky. Text copyright © 1984 by Jack Prelutsky. By permission of Greenwillow Books (A Division of William Morrow)

Harper & Row, Publishers, Inc., for "Wagon Wheels" from *Wagon Wheels* by Barbara Brenner. Text copyright © 1978 by Barbara Brenner. Used by permission of Harper & Row, Publishers, Inc.; for "The Acrobats" from *Where the Sidewalk Ends* by Shel Silverstein. Copyright 1974 by Shel Silverstein. Used by permission of Harper & Row, Publishers, Inc.; for "Escape" from *Charlotte's Web* by E. B. White, illustrated by Garth Williams. Copyright © 1952, 1980 by E. B. White, illustration copyright renewed 1980 by Garth Williams, all by permission of Harper & Row, Publishers, Inc.; for "Anchored" from *A Light in the Attic* by Shel Silverstein. Copyright © 1981 by Shel Silverstein. Used by permission of Harper & Row, Publishers, Inc.

Hastings House Publishers, Inc. for "Summer Challenge" from *Yours Till Niagara Falls, Abby* by Jane O'Connor. Copyright © by Jane O'Connor. Published by Scholastic Inc. Used by permission of Hastings House Publishers, Inc.

Henry Holt and Company, Inc. for "Fog" from *Chicago Poems* by Carl Sandburg. Copyright 1916 by Henry Holt and Company, Inc. Copyright 1944 by Carl Sandburg. Used by permission of the publisher.

Houghton Mifflin Company for "The Fisherman's Wife" by Amy Lowell from *The Complete Poetical Works of Amy Lowell*. Copyright © 1955 by Houghton Mifflin Company. Reprinted by permission of the publisher.

Alfred A. Knopf for "On My Own" from *The Bad Dreams of a Good Girl* by Susan Shreve. Copyright © 1982 by Susan Shreve. All Rights reserved. Used by permission of Alfred A. Knopf.

Little, Brown & Co., Inc., for "The Enormous Egg" from *The Enormous Egg* by Oliver Butterworth. Copyright © 1956 by Oliver Butterworth. Used by permission of the publisher.

Macmillan Publishing Company for "Curious Something" from *Skipping Along Alone* by Winifred Welles. The Macmillan Company, New York, 1931. Used by permission of James Welles Shearer.

Josephine Curry McNatt, for "Smells," from *Poems for Josephine* by Kathryn Worth. All efforts to contact the author for permission to use this poem have been to no avail.

Prentice-Hall, Inc., publisher, for "The Story of Paul Bunyan from *The Story of Paul Bunyan* by Barbara Emberley, illustrated by Ed Emberley. Copyright © 1963 Used by permission of the publisher, Prentice-Hall, Inc., Englewood Cliffs, NJ.

Random House, Inc., for "Fernando" by Marci Ridlon; for "Driving to the Beach" by Joanna Cole. Copyright © 1973 by Joanna Cole. Used by permission of Random House, Inc.; for "Long Trip" from *Selected Poems of Langston Hughes* by Langston Hughes. Copyright © 1959 by Langston Hughes. Used by permission of Random House, Inc.

Henry Regnery Company for "Bunches of Grapes" excerpted from *The Golden Journey* by Walter De La Mare. Copyright © 1965. Used by permission of The Society of Authors Ltd.

Scholastic Inc. for "Summer Challenge" from *Yours Till Niagara Falls, Abby* by Jane O'Connor. Copyright © 1979 by Jane O'Connor. Used by permission of Scholastic Inc.